SHORT-TERM COUNSELING

A Humanistic Approach for the Helping Professions

SISTER KATHLEEN BLACK

Emeritus Professor, School of Nursing,
State University of New York at Binghamton

Addison-Wesley Publishing Company, Inc.

Medical/Nursing Division
Menlo Park, California • Reading, Massachusetts
London • Amsterdam • Don Mills, Ontario • Sydney

Sponsoring Editor: Deborah Gale
Associate Editor: Thomas Eoyang
Production Editor: Nancy Sjoberg
Copyeditor: Andrea Matyas
Book Designer: Nancy Sjoberg
Cover Designer: Robin Gold
Cover Photo: George B. Fry III

Epigraph on p. xi taken from Gassner, John, ed. *Best Plays of the Modern American Theatre.* Second Series. New York: Crown, n.d., p. 543. Reprinted by permission of Random House, Inc.

Library of Congress Cataloging in Publication Data

Black, Kathleen.
Short-term counseling.

Bibliography: p.
Includes index.
1. Counseling. 2. Problem-solving. 3. Self-perception.
4. Humanistic psychology. I. Title.
[DNLM: 1 Counseling. WM 55 B627s]
BF637.C6B45 158'.3 82-4063
ISBN 0-201-00073-3 AACR2

ABCDEFGHIJ-MA-898765432

Addison-Wesley Publishing Company, Inc.
Medical/Nursing Division
2725 Sand Hill Road
Menlo Park, California 94025

FOREWORD

People need people. That is the warm and eloquently simple message Sister Kathleen Black conveys in this book. It wholeheartedly reaffirms the spirit of caring and sensitivity toward others and the appreciation of characteristics that are uniquely human.

The author's basic optimism about people is crucially important to everything said in this book. The convictions that every person is fundamentally good and that every interpersonal relationship has elements that foster personal growth for both helper and client make their presence felt on every page.

Humanistic-existential premises, concepts, and values are delicately but thoroughly blended in the client-centered, problem-solving, and behavioral approaches to counseling presented here. Curricula in schools that educate helping professionals increasingly reflect the primary importance of humanistic psychology in contemporary society. Survival in a technological society demands the humanizing of our person-to-person contacts. This is the reason this book is particularly relevant.

Helping professionals will appreciate being helped to enter into the private world of the client. They will find the skills and understandings that will enable them to do so in the pages that follow. Practice exercises are designed to raise the helper's consciousness through achieving inner vision and affirming the self. Case examples consistently demonstrate responsible and responsive caring.

Clients will appreciate counselors who, because of this book, have cultivated a sensitivity to their physical and emotional states, facilitate their right to take charge of their own lives and to assume responsibility for the outcomes of their decisions, and engage with them in I-Thou encounters based on mutual respect.

As Abraham Maslow once put it, "History has practically always sold human nature short." Sister Kathleen Black has *not* sold people short. She presents much more than a system for counseling others. She presents a way of being in the world.

Carol Ren Kneisl
Graduate Psychosocial Nursing Program
School of Nursing
State University of New York, Buffalo

PREFACE

AUDIENCE

This book is designed to meet a growing need among students, teachers, and practitioners in the helping professions to develop the skills and understanding that will allow them not only to feel personally comfortable in their relationships with clients and client groups, but also to provide support and facilitative guidance. Helping professionals may have limited contact with their clients—perhaps only a single interview—or the counseling relationship may extend over a considerable period of time. In either case, the helping professional will need concrete counseling skills grounded in a solid theoretical foundation. Although primarily addressed to nurses, this text will be useful for all educators, students, and practitioners in fields that include counseling as an important but not necessarily central component: nurses, physicians, and other health care workers; teachers, trainers, and tutors; clergy; law enforcement officials; guidance counselors and youth workers; employment and personnel workers; and rehabilitation, child care, and social workers.

PURPOSE

In integrating counseling theory and practice, this book takes its perspective from humanistic psychology, viewing the human being as a whole and potentially healthy person. As the text discusses the various concepts that bear on the counseling situation, continued emphasis is placed on the practitioner's growth as a helping person and on counseling as a process that fosters growth in the client. Self-awareness, with self-affirmation as its corollary, is at the core of the humanistic counseling model. This core must be consistently nurtured within helper and client alike if continued personal growth is to be assured.

The helping professional can expect to grow as a result of internalizing—both emotionally and intellectually—his or her observations of the self and others. Material for this understanding is found primarily in one's personal relationships, but a rich vein is also available in literature of the imagination, as well as of the behavioral sciences.

For the client, the helper can stimulate personal growth by offering the experience of being unconditionally accepted by another, which in turn enhances the client's capacity for self-acceptance. The client is thus assisted in the moving toward that unique person he or she is alone capable of being.

CONTENT

In this text approaches to counseling are grouped and discussed in detail as client-centered, problem-solving, and behavioral counseling. The process of psychologic interviewing is included for each approach. Whether helping professionals interact with their clients on only one or two occasions or repeatedly over a prolonged period, they will expect to draw from the same fund of counseling knowledge and skills for each encounter.

The book begins by focusing on understanding the self and its relationship to others. Without reviewing the material often presented in college courses such as general psychology and psychology of personality, Chapters 1 and 2 encourage the reader to take a fresh look into the primary sources of personality theory and theories of the self. It is assumed that the reader, as one who expects to work professionally with people, will have already acquired the rudiments of psychology, as presented in courses such as those mentioned. Models of human behavior and human development are therefore discussed in light of understanding and using them in counseling. Humanistic-existential concepts form the frame of reference for the discussion of counseling throughout the text. A nonjudgmental view of the dynamics of human behavior and an appreciation of human differences are consistently encouraged.

In Chapter 3, sensitivity and self-awareness are further stimulated through a combination of consciousness-raising concepts and practice exercises. These early exercises, and what the reader learns from them, are cumulative in that each new experience and each new discussion builds on the pertinent information that has preceded it.

The counseling of individual clients is the subject of Part II, with the approaches grouped under client-centered (Chapters 4 and 5), problem-solving (Chapters 6 and 7), and behavioral counseling (Chapter 8). All the approaches are presented in relation to the individual, one-to-one relationship central to the work of the helping professional. Although each approach is examined separately, the reader is reminded that professional counselors and therapists do not usually remain within the confines of a single school of thought.

Problem-solving counseling, for example, incorporates concepts and skills described in the previous chapter on the client-centered approach. Similarly, aspects of both methodologies are applied along with behavioral principles to meet other kinds of client needs.

Part III applies the principles of group and family counseling and therapy to humanistic short-term counseling.

A number of exercises and case examples, suitable for either classroom use or self-motivated study, are introduced and highlighted throughout the text to provide frequent opportunities to apply both principles and techniques. Enough technical terminology is introduced and defined under each topic to prepare the reader to engage intelligently in related reading and discussion.

Basic constructs are explained in readily understandable language and with examples. References to primary and secondary literature are provided for further study. To aid novice counselors who are apprehensive about what to say and how to say it, verbatim dialogues are used to illustrate the differences between more and less helpful responses in typical counseling situations.

* * *

Humanistic helping is presented throughout this book as a means to an end that extends beyond assisting clients to meet the problems of everyday life: the fundamental humanistic aim of human progress toward personal integrity and interpersonal support. To the extent that both clients and helpers share in this aim and allow humanistic principles to take on meaning in their lived experience, they will resist the dehumanizing features found in social institutions, traditions, and practices.

ACKNOWLEDGEMENTS

I am indebted to a number of counseling specialists for their critical reviews of the manuscript at various stages of its development. They include Ann Herrick, RN, PhD, a valued colleague and friend, a teacher at Russell Sage College, and a private practitioner of counseling, Albany, New York; Donna C. Aguilera, PhD, FAAN, Chairman and Professor, Graduate Division, Psychiatric Nursing, University of Maryland, Baltimore; David S. Bailey, EdD, Director, Mental Health Division, Northeast Georgia Medical Center, Gainesville, Georgia; Jane Chapman-Gallan, PhD, Assistant Clinical Professor of Clinical Psychology, University of Colorado Medical Center, Denver; Vincent J. D'Andrea, MD, Staff Psychiatrist, Clinical Associate Professor of Psychiatry and Behavioral Science, Palo Alto Medical Foundation, Student Health Division, Stanford University; Patricia I. Johnson, PhD, Clinical Psychology, St. Joseph's Hospital Mental Health Center, Phoenix, Arizona; Carol R. Kneisl, RN, MS, Graduate Psychosocial Nursing Program, School of Nursing, State University of New York at Buffalo; Rae Sedgwick, RN, PhD, Clinical Psychologist, Child and Family Therapist, Clinical Specialist in Psychiatric and Mental Health Nursing, Bonner Springs, Kansas; and Martha L. Stockwell, RN, MN, Associate Professor, College of Nursing, The University of Oklahoma Health Sciences Center, Oklahoma City.

I am sincerely grateful to Thomas Eoyang of Addison-Wesley and James Keating for their encouragement and editorial assistance, and to numerous friends for their supportive interest.

My love and heartfelt thanks are extended to my brother Ted for his persevering help with editorial detail and with typing and retyping the manuscript. Above all, I thank him for his sustaining faith in me, a faith that has never faltered throughout our combined efforts.

Sister Kathleen Black

CONTENTS

PART II
HELPING INDIVIDUAL CLIENTS 49

PART III
HELPING PEOPLE IN GROUPS 163

As a human being . . . I'm the people I've met. I'm a mixture of everything I've read and seen. I've stolen a virtue here—and a weakness there. I'm everyone I ever loved.

JOHN PATRICK
The Hasty Heart, 1945.

PART I

Understanding Self and Others

CHAPTER 1

Personality and Person in Counseling

COUNSELING AS HELPING

People who work with people find themselves greatly in need of short-term counseling and interviewing skills. This is particularly true of practitioners in the **helping professions**: nurses and other health practitioners, social workers, ministers, and guidance counselors. Others, such as teachers, personnel workers, and law enforcement agents, may also consider counseling a significant skill to exercise in their various functions. This text is addressed to practitioners in these and other fields whose practice would benefit from applying the principles and skills of short-term counseling. The respective workers are herein addressed using catch-all terms such as *helping professionals, professional helpers,* or simply *helpers, practitioners,* or *workers.* In most of the illustrative case examples, a nurse is featured as the practitioner prototype.

In recent years, the terms **helping** and **the helping process** have come to denote psychologic intervention (counseling) engaged in by a variety of workers who are not specialists in psychotherapy (Rogers, 1961; Brammer, 1979). Because the functions of any helping professional usually include many other kinds of helping, the interpretation of the term as a form of counseling usually depends on its context.

The days and years of the average person's life bring an uneven mixture of contentment and anxiety. There are periods when anxiety threatens to become overwhelming. The services of a professional whose sole function is counseling or psychotherapy are not always available at such times. They may not be needed. The troubled person may find it sufficient to confide in a member of the family, a friend, or a stranger met quite casually. The contents of "Dear Abby" and similar news media features attest to the ubiquity of personal problems and to the widespread recognition of the need for aid in solving them.

When such sources fail or when the problem seems to be related to the specialized field of knowledge of a given helper, one is likely to turn to that person for help. Clients increasingly look to people who are members of the helping professions as the persons with the answers. Helpers, however, find that having answers is not enough, because answers are seldom what the seekers need. Clients may know the best course of action but be unable to take it. They may vacillate among several alternatives among which it is impossible to choose. The identified problem may be such that there is no solution available; the real answer may be to discover new directions in which to look for avenues to satisfaction.

Practitioners in the helping professions discover that their basic professional knowledge and expertise are often insufficient to be of psychologic help in the multiplicity of situations they face with their clients. They find themselves in urgent need of a sound theoretic framework and a selection of skills to draw from in exercising their counseling function.

Practitioners such as social workers and clinical nursing specialists in the psychiatric–mental health field have interviewing and counseling as their principal function and have been educated to assume it. Together with clinical and counseling psychologists and psychiatrists, they are referred to in this text as **professional counselors**. Professional counselors are likely to receive clients in an office by appointment and engage in interaction over a specific period of time with a view to goals that are mutually agreed on. The client may have previously gone through some type of selection process to reasonably insure that a suitable client-helper match is attained.

The counseling sphere of helping professionals tends to be considerably less circumscribed. Clients may be encountered in a clinic, in any part of a health or social agency, in a classroom or a rectory office, in their own homes, or even at the scene of an accident. Persons in need of help may not be clients in the strict "consumer of services" sense of the word. Instead, they may be victims, neighbors, derelicts, or patients assigned to any number of helpers with a variety of professional identities.

Helpers need, then, to possess the basic skills of counseling. Short-term counseling aimed toward enabling each client to utilize all available inner and outer resources in coping with problems, and thus grow in the process, can become a built-in feature of their helping function.

Because the demands on them are so varied, helping professionals must prepare to move comfortably from one scheme of theoretic constructs to another as the occasion demands. They must deftly draw from a mixed bag of intervention skills those that most efficiently and effectively serve their clients under a given set of conditions. No less than full-time professional counselors, helping professionals require the inner confidence provided by a sense of knowing what they are doing and why they are doing it. Their self-confidence and self-respect will be communicated to their clients, and their potential to help will be strengthened accordingly.

THE THEORETIC BASE FOR COUNSELING

Although full-time professional counselors hold some theoretic views in common, most follow a set of tenets adhered to by members of a fairly definable school of thought. Whether the practice in question is called counseling, psychotherapy, or any other name likely depends on the professional category of the practitioner. Psychiatrists and many clinical psychologists use the term *psychotherapy*. Counseling psychologists usually designate their work as *counseling*. Nurses with specialized preparation use both terms, sometimes interchangeably. In the practice of social work, the term *interviewing* is often used to embrace counseling and psychotherapeutic techniques, as well as other related elements of work with clients.

The way that specialists in professional counseling approach their collaborative tasks with clients differs according to the philosophy on which their intervention strategy is based. Decided differences in philosophy are found. For many, there is an underlying premise that the human individual develops along reasonably predictable lines and that growth occurs from within. Although change may be moderated or fostered as a result of outside influences, the actual impetus for change is an integral aspect of what it means to be human. Counseling, therefore, is related directly to persons as they inwardly are, were, and will be, and only tangentially to the various segments of their outward behavior.

Other professional counselors operate from a radically different set of assumptions. In their view, the idea of self is fiction, and overtly observable behavior is the only reality the counselor can deal with. Furthermore, behavior is the direct result of environmental influences and can therefore be changed or eradicated by other environmental conditions, of which counseling is one.

The special bias of each professional counselor rests on the growing body of theoretical postulates that he or she considers scientifically sound. This theory is studied in great depth and tested repeatedly in various ways in practice. The particular theory of a given field provides a base for building a body of principles to guide the choice of aims, methods, and techniques and provides a scale for the evaluation of counseling effectiveness with each client. This fund of knowledge provides the counselor with a dependable source of continuing growth as a professional expert and confidence in the ability to perform adequately in this role.

As a result of particular interests, background, and propensities, an individual professional counselor feels drawn more to one school of thought than another. By subsequent study and practice the counselor keeps in close touch with developments in this area especially, but at the same time remains aware of the advantages to be gained from choosing the best from a variety of sources. Very few currently active counselors choose to narrow their counseling approach to fit an exclusive school of thought. Each tends to rely on an ever-expanding body of interrelated theory. From this a broadly based fund of validated knowledge about human beings and a wealth of intervention skills are gradually accumulated. Study of theoretical developments and the effectiveness of different forms of treatment is a lifelong task (Nye, 1975; Lewis, 1978; Liebert and Spiegler, 1978; Brammer, 1979; Maddi, 1980).

Like professional counselors, helping professionals who wish to incorporate effective counseling into their daily work find that continual study is the price to be paid for the requisite knowledge and skill. The aim of this book is to encourage the student or practitioner in any helping profession to build a foundation for developing an eclectic, or broadly based, theoretical and practical approach to the counseling aspects of his or her professional work. Several leading systems of professional counseling and psychotherapy are outlined. Some models are more readily adaptable than others to short-term interviewing and counseling. Each, however, has something of value to offer in methods and techniques or in the basic philosophic elements from which methods and techniques are derived.

The counseling activities of helping professionals may with some justification be categorized as short term. This contrasts with the work of private practitioners of psychiatry and, in some instances, of clinical psychology, who carry out a planned treatment procedure intended to effect an extensive reorganization of the client's personality. The counseling work of others is likely to be confined to a much less time-consuming and intensive endeavor. This is not to suggest that the worker and client may not have a relationship that lasts for months or years. In schools, in long-term institutions, in the ministry, and in other such settings, there may be a long-lasting association. **Short term** denotes *a relationship that focuses on the client's current difficulties and strivings rather than deep-seated problems of personality structure.* Helper-client relationships, as is made clear in every chapter of this text, are developed to put clients' difficulties and strivings into the service of their personal growth.

Counseling, wherever and in whatever mode it is practiced, is centered on a person or group of persons. Helping professionals face many questions about what people are like, why they behave in certain ways, whether they can change their ways of being and behaving, and how. The works of recognized theoreticians offer us valuable generalizations from their own insights to answer some of these questions. Their findings are based on long experience in observing and inquiring into human behavior and its motivations.

Wide but selective reading and discussion, combined with continual self-questioning and speculation, will lead to further understanding of ourselves and of others we know in our study and work. These are some general questions we must ask ourselves and our study sources as we attempt to make practical use of theoretical findings:

- What evidence is there to indicate that this idea is valid?
- To what extent does it apply to people in general?
- In what particular ways does it apply to me?
- Does it point to something in me that hampers my personal development?
- How can I work with my relevant qualities in order to move in the direction of optimum self-realization?
- When I recognize that a client is impeded by similar or related factors, how can I help him or her to progress toward self-understanding and self-actualization?

To illustrate the ideas and applications referred to in the first and more basic questions previously posed, selected psychologic and philosophic concepts particularly significant to the practice of counseling are discussed in the remainder of this chapter. The concepts are purposely divided under headings denoting a contrast between the terms personality and person.

Personality, derived from the Latin **persona**, or mask, refers to an integral set of individual characteristics that are dynamic in nature, and are to some extent objectively observable. Under "Using Personality Theory," some examples of conventional psychoanalytic concepts are discussed. With Freud as their pioneering exponent, they are presented first in recognition of their primary historical significance in the psychology of personality.

The final section of the chapter presents an orientation to philosophic-psychologic ideas associated with the more subjective term **person**. The concepts described and defined here are essential to the humanistic knowledge base that this book intends to develop.

In Chapters 2 and 3, humanistic concepts of the person are elaborated and applied as the notion of **self** is examined. This key idea is developed with attention to the importance of self-awareness and self-understanding for the professional helper as counselor.

The concepts introduced in all three chapters are illustrated by frequent use of the first person, singular or plural. This device, repeated at intervals throughout the text, exemplifies the meaningful application of theory to further our understanding of self and others.

USING PERSONALITY THEORY

The Psychoanalytic Tradition

As a result of his background in human biology, Freud was accustomed to thinking of organisms in terms of the structure and functions of their parts. In his delineation of the personality, he offers an interpretation of the warring elements within us, which strikes a responsive chord in the thoughtful observer of self and others. We are frequently aware of inner realities such as the love-hate dichotomy, the antagonistic components of private needs and impulses versus outer pressures from people and events, the day-by-day anxiety that signals the presence of threatening conflict, or guilt feelings that inhibit or follow pieces and patterns of behavior.

The concept of the **unconscious** is undoubtedly one of Freud's greatest contributions to human self-understanding (1949). The idea that there is an area of mental functioning beneath the level of our awareness did not originate with Freud. Throughout the ages it has been recognized in all of the great religions and by philosophers of many different persuasions. Freud, however, was the first to attempt to plot the workings of this hitherto unmapped expanse of the human personality. He heightened our appreciation of the fact that much of our motivation arises from sources we can only minimally perceive. All of our experiences, from our dreams and fantasies to the successful discharge of our responsibilities to family and society, are shot through with the push and pull of inner forces we are at best only dimly aware of.

The stamina with which we face life's vicissitudes and overcome its obstacles can be seen to relate as much to our ego strength as to our genetic and environmental endowments. A rough estimate of the health of the ego can be made by measuring this stamina. A healthy ego makes for a productive, relatively comfortable adjustment to work and play and to family and wider social relationships. It is not driven into compulsive responses by the hedonistic demands of the id or the perfectionistic claims of the superego. It assures a quiet confidence in one's identity and integrity that is not shaken by any but severely traumatic, externally induced stresses. It enables its possessor to meet the inevitable recurrence of anxiety without utter defeat or unduly hostile action (Freud, 1949; Waelder, 1960).

We can observe in ourselves the continuing undercover action of the superego as a necessary monitor of our behavior. At the edge that touches our consciousness, the action of the superego is so vivid at times that we can almost hear a returning admonition of one or the other parent—a residual of our childhood experience. If early parental responses to our mistaken enterprises were especially punishing or inhibiting, we may be hampered later by a superego embodying similar attitudes. We may find ourselves overly apprehensive about entering into new experiences. We may be guilt-ridden concerning errors made in our work or our relationships. Or sexual interest may have had such a strong taboo that we are crippled in our attempts to develop a healthy sexual identity. A gamut of gratifying sensory and interpersonal experiences may also be forbidden as a legitimate part of our existence. Such inhibitions may be largely due to an early spreading of affect, or emotion, from one experience to another on our own part. A general poverty of identity, of ego strength, and of interpersonal competence may nevertheless result. On the other hand, a normally strong superego has a steadying effect on both our development and our current status. It assures that we will be able to cope with our inner drives to a socially acceptable extent and fit constructively into our sociocultural niche with no more than a moderate degree of stress and strain.

As we sharpen our understanding of the many pressures and incentives that determine the direction and quality of human responses, we are confirmed in our recognition of the uniqueness of the individual. We also deepen our appreciation of the difficulties encountered by the person who struggles through a succession of impediments to being and becoming—impediments placed there first by the unknown forces within the self and, second, by other people who are also struggling to find their own best way among the hazards that beset every life, however favored it may be. Along with an increase in understanding, we gain a parallel capacity for acceptance of self and, correspondingly, of others.

Erik Erikson is widely known for his modification and extension of Freud's well-known psychosexual stages into a series of eight **psychosocial crises** (1959), which he whimsically characterizes as the "Eight Ages of Man" (1963). The age that Erikson most completely and brilliantly delineates has become a significant part of the language and literature of our time: the familiar **identity crisis.**

Erikson has been involved for many years in a study of the human life cycle, extending his investigations to cultures and societies outside the milieu of middle-class America. While his psychoanalytic background and experience give him the advantages of a thorough grounding in psychology, he also takes into account the many outer forces that affect the person, and that, in turn, are affected by the person. Erikson's findings have helped us view individuals as existing, throughout the totality of a life span, in continuity with all the others who constitute their world and with all the significant happenings that in any way touch their lives.

In our counseling endeavors, the characteristics of the eight crises can serve as helpful criteria in estimating the level of psychosocial maturity and special ego strengths (trust, autonomy, and so forth) and weaknesses (mistrust, self-doubt, and so forth) that can be attributed to our clients and to ourselves as well. Such assessments can only be made when we attain depth in both theoretical and experiential understanding of the many facets of the growth model (Schultz, 1977). The helper must also reach a profound understanding of the individual concerned, whether self or client. Any of the concepts included in Erikson's scheme may trigger the type of reflection that every counselor must engage in to enhance comprehension. Much can be accomplished, for instance, by thinking of one's own experiences in moving through each developmental stage up to the present and of the manifestations observable in others who are presently facing the choices to be made at the crossroad each crisis symbolizes.

The term **cycle** has a special set of meanings in Erikson's theory. First, there is a cyclic aspect to the series of crises in the life of the individual. As each crisis occurs, the ascendant quality picks up each of the preceding qualities for further development parallel to its own. To the extent that there has been failure of development at the time of any previous crisis, there is a gap in the foundation on which subsequent qualities must build. Persons who mistrust themselves and others, for example, will undoubtedly have difficulty in moving toward autonomy in action and decision making. And those whose identities are not clearly evident to themselves will have problems in establishing satisfactory intimate relationships with others and, later, in becoming truly generative in their attitudes toward the young.

In Erikson's thinking, individual development not only moves in a cyclic process through a single life span, but there is also a cyclic movement that joins one generation to those succeeding it. The first of the eight ages features a crisis of trust; the last a crisis of integrity, or complete inner and interpersonal trustworthiness. Erikson views human beings as having the potential to progress, over the span of a lifetime, from an early relationship of trust to final integrity. Trust is mutually established between children and parents or parent substitutes who are themselves in the process of moving toward integrity. The children can then begin to move toward the eventual point of attaining integrity of their own. If the circle of relationships includes an elderly person of integrity in whom parents and offspring can repose their full trust, both will thereby advance in the direction of attaining their own integrity. Thus, as the life cycle of the elderly person nears completion, its fruits contribute to the early phases of the cycles of succeeding generations.

Transactional Analysis

Whereas Freudian personality theory emphasizes the role of the id instincts in impelling and shaping human growth, Erikson's theory centers on the functions of the ego. Drawing on the sciences of sociology and anthropology, Erikson recognizes those forces in the larger milieu that influence individual development either directly or indirectly through the family. Eric Berne's (1961) **transactional analysis** (TA) also concentrates on ego development and function as the predominant aspect of personality. Like Freudian analysts, however, Berne narrowly dwells on the quality of very early parent-child relationships and their influence on personality in later life.

In Berne's model of personality structure and function, the interacting id, ego, and superego postulated by Freud are replaced respectively by **Child** (C), **Adult** (A), and **Parent** (P) ego states. The transactional aspect of transactional analysis explains, in a familiar manner, many commonly encountered interpersonal interactions inside and outside the counseling situation. The formulations introduced by Berne bring into focus the irrational values that determine many of our attitudes and, therefore, much of our behavior in relation to self, to other persons, and to the existential world created by each of us to live in. Because key TA concepts are less commonly encountered by most helping professionals than those of Freud and Erikson, they are mapped out in some detail in the remainder of this section.

We respond to other people, to ourselves, and to events and circumstances in our lives from the ego state in which energy is aroused. At the moment of response, the real self is experienced as residing in the currently energized state: Parent, Adult, or Child. We are likely to shift from one state to another with different persons, and even from moment to moment with the same person.

Within each of us, one ego state tends to predominate and to therefore become our usual window on the world. The person who generally responds from the Parent state is the one who gives advice freely, is critical and judgmental, and assumes responsibility for what is conceived as the well-being of self and others. The constant Adult is objective, reasoning, and reasonable, and expects others, for the most part, to be responsible for themselves. The habitual Child looks to others or to the internal Parent for approval or disapproval, tends to avoid responsible choices, and longs for a future free of work and worry.

When two people interact, the ego state in control (P, A, or C) of each person can be identified by observing the **transaction**, or unit of communication, that takes place. A transaction may take a course that is parallel or crossed. A **parallel transaction**, also called complementary, travels back and forth between like ego states in the two participants. For example:

A to A_1: *Did you enjoy the lecture last night?*
A_1 to A: *Yes, but there were some statements I didn't agree with.*

A **crossed transaction** occurs when the response, instead of coming from A_1 as addressed, comes from C_1 or P_1. For example:

C_1 to A: *I wish you hadn't persuaded me to go. I was too tired to get anything from it.*

or

P_1 to A: *Yes. It would have done you good to hear it too.*

A crossed transaction is inimical to openness in communication because it conveys that the second speaker is not really listening. Contrary to the first speaker's intention, it activates a different ego state from the one addressed. Complementary or crossed transactions may contain ulterior verbal messages or may be accompanied by nonverbal signs that carry unspoken communications. Such hidden, emotionally expressive messages are generally classed as **metacommunication**.

By examining our own transactions with others and with events, we can recognize which of the three inner states is in the driver's seat at any given moment, or perhaps most of the time. We may note that we allow some people to bring out the Child in us, others the Parent, and still others the Adult. Quite apart from our interactions with others, we may find the Child steering us into a tearful or rebellious response to frustrating circumstances or the Parent charging us with needless trepidations when we undertake a difficult task or with feelings of guilt over the possibility of an inadequacy. Then again, we may be encouraged by finding our Adult in competent control. The gratification that this recognition gives us acts as its own reinforcement.

As developed by Harris (1973), the TA concept of **life positions** enables us to identify our prevailing view of self in relation to other people and to life in general. One's life position represents a summation of one's system of values as well as the type and extent of one's commitment. The four life positions are:

1. I'm Not OK–You're OK
2. I'm Not OK–You're Not OK
3. I'm OK–You're Not OK
4. I'm OK–You're OK

The first position, if it obtains in adult life, is an immature stance—a carry-over of the dependent, insecure position of the young child. The Child ego state is, therefore, the major source of "I'm Not OK–You're OK" energy, and from it relationships are formed and decisions made with Child characteristics in ascendancy.

The second and third positions are seen by transactional analysts as indicative of psychopathology. The second, or "I'm Not OK–You're Not OK" position, is that of the all-time loser and blamer of others for failure. From this position reality is distorted, sometimes to the extremes of neurosis or psychotic withdrawal or depression. A continuing conflict between the Parent and Child states within the personality is basic to this position. In the third position, "I'm OK–You're Not OK," the child dethrones the Parent entirely and is completely in control. Criminal, sociopathic, or paranoid trends are likely to result.

In the fourth position, the ideal "OK" position, the Adult state is energetic and dominant. The "I'm OK–You're OK" concept corresponds to Rogers' notion of fullness of functioning (Chapter 4). The feeling-based egocentricity and dependence of childhood gives way to the conceptually validated self-responsibility and work-centered and other-centered commitment of the mature adult.

The "I'm OK–You're OK" person does not look at life through a rose-colored dream. Rather, from this position he or she is able not only to realistically assess the good in self, in others, and in life in general, but also to be painfully aware of life's tragedies and injustices. Energy is devoted to changing what should and can be changed; one avoids wasting one's powers on what cannot be altered. The fourth position, like fullness of functioning, can be attained and maintained only as the result of a gifted genetic and developmental heritage combined with socialization to a responsible self-awareness and to participation in being and becoming in relation with others.

Obviously, many factors are involved in determining one's life position. A component given prominence in TA theory is the interpersonal act of **stroking**. The behavioral equivalent of stroking is positive reinforcement. Stroking includes the many signals a person uses to convey attitudes of liking, interest, acceptance, concern, approval, respect, and esteem to another. The signals range from actual stroking and touching (of an infant, child, or other loved person, for example) to awards, kudos, and applause accorded a public figure (Harris, 1973; Jongeward and James, 1973).

From birth to death, every individual needs "You're OK" strokes, or narcissistic supplies. The infant and child are powerless to progress from a "Not OK" position to an "OK" position without them. Stroking plays an essential part in the interdependence and intimacy of later relationships; its presence or absence is a feature of the games described here and of the psychologic life scripts chosen. Parents teach their children the games that they will play in life and help them write their scripts.

The attainment of authentic intimacy in relationships is essential to one's progress toward the fourth stage or position. Intimacy, as a TA concept, denotes an interaction pattern between people that is free of **psychological games** (Berne, 1964). Games involve ulterior transactions that are partly unconscious. They are directed, not toward intimacy, but toward exploiting the other person in a relationship. The game is made up of complementary transactions that ostensibly take place between two Adult states. But on a metacommunicative level, the transactions go back and forth between Parent and Child or Child and Child.

The ulterior message contains a gimmick, a deceptive snare, to which the concluding transaction supplies an expected payoff—the response sought in the gimmick. The gimmick provides the name of the game: "Yes, But" (I would do better if it weren't for this bum elbow of mine.), "Ain't It Awful," "You Got Me into This," "Kick Me," "If It Weren't for You," "Let's You and Him Fight." Perhaps the commonest game is the childhood source of all the others: "Mine Is Better Than Yours."

The "Yes, But" game proceeds something like this:

A to A_1 (actually C to P_1): *I suppose I should take the sherbet salad.*
A_1 to A (actually P_1 to C): *Well, it's less fattening than the sandwich.*
C to P_1: *I know. I only had one piece of toast for breakfast, though. (gimmick)*
P_1 to C: *Well . . . It's your funeral. (payoff)*

Ulterior to the A to A_1 transaction is an appeal from the Child to the nurturing parent of the second speaker. P_1 is hooked and offers a P response, which C obviously did not want in the first place. C rejects it and finishes the gainer with a type of parental permission. The game might have been prolonged with many "Why Don't You" (P_1 to C) transactions.

Berne (1964) suggests that some games, although exploitative, are more good than bad. He calls one example "Cavalier," in which an older man offers obvious blandishments to a younger woman in the expectation of receiving reciprocal strokes. Other similar games are "Happy to Help," and "They'll Be Glad They Knew Me."

Game playing often becomes a stereotyped mode of communication between two people involved in marital, sibling, parent-child, or work relationships. Game playing can be ended by the initiator, who becomes aware of the significance of the activity, or by the partner, who refuses to reinforce the first move and furnish the payoff.

TA theorists liken the idea of intimacy to Martin Buber's (1970) concept of the I-thou relationship in which each participant fully respects the worth and dignity of the other. Not under compulsion to play games, a person capable of such a relationship is open and therefore vulnerable. To refuse to use others for one's own ends is to expose oneself to the risk of being used by others. But concomitantly, the possibility of a deeply authentic interpersonal encounter exists. Learning that develops a capacity for intimacy in this sense is a major goal of the transactional method of psychoanalysis, as it is for most programs of human relations training and for most other psychotherapies.

One's **psychological script** provides the text for the role one chooses to play in life vis-a-vis the roles one ascribes to other players. Like games, scripts are colloquialized according to their main themes: "Losing My Mind," "Being the Best," "Carrying My Cross," "Putting People Down," "Getting Even," "Being Miserable," "Trying Harder," "Being Trapped," "Getting Stepped On," "Being a Loser," or "Looking for a Pot of Gold" (James and Jongeward, 1971). Perhaps more constructive and more realistic themes exist: "One Day at a Time" or "Win One, Lose One." But the person who is open to existence in its entirety does not need to play games, take on a role, or live out a rigidly predetermined scenario. In TA terms, one is capable of reparenting oneself, thereby liberating the natural originality of the inner Child, developing the nurturing capabilities of the Parent, and replacing games and scripts with honest and complementary Adult transactions with others (Berne, 1972; Steiner, 1974).

THE PERSON–A HUMANISTIC FRAMEWORK

Humanistic psychology and psychotherapy represent a recent departure from prevailing thought in both fields of study. Theorists and practitioners from William James to contemporary writers such as Gordon Allport, Abraham Maslow, and Carl Rogers previously formulated many of the assumptions on which the new movement was based. But it was not until 1962 that a group of psychologists, under Maslow's leadership, agreed to form an organized group designated humanistic psychology (Buhler and Allen, 1972; Nevill, 1977).

The group was primarily interested in developing a science centered on the human being as a whole person–a potentially healthy person (Schultz, 1977). This idea contrasted with behaviorism's atomization of the individual into discrete behaviors and the psychoanalytic view of almost all human behavior as pathologic. Maslow characterized the new approach as a third force in psychology, beyond classical Freudianism and behaviorism. Its emergence signaled a rapprochement between psychology and philosophy–an alliance that had once endured without question. The partnership was strongly repudiated at the turn of the present century as psychology struggled for respectability in the scientific community as a science in its own right. The following brief historical review discloses the origin of a number of themes that characterize the new humanistic movement.

In its original form, the philosophy of humanism flowered during the Renaissance. Erasmus was esteemed as its leading light. Followed by literature and the arts, humanistic philosophy then symbolized the primacy of human beings over abstract principles. Modern humanistic psychology adopted this premise. It borrows from two branches of modern philosophy: phenomenology and its near relative, existentialism. Existentialism stems largely from the mid-nineteenth-century Danish writings of Søren Kierkegaard, which passionately defend subjective, intuitive thought as a more reliable source of knowledge than accumulated facts. Feelings are valued as trustworthy barometers of the significance of experience. Kierkegaard gives vigorous testimony to the obligation of individuals to live out their own truth in their day-to-day existence. Truth as an abstraction is meaningless; the person's relationship to truth gives it significance.

Edmund Husserl is credited with founding phenomenology as a strand of philosophic thought in the second quarter of the present century. Its further development was led by Husserl's pupil in Germany, Martin Heidegger, who was also influenced by Kierkegaard. The essential concern of phenomenology is **meaning**, or intentionality. All one's experience is mediated through one's intentionality–the particular conscious and unconscious meanings which influence one's perceptions and reasoning as well as one's choices and actions (Frankl, 1978; Shaffer, 1978; Yalom, 1980). The only truth that is of moment to me as an individual is my version of it–what it means to me in the here and now of my existence. The most reliable source of further meaning is found in beings and experiences as they present themselves to me as directly discernible phenomena.

Currently, existentialism and phenomenology merge, especially as they are incorporated into humanistic psychology and psychotherapeutic counseling. The French writer Jean-Paul Sartre devoted himself to building a bridge between existential philosophy and psychology. He popularized existential thought, not only in psychological essays, but in novels and plays. Karl Jaspers, a German philosopher-psychopathologist, brought psychiatric insights to bear on the study of philosophy. In this country, Rollo May wrote as an existential psychologist for both professional and popular audiences. The work of Combs et al. (1976) on individual behavior is essentially phenomenological in character. Yalom (1980) examined the relevance to psychotherapy of four basic existential concerns: death, freedom, isolation, and meaninglessness.

Humanistic Concepts

The following overview of key humanistic concepts, drawn mainly from existentialism and phenomenology, will bring the general framework of the model into focus. Because the terms do not generally lend themselves to precise definition, brief descriptive interpretations are included.

The reader will recognize that existential conceptualizations of reality characterize the world view of many in present-day Western culture. They strike a responsive chord, particularly in the young. By symbolizing the person as a total functioning organism interacting intentionally as well as unconsciously with environmental forces, they transcend many dichotomies: body-mind, inner-outer, conscious-unconscious, thought-feeling, subjective-objective (Shaffer, 1978). They are eminently relevant to our study of persons, including ourselves, and to our helping relationships.

Existence vs essence Existentialism was named for its emphasis on existence, rather than essence, as the locus of identity. Earlier philosophies locate the identity of a being in its essence. In that framework, the human individual was seen as a static representative of "man"—one of a class of beings with an essence that shared specific properties common to all members of that class. In contrast, the existentialist view holds that the existing person stands forth (*ex-ists*) as unique. The unique possibilities of each individual's existence are of far greater significance than the properties the individual shares with all others of the same species.

Dasein Dasein literally means "being there" as a unique ontological entity—a person. Dasein is Heidegger's term for existence (Shaffer, 1978). I am the person who is there, not static, but "be-ing," experiencing. I am also growing, becoming, and able to transcend myself in the future of my becoming.

Being-in-the-world Being-in-the-world was coined as a single German word by Heidegger. My dasein can be known only as a total phenomenon engaged in my experiencing of my world. It is a world of my own construction.

There are three modes of being-in-the-world, and the person exists simultaneously in all three. The *world of things* includes things, places, events, and circumstances. The *world of others* refers to the realm of interpersonal, social, and institutional relationships. Finally, *one's own world* is the inner sphere of awareness, perceptions, feelings, meanings, and values peculiar to the self. A human being lives in all three worlds simultaneously and cannot be understood apart from them. Each person, being and becoming and existing in the three worlds that make up his or her one world, is unquestionably unique.

Authenticity To be fully authentic is to be fully intentional, fully human. The authentic person is a *real* person. In being present to the three worlds in their entirety, the authentic person accepts a particular place in the total scheme of things. This person is open to all that experience brings and views it as concrete and clear. The inauthentic person, in contrast, has problems with identity. Consequently, this person experiences disorder and nothingness.

Existential value Individuals are free, within the constraints of the givens of a human life, to define their own existence. They become the persons they are as a result of the sum of their choices. Their three worlds are organized in large part around their own meanings and where each meaning lies with reference to their scale of values. Among a host of relative values, people select and commit themselves to one paramount value (Chapter 3). The key value may be a significant other, an idea, an ideal, or an accomplishment. For some it is a possession or many coveted possessions.

Authentic persons translate their values into a coherent project of existence. Their identity is assured, even in the face of severe threat or loss. With maturity, they grow to integrate the ultimates of existence as values: life, death, good, evil, joy, and suffering. A major source of the alienation, emptiness, and despair that plague our present-day society is the absence, in the experience of many, of a sense of values and commitment to responsibility that gives meaning and purpose to existence.

Commitment and responsibility Authentic persons are committed to action. Based on their values, their choices and actions create their identity and their existence. And in thus choosing themselves, they are responsible, not only to themselves but to all of humanity as well. "In creating the man we want to be, there is not a single one of our acts which does not at the same time create an image of man as we think he ought to be" (Sartre, 1957). The authentic person is therefore committed in self-transcendence to all of humanity.

Existential encounter The individual's existential relationship with another person is characterized by Heidegger as **being-with-another.** An authentic encounter is an articulation of two beings-in-the-world in a relationship of mutual concern, mutual commitment, and mutual responsibility. Buber (1970) distinguishes between **I-thou** and **I-it** relationships. Many of our encounters are of the latter variety. The individual behind the counter or next in line is not a person to us, but merely an "it." Too often, the acquaintance passed by with the usual *How are you?* is unnoticed, except as a thing. A client, a friend, or a family member may be used as an it—someone to be exploited as a means to secure an objective, rather than to regard as a "thou"—an esteemed person.

Through relationships of mutual respect, commitment, and responsibility with others I am capable of creating my authentic existence. Reciprocally, I enable others to fashion their own freedom as separate, authentic persons.

The essentially humanistic nature of Rogers' client-centered approach to counseling is apparent in the discussion in Chapter 4. Rogers' original conceptualizations set the stage for the introduction of existential therapy in this country. His theoretical base continues to be developed by successive generations of psychological counselors. For those who base their approaches specifically on existential concepts, cohesiveness around a separate body of existential theory is unlikely to develop.

The humanist uses, as a point of departure, the existential assumption that experience can only be known directly. If examined through the screen of a theoretical structure, experience is not apprehended as an existing reality. Rather than dwelling on a client's past, counseling focuses on the client's present mode of experiencing. The causes of a client's difficulties are only important to the extent that they hold meaning for the client in the present. Intellectualizing about past cause-effect relationships does not make for forward movement in experiencing. Expressing present feelings about past events may indeed help in finding new meanings in the here and now of existence. But the client's becoming must start from his or her position of being-in-the-world at the present moment.

Another premise that is relevant to humanistic helping is that, being human, the individual is free to make choices and is responsible for their outcomes. No helpful purpose is served if the counselor undermines this realistic connection by appropriating the client's freedom to choose or the client's accountability for the outcomes of his or her choices (Yalom, 1980).

The aim of humanistic helping is to advance the client's becoming toward unique authenticity and commitment. Accordingly, helper and client work together to preserve and enhance the client's singular mode of experiencing. The principal helping modality is existential encounter, an I-thou relationship. The helper, by virtue of personal authenticity, creates a climate in which the client can freely examine experiencing and openly express its all-important feeling and value content. The indispensable skill demanded of the helper is that of **presence** (May, 1961). To be present is to be fully there, an entire person (dasein) to the client. In the authentic encounter of the helping relationship, the humanist reaches out in every possible way to meet the client on the threshold of intentionality.

Whenever two people participate with openness in sharing the meanings that are truly significant to them, each becomes more uniquely human in the process. The client's sense of values is central to the helping encounter. The humanistic helper does not expect that his or her own values will be adopted, but there are times when those values may become a topic of discussion. In any human encounter, this mode of sharing is a vital factor in our growth as persons. To know how another reacts to what we are and what we value moves us along in experiencing. It reveals interpersonal and situational nuances that we have not heretofore taken into account. Efforts may sometimes be needed to awaken the client's esteem for the meaning lent to life by an appreciation of its enduring values and by a sense of one's responsibility for translating them into action (Frankl, 1978).

Consistent with the humanistic ideal, humanistic counseling is not in itself a system of psychologic treatment. Rather, it is a frame of reference, a value structure that may be adapted to any framework, whether theoretic or existential. In keeping with the attitudes conceptualized in this section, no further portion of this book offers a body of tenets for the professional helper to follow in a humanistic approach to counseling. The author's intention is to make humanism a theme running through all of the remaining chapters. Each aspect of counseling treated here is approached from a humanistic-existential point of view.

References

Arbuckle, D. S. 1975. *Counseling and psychotherapy: An existential-humanistic view.* 3rd ed. Boston: Allyn and Bacon.

Berne, E. 1961. *Transactional analysis in psychotherapy.* New York: Grove.

——. 1964. *Games people play.* New York: Grove.

——. 1972. *What do you say after you say hello?* New York: Grove.

Brammer, L. M. 1979. *The helping relationship: Process and skills.* 2nd ed. Englewood Cliffs, N. J.: Prentice-Hall.

Buber, M. 1970. *I and thou.* New York: Scribner.

Buhler, C., and Allen, M. 1972. *Introduction to humanistic psychology.* Monterey, Calif.: Brooks/Cole.

Child, I. 1973. *Humanistic psychology and the research tradition: Their several virtues.* New York: Wiley.

Combs, A. W.; Richards, A. C.; and Richards, F. 1976. *Perceptual psychology: A perceptual approach to behavior.* New York: Harper & Row.

Erikson, E. H. 1959. *Identity and the life cycle.* New York: International Universities Press.

——. 1963. *Childhood and society.* 2nd ed. New York: Norton.

Frankl, V. E. 1978. *The unheard cry for meaning: Psychotherapy and humanism.* New York: Simon & Schuster.

Freud, S. 1949. *An outline of psychoanalysis.* Translated by James Strachey. New York: Norton.

Harris, T. A. 1973. *I'm OK–You're OK.* New York: Harper & Row.

James, M., and Jongeward, D. 1971. *Born to win: Transactional analysis with gestalt experiments.* Reading, Mass.: Addison-Wesley.

Jongeward, D., and James, M. 1973. *Winning with people–Group exercises in transactional analysis.* Reading, Mass.: Addison-Wesley.

Lange, S. P. 1978. Transactional analysis in nursing. *Behavioral concepts and nursing intervention.* 2nd ed. C. E. Carlson and B. Blackwell, editors. Philadelphia: Lippincott.

Lewis, J. M. 1978. *To be a therapist: The teaching and learning.* New York: Brunner/Mazel.

Liebert, R. M., and Spiegler, M. D. 1978. *Personality: Strategies for the study of man.* 3rd ed. Homewood, Ill.: Dorsey.

Maddi, S. R. 1980. *Personality theories: A comparative analysis.* 4th ed. Homewood, Ill.: Dorsey.

Mahrer, A. R. 1978. *Experiencing: A humanistic theory of psychology and psychiatry.* New York: Brunner/Mazel.

May, Rollo, editor. 1969. *Existential psychology.* New York: Random House.

Mellecker, J. 1976. Transactional analysis for non-TA counselors. *Counseling directions in theory and practice.* G. S. Belkin, editor. Dubuque, Iowa: Kendall/Hunt.

Nevill, D. D. 1977. *Humanistic psychology: New frontiers.* New York: Gardner.

Nye, R. D. 1975. *Three views of man: Perspectives from Sigmund Freud, B. F. Skinner, and Carl Rogers.* Belmont, Calif.: Wadsworth.

Paterson, J. G., and Zderad, L. T. 1976. *Humanistic nursing.* New York: Wiley.

Rogers, C. R. 1961. *On becoming a person.* Boston: Houghton Mifflin.

——. 1980. *A way of being.* Boston: Houghton Mifflin.

Sartre, Jean-Paul. 1957. *Existentialism and human emotions.* New York: Philosophical Library.

——. 1965. *Essays in existentialism.* New York: Citadel.

Schultz, D. 1977. *Growth psychology: Models of the healthy personality.* New York: Van Nostrand Reinhold.

Shaffer, J. B. P. 1978. *Humanistic psychology.* Englewood Cliffs, N. J.: Prentice-Hall.

Shertzer, B., and Stone, S. C. 1981. *Fundamentals of counseling.* 3rd ed. Boston: Houghton Mifflin.

Steiner, C. M. 1974. *Scripts people live: Transactional analysis of life scripts.* New York: Grove.

Waelder, R. 1960. *Basic theory of psychoanalysis.* New York: International Universities Press.

Welch, D. I.; Tate, G.; and Richards, F., editors. 1978. *Humanistic psychology: A source book.* Buffalo, N. Y.: Prometheus.

Yalom, I. D. 1980. *Existential psychotherapy.* New York: Basic Books.

CHAPTER 2

Concepts of Self and Becoming

THE SELF-CONCEPT

FACETS OF SELF

SELF AS BECOMING

COGNITIVE ASPECTS OF BECOMING

THEORY AND HELPER ATTITUDES

This chapter further develops the idea of self and contrasts it to the concept of personality. In psychoanalytic thinking, touched on in Chapter 1, the analyst sometimes views the individual as an organismic object of external observation, diagnosis, and curative ministrations. From a more humanistically oriented viewpoint, the counselor engages in interaction with a client who is a self-observing and self-monitoring agent. The client's subjective self is central to the counseling process.

THE SELF-CONCEPT

To go back a little in time from the emergence of the American existential movement, two psychologists who fully explored the notion of **self** were Carl Rogers and Gordon Allport. Their findings provide guideposts for the cognitive self-observation of both counselors and clients. The Rogerian **self-concept** and **self-ideal** (1959) are "here-and-now" phenomena potentially available to a person's experiencing at any given moment. Combined, yet sometimes at odds with one another, they respectively represent a total self-image of the *I* or *me* as it now exists and that part of a visualized I or me that I desire to bring into being.

As an existential phenomenon, the self-concept embraces within its borders the individual's experiencing of his or her private world of the moment. The process may be thought to include recurring elements of the self-ideal. Although this perceptual gestalt possesses consistency and continuity, it is at the same time fluid and changing. It may be characterized as a process internal to the individual and as a structure with elements that are to some extent externally identifiable.

The self-concept functions to maintain one's identity in its stability, its unity, and its separateness within one's own world of perceptions. Because it is the growing edge of potential self-actualization, it is central to becoming. It pushes in the direction of fullness of functioning as a person. A self-actualizing tendency is present at birth and operates throughout life. If a given experience appears to the self-concept as potentially maintaining or enhancing the self-concept and therefore conducive to self-esteem, or positive self-regard, it is received with openness and integrated into the total structure. The consequent enrichment and enlargement of the self-concept signifies growth of the person.

If, instead, an experience is viewed as incongruent with the self and therefore a threat to positive self-regard, a state of anxiety ensues. Using various mechanisms of denial or distortion, the self-concept rejects this experience by defending itself, in which case shrinking and hardening of some part of the border of the self-concept occurs. Note that, within limits, defensiveness as a response to anxiety serves an adaptive purpose to the organism. It functions to define the separateness and individual distinctiveness of the self-concept. Complete assimilation of all experience, if it were possible, would provide no direction for growth. One would be entirely at the mercy of one's inner dynamics and outer circumstances. Nevertheless, a relative degree of openness and flexibility of the self to experience are supremely necessary conditions of becoming.

With a succession of habitually defensive, rejecting responses, the self-concept becomes constricted, inhibited, and rigidified, and the person's functioning and growth are impeded. One becomes a prisoner behind a self-constructed, thick-walled, defensive facade. To some extent, each of us is already trapped behind, or perhaps occasionally tripped up by, defensive blocks we place in the way of our own growth toward maturity. Of these, the tendency to place blame outside ourselves for our mistakes is probably the most common. The first step toward breaking through this or any similar barrier to openness is recognizing and naming it for what it is. Only thus do we become alert to our ways of using it. With awareness and use of a **secondary process**—cognition—we may eventually recondition ourselves to face our blunders with more open, authentic responses.

FACETS OF SELF

Allport's conceptualization (1955) of the **functions of the proprium** (Latin for one's own) offers a taxonomy that is useful in segmentally describing our sense of self: our subjective impression of what is peculiarly our own. Because his concepts have also been recognized as adding to the theory of personality psychology, they have been further developed by numerous authors, usually as somewhat separate entities. The most widely exploited is Allport's notion of **bodily sense**, or bodily self, often called *body image.* Allport, however, considered the various functions fused together. Taken as a whole, they represent an inner view of the self. Studying Allport's model offers food for reflection to add to our self-awareness and to our understanding of the inner world of our clients (Schultz, 1977).

The propriate functions are value-oriented aspects of self and its becoming. We see ourselves functioning in relation to our values—what we become is what we inwardly value. The fact that bodily sense is a value-oriented function is evident. Estimation of the bodily self—from infancy the most concrete aspect of the *me*—is the foundation for and a continuing influence on other evaluative aspects of the proprium such as self-image, self-identity, and self-esteem. Bodily sense is the impression of separate organic unity. Human beings, in developed countries at least, value aspects of the bodily self, devalue others, and reject others outright. Although most of us accept and esteem certain aspects of our physical makeup, there are sure to be elements we are reluctant to own. To a greater or lesser degree, we are not at ease with our bodies. We resent aspects of our bodily configuration, appearance, or processes, and above all, symptoms of bodily "dis-ease."

For example, I may appreciate the fact that my complexion is clear, but I hate my stringy hair. I'm too thin, too fat, too tall, too short, but at least I have good legs. I am luckier than people who are born with kidney disease or epilepsy, but when I have a headache, I tense myself against it as if it were something apart from myself, inflicted by a hostile force from outside. All such responses are determining factors in self-identity, self-esteem and self-image—in short, in all facets of the proprium. All are potent influences on becoming.

Self-identity may be defined as the sense of one's continuity and physical separateness. It is related to bodily sense, which delimits our organic separateness. We have already examined Erikson's elaboration of the concept of identity crisis. Bugental (1976) focuses on identity as an existential theme. The sense of one's continuity and separateness develops gradually in the early years of life and becomes of crucial importance, as we can all attest, during adolescence. Because it involves an impression of separateness, its development is, to a great extent, an outcome of our relationships with other people. As I gradually disentangle my feelings, thoughts, attitudes, and values from those of family members and of my immediate world, I develop strength and confidence in myself as a unique person. In the colorful slang expression, I move in the direction I must take to get myself together.

The transition will never be complete. A degree of separateness is necessary, but so is a degree of connectedness. I need enough closeness to others to enable me to recognize the validity of feelings such as anger or grief as motivators of their behavior. But in order to develop and maintain the continuity of my unique identity, I also need enough distance to keep me from responding automatically to the expression of another's anger or grief with similar, involuntary emotions.

The propriate function of **ego-enhancement**, or self-esteem, has much in common with Rogers' (1959) notion of **positive self-regard**. Rogers relates self-regard to the degree of congruence between one's self-concept and one's self-ideal. In Maslow's scheme (1970), **self-esteem** ranks high in the hierarchy of human needs. Our experience bears out the commonly held theory that self-esteem is a precondition of becoming—of growth toward self-actualization. In any intercurrent endeavor, we are more likely to be successful if we hold our own capabilities in high regard.

The degree of our self-esteem is directly related to the esteem we receive from others. This is especially true in childhood, when our self-evaluation largely depends on the evaluations made of us by our parents and parent surrogates. But if self-esteem remains too much an outcome of positive regard received from others, our experiences as adults lead us to repeated defensive denial and distortion, with their attendant anxiety and consequent narrowing and solidifying of the boundaries of the self.

Lack of self-esteem can be readily recognized in the behavior of people who continually belittle themselves and in self-aggrandizement and other self-promoting conversation and action. Persons who value themselves can afford to accept themselves largely as they are. They are relatively at ease with themselves and, therefore, with others without having to assert or disparage themselves publicly.

Allport's concept of **ego-extension** is another value-connected self-function. We acknowledge ownership according to whether things represent assets or liabilities to us. In the process of becoming, we annex to ourselves not only material possessions, but ideals, causes, loyalties, and other such deep-seated motivators. We also claim ownership of people: *my* brother, *my* boss, *my* doctor. Several authors have developed a specific aspect of self-extension under topics such as *territoriality* and *personal space.* They demonstrate that the size of the area available for living and acting is as important as people and possessions to being a complete person.

There is also interchangeability among the various components of self-extension. In long-term care facilities and in the single rooms or apartments of the solitary elderly, the tendency to clutter is recognizably typical. As physical, interpersonal, and cultural deprivation occurs, the satisfactions that were formerly attainable are often replaced by a multitude of valueless possessions to which the residents become inordinately attached.

However the notion is categorized, the self-concept in all its facets is given key significance by humanistic theorists. Combs (1971) labels the self-concept "the product and producer of experience," and the "basis of reality." It provides a transparent screen through which to see, hear, understand, and evaluate everything in terms of the real and the ideal. The self-concept is, as it were, one's window on the world. Consequently, one's image of oneself is well worth examining and reflecting upon. Growth in self-awareness makes up much of the process of learning the art of counseling and the interactive process of counseling itself.

SELF AS BECOMING

Three authors may be primarily credited with enhancing our understanding of the significant processes involved in becoming. Each has described and categorized a different thread that intertwines with the others throughout the lifespan of the individual. A. H. Maslow (1970) is widely known for his theory of human motivation, organized around his familiar hierarchy of five sets of basic human needs; Jean Piaget traces the course of cognitive development (Brainerd, 1978); and Lawrence Kohlberg is engaged in a long-term study of the development of moral reasoning (1973).

The following discussion presents an idealized picture of the higher reaches of becoming. Note that becoming is not entirely a matter of willing to become. In actuality, the self is engaged in the complexities of being-in-the-world.

Counselor and client alike have arrived at a momentary present through processes that are facilitated or impeded by elements of genetic and biologic inheritance, by familial and other sociocultural determinants, as well as by their own volition.

In Maslow's theoretical scheme, the self is potentially capable of developing from infantile dependence on immediate physiologic gratification to a stage of relatively mature **self-actualization**. Paramount motivators at this point of fullness of functioning are the needs for self-identity, self-realization, and self-direction. They represent an ideal phase of becoming beyond the anxious search for security, love, and esteem. Self-actualizing people largely take on the task of their own being and becoming and make themselves actual, real, creative parts of the world in which they find themselves. They are less preoccupied with the Child within them who clings in dependent relationships with other Parents to ensure that childish needs are met, and they are more open to Adult to Adult transactions.

Maslow searched for and extensively studied people he considered self-actualizing. He calls this branch of study **the psychology of being**, contrasting the term *being* with the word *becoming* (1962). The objects of his study are people whose becoming is so nearly complete that they have reached a state in which they are more able than most to simply *be.* What have such persons become? They have become themselves—real persons because they are *realized* persons. They are genuine, authentic.

The term self-actualization may be used to denote attaining an apex in progress toward becoming fully human. To be fully human is to excel in all the traits that distinguish homo sapiens from other creatures. Like fullness of function, self-actualization is a relative term. Perfection is of course not attainable in anyone's life. Self-actualizing people are more highly ethical than most—people of integrity who make judgments and choices according to definite principles and sharply differentiated values. Moreover, these values are essentially affirmative in nature. Such persons, who may be encountered in all walks of life, are singularly free of petty hostilities, intolerances, and prejudices. They regard others as equals. Hence, they neither act nor feel that they are superior or inferior to others because of status differences or because of others' inherent attitudes of preeminence or inadequacy.

Self-actualizing people possess a marked degree of autonomy; they assess situations and arrive at decisions with minimal regard for popular opinions or popular taboos. They are secure enough to be real, to rely on themselves even in times and situations of insecurity, and tend to enjoy the unfamiliar rather than fear or blindly oppose it. They look for adventure in the unexpected rather than being dismayed by it and creatively approach whatever they may engage in. They have an appreciative sense of humor and enjoy the ridiculous, yet have no need to use humor at others' expense.

The self-actualizing person is a committed person—committed to creative work and accomplishment as an essential part of the rhythm of existence—but he or she is committed first and foremost to other persons. Because humans are social beings, they can never become fully realized or fully functioning, except in intimacy with other persons. The person who is moving toward wholeness, integration, and fulfillment recognizes that being a person in the fullest sense means being open to relating with other persons, not refusing to enter into the being of another, and not refusing another entrance into one's own being. This is authentic encounter—the intimacy characteristic of maturity. Such people are well on their way toward the self-transcendent consummation of all their powers, toward virtue in the original meaning of the word.

COGNITIVE ASPECTS OF BECOMING

The discussion of self has thus far focused mainly on the affective components of being and becoming. The remainder of this chapter offers a sample of the ideas of two contemporary theorists who describe the rational, or intellectual, attributes of self. These capacities do not possess an independent existence. It is obvious that their effectiveness may be enhanced or diminished by emotional states. Likewise, our feeling states are amenable to modification resulting from our use or misuse of powers of reasoning. As helping professionals, grasping the salient factors involved in cognitive functioning provides us with a basis for adjusting our expectations of rationality in ourselves and our clients.

The humanist is convinced that most individuals can bring about change in their behavior and attitudes, and even in the underlying system of values that determines them, as an outcome of rational intention on their part. I am a human person, and I am, therefore, much more than an organism actuated by blind instincts, prejudices, and irrational affect. Unless my circumstances are severely limiting, I am capable of recognizing the effects of such inner dynamisms and of making reasoned choices and modifications among them.

Jean Piaget, a Swiss psychologist, has achieved world-wide recognition for his studies of cognitive development. Piaget's interest has focused mainly on the processes involved in concept formation and its relationship to the gradual moral development that occurs throughout the formative years of human life. Lawrence Kohlberg, a professor of education and social science at Harvard University, using Piaget's method of posing cognitive and moral problems to children of different age levels, has identified and described a series of stages of moral reasoning.

Piaget and Kohlberg have thus concerned themselves with aspects of the self such as the capacity for rational thought and the consequent acquisition of a belief system that guides a person's choices. Recall that Erikson views **ideological perspectives** to be of vital importance in establishing one's identity. Beginning with Freud, psychologic theorists have designated cognition and decision making (a partly conscious and partly unconscious process) as functions of the ego or, in Allport's terminology, of the self as **rational coper**. All the cognitive-emotive choices an individual human being makes are based on his or her individualized system of values. Our choices determine what we are and what we will become.

Piaget's studies led him to conclude that a capacity for mature cognitive functioning normally develops during the adolescent years, making **hypothetico-deductive reasoning** possible. A teenager can be expected to utilize **formal operations**—the kind of thought used in thinking about thinking and ideas. Cognition, previously limited to more concrete, inductive operations, now relies on conscious symbolization. When a hypothesis is advanced, facts and events are analyzed to support or contradict it, and conclusions are drawn in accordance with the results. Metaphors become understandable.

Piaget's conclusions rest on the notion that formal operations consist essentially in the process of problem solving. Ongoing studies of cognition show that analogic reasoning is more likely to be used than deductive reasoning. We reach our conclusions mainly by an intuitive process of comparing what is new in our experience with something we have already found to be plausible. Decisions are then made on the basis of probability, not logical certainty (Hunt, 1982).

As adolescents gain in social awareness and objectivity, reasoning of both types is enhanced. Associations between behavior and social expectations take meaningful shape, as do those concerning space, time, and causality. If the environment stimulates them, concepts of tolerance and justice are developed, and relative valuation is used in reasoning that has social and political concomitants.

But the capacity for formal operations, like other human capabilities, develops only insofar as it is adequately nurtured. In an intellectually and ideologically impoverished environment, the adolescent's cognitive choices remain dependent on his or her previously emergent capacity for **concrete**, or externally triggered, **operations**. Rather than being based on reasoning, decision making may continue to be guided entirely by the accumulated prejudices and catch phrases that combine to form parochial chauvinism and bigotry.

Kohlberg's model offers a means to categorize the various value orientations that determine the person's moral-ethical choices. Here again, the actual human norm probably lies half-way through the developmental series. Most adults continue to base their moral choices essentially on identification with the absolute values held by family or other social reference groups or held as a national average. The relative few considered to have attained a fully mature state of moral discrimination are guided by universal ethical principles such as the Golden Rule. Their ideas of universal justice carry them beyond the values of their immediate social milieu. They accept different ideologies and mores as right for different individuals, social groups, and peoples.

Both Piaget and Kohlberg find the subject of transition or progress from one stage to another a very complex developmental phenomenon requiring the gradual transformation of one somewhat painfully built structure of reasoning to another that eventually supplants it. Like any accomplishment in human growth toward maturity, mastery can be attained only at the expense of anxiety-laden effort to open up and rebuild the previously safe, protective borders of the self-concept. In the models of both theorists, the cyclic relationship between value systems and achievement of mature identity—movement in the direction of becoming fully functioning, self-actualizing persons—is evident. Interactions with people, things, and events result from choices, whether or not these choices are made on a completely rational level.

Each of us makes innumerable decisions, arranged in an extended chain that only ends with death. In every choice, we select, on the basis of what we value, from among two or more alternatives. The type and number of alternatives available to us depend on many factors, among which are biological inheritance and the many influences that we encounter in life up to the point a given choice is made. In humanistic thinking, the person's value system is not shaped entirely by a random combination of genetic and environmental factors. Rather, in the choices made throughout the course of a life, the individual is an active participant in molding a personal set of moral standards (Child, 1973).

THEORY AND HELPER ATTITUDES

Reflection on observed patterns of thinking, feeling, acting, and interacting, enlightened by the findings of other observers of human behavior, is essential to the growth and artistry of counselors. This becomes a way of life for helping professionals, and embraces both the professional and personal aspects of our experiences. As participant-observers of our own and our clients' behavior and relationships, we are persistently alert to the fact that the influence that is operating is a two-way process. And to the extent that each of us is an authentic and unified person, we do not turn off this awareness in the transition from professional to personal transactions. Through interaction with others all human beings come to define and redefine themselves as persons. As counselors, we strive to continually grow in self-knowledge and in our ability to use it as an analogous means of knowing others.

There are limits, however, to the extent that knowledge of self or knowledge derived from theorists can be applied to a given individual. In considering the natures of our clients, we must repeatedly remind ourselves that each person is unique. Because this chapter deals with theoretical findings that apply to some degree to all human beings, we must be alert beforehand to the limitations inherent in such data.

Some characteristics in each individual we relate to differ from those of everyone else we know. Many human problems arise from the lack of esteem people tend to have for those who differ from themselves in obvious ways. We are inclined to think and act as if *our* way were the only way. In individual and group relations we readily accept only those who comply with the behaviors expected in *our* social set or in *our* religious, national, racial, or professional groups. There is need fulfillment, of course, in the assurance that we are part of an in-group or that we are acceptable to a given reference group. But when we exclude others because they are different, we narrow our experience and, ultimately, ourselves.

As humanistic helpers, we recognize that innumerable personal differences exist in physiology, capability, values, and interests. Even when similarities among qualities exist, they continually undergo modification from differing cultural, educational, social, personal, and interpersonal influences. We must appreciate that these myriad differences exist, and we must value the resulting "different-ness" of the individual. Only thus can we expect to help our clients appreciate their existential uniqueness and, ultimately, that of others. They, too, can learn to relate only by beginning where each person is at the moment of encounter.

References

Allport, G. W. 1955. *Becoming: Basic considerations for a psychology of personality.* New Haven: Yale University Press.

——. 1965. *Pattern and growth in personality.* New York: Holt, Rinehart and Winston.

Berscheid, E.; Walster, E.; and Bohrnstedt, G. Body Image. *Psychology Today,* November 1973, pp. 118–131.

Brainerd, C. J. 1978. *Piaget's theory of intelligence.* Englewood Cliffs, N. J.: Prentice-Hall.

Bugental, J. F. 1976. *The search for existential identity.* San Francisco: Jossey-Bass.

Child, I. L. 1973. *Humanistic psychology and the research tradition: Their several virtues.* New York: Wiley.

Combs, A. W.; Avila, D. L.; and Purkey, W. W. 1971. *Helping relationships: Basic concepts for the helping professions.* Boston: Allyn and Bacon.

Elkind, D. Giant in the nursery—Jean Piaget. *New York Times Magazine,* 26 May 1968.

Evans, R. I. 1973. *Jean Piaget: The man and his ideas.* Translated by Eleanor Duckworth. New York: Dutton.

Heatherington, E. M., and Parke, R. D., editors. 1981. *Contemporary readings in child psychology.* 2nd ed. New York: McGraw-Hill.

Hunt, M. How the mind works. *New York Times Magazine,* 24 January 1982.

Kohlberg, L. 1973. The claim to moral adequacy of a highest stage of moral judgment. *J. Philos.* 70:630–646.

Maslow, A. H. 1962. *Toward a psychology of being.* Princeton, N. J.: Van Nostrand.

——. 1970. *Motivation and personality.* 2nd ed. New York: Harper & Row.

Rogers, C. R. 1959. A theory of therapy, personality, and interpersonal relationships as developed in the client-centered framework. *Psychology: A study of a science.* Sigmund Kock, editor, vol. 3. New York: McGraw-Hill.

Schultz, D. 1977. *Growth psychology: Models of the healthy personality.* New York: Van Nostrand Reinhold.

Sutterly, D. C., and Donnelly, G. F. 1973. *Perspectives in human development: Nursing throughout the life cycle.* Philadelphia: Lippincott.

CHAPTER 3

Self-Awareness in Counseling

The preceding chapters form an essential prologue to investigating self-awareness and its significance in counseling. The thinking of the theorists cited in Chapters 1 and 2 continues to demand interpretation and reinterpretation throughout the helping professional's career. A thoroughgoing eclecticism broadens the possibilities open to the professional for depth of human understanding, deters adherence to one-sided categorizations and dogmas, and encourages viewing a client as a person rather than a personality type, with motivations and responses peculiar to him or her alone.

The insights of theoreticians only provide us with a platform from which to launch our own personal quest for tested and internalized knowledge and wisdom. When we make ourselves the subjects of our own observation and meditation, we have an added source of data that is always available, convenient to use, and economically feasible–ideal qualities in a subject.

SELF-AWARENESS AS A COUNSELING VALUE

Largely through the influence of humanistic psychology, the concept of **self-awareness**, or more popularly, **consciousness raising**, came into prominence. Whereas consciousness raising often denotes an orientation of the self toward a specific issue, self-awareness has much broader connotations. The self-awareness the humanistic helper aspires to for both self and client is an authentic openness to the perception of experiencing. The participle *experiencing* is sometimes used to indicate that perception is an ongoing process. It is not static in content. Experiencing includes both internal and external events–one's own feelings and values as well as one's perceptions of external behavior, situations, and circumstances. Authenticity lies in the correspondence between one's perceptions and objective reality. And to be open implies receptiveness–an acceptance of reality comparatively free of defensive self-deception.

Self-awareness is not self-consciousness. The self-acceptance that authentic self-awareness brings precludes excessive concern with the impression one makes on others. The self-conscious individual lacks the freedom that openness confers and is enclosed in a defensively armored self-concept. The real self is shut away from others, and others are shut out of the real self.

An adequate degree of self-acceptance must be achieved before open acceptance of others–an essential characteristic of the humanistic helper–is possible. Persons who stringently deny their self-worth are constantly on the defensive against themselves and others, hence rigid, unyielding persons. They bring to their relationships the anxiety and resentment that arise from self-blame within, and they are fed by the accompanying need to project blame to others without. In TA terms, *I'm not OK, so you're not OK either.* It is apparent that professionals fixed at this level of growth as persons need more help than they are able to give to clients.

In the education of a psychiatrist or a psychiatric nurse clinical specialist, and in some instances of a clinical psychologist, a course of personal psychotherapy is commonly recommended as part of the professional curriculum. Humanistic counseling students who begin to realize that they are hampered by inadequacies that render them incapable of the unconditional acceptance of people that is the hallmark of humanistic helping are well advised to seek counseling or psychotherapy themselves. Their experience as clients will be invaluable in enabling them to judge their ultimate fitness for the counseling function.

Before one can recognize one's emotional capacities in their various ramifications, a degree of general self-awareness must exist. Much of the content and methodology of any program of counseling education is therefore aimed at cultivating self-awareness in the student. The breadth and depth of self-understanding that is ultimately desirable can be attained only over a period of years of gradual growth. But even in a comparatively brief course of study, a good beginning can be made. It provides the necessary momentum for the sincerely motivated student to proceed thereafter largely alone, but always with continued study, and with the help of colleagues as needed. The remaining sections of this chapter offer a means of embarking on a modest beginning.

ACHIEVING SELF-AWARENESS

Fully functioning persons in the humanistic model are individuals who consciously experience and accurately communicate the full range of emotions, both negative and positive. They engage in examining their values and are able to identify their major guiding principles. This represents an ideal that is pursued conscientiously by the humanistic counselor. For students of counseling, the early steps toward achieving awareness and acceptance of their own feelings and values and communicating them without distortion are here ordered in a logical sequence. The following breakdown of self-awareness into working components outlines the main topics of this chapter:

1. Identifying one's present feelings accurately
2. Owning feelings as part of oneself
3. Identifying and owning values
4. Communicating feelings and values objectively

Identifying Present Feelings Accurately

Only through long-term study and practice can we learn to identify our own feelings accurately. To be able to name feelings is a necessary preliminary to the more difficult task that follows. A productive first step for the student is to abstractly identify as many positive and negative emotions as possible. A group of students will be able to come up with many more classes of feeling than an individual can. Individuals or groups can greatly expand the list by using a thesaurus. Once a working list is under way, it takes on meaning only insofar as the individuals concerned continue to reflect on the part played by each type of feeling in their own existence. This exercise leads naturally into the second phase of developing self-awareness: identifying present feelings.

Experiencing the totality of one's current feeling life includes all shades of the physical and emotional, as well as the positive and negative emotions. Physical and emotional states cannot be separated for theoretical examination as readily as feelings identified as positive or negative. Every emotional state has its accompanying physiologic phenomena. Physical changes and sensations often provide us with clues that enable us to recognize their emotional concomitants. The universal complex of feelings we call anxiety (Chapter 6) is a prime example of this type of concurrence.

Joy may be looked on as anxiety's opposite. It, too, is a composite of feelings: delight, fulfillment, and refreshment, along with the warm glow that comes with an increased heart rate, deeper breathing, and a general relaxation of muscular tension. When we are in the midst of an experience as pleasantly exhilarating as joy, we are likely to identify it in an inner conversation with ourselves as a wonderful feeling. Whether the diagnosis has a positive or a negative slant depends on our individual temperament and life history and our prevailing mood. For example: *If only this could last forever!* or *This is too good to last* or *I must be ready for the bad luck that is sure to follow.* Other intense emotions such as grief, rage, the ecstasy of a peak experience, or relief from extreme stress recognizably combine physical and emotional components.

Low-level states, whether in the pleasurable or unpleasurable half of the continuum, are less likely to command recognition. Jourard (1964) writes of the enculturated attitudes that keep us from acting on the low-level discomfort signals that may warn of impending illness. Low-level states such as fatigue, minor headaches, and changes in appetite and sleep patterns may indicate danger to be avoided or reward to be sought after. In sectors of society that prize independence and fortitude, they may be disdained and dismissed as signs of weakness or neuroticism. It is important that counselors be alert to the low-level signs of their own rising anxiety in counseling relationships. If they are not aware when anxiety begins to mount, as is inevitable at times, they will counter with defensive maneuvers that concentrate their energies on meeting their own needs rather than those of their clients. The receptive self-concept eventually comes to welcome those features that add to its fullness of functioning from both pain and enjoyable experiences.

Self-actualization, as operationally described by Maslow (1970), has, among other qualities, "superior perception of reality, increased acceptance of self, of others, and of nature" and "greater freshness of appreciation and richness of emotional reaction." All these traits place the self-actualizing person in the here and now. Such persons are drawn completely into the presently active, eventful experience of being. Their becoming progresses in and through involvement in reality as it is given, not as a result of desiring untroubled pleasure as the illusory center of attention.

Recognizing physical states The field of sensory perception is both a useful and an expedient point from which to begin cultivating self-awareness. The effort stretches the limits of the self-concept and provides clues to additional areas of perception still to be explored. A few fortunate individuals may not need practice in self-awareness. For most of us, conditioned as we are to the pressures and restrictions of our rigidly structured society, it offers liberating possibilities. Ordinarily we have a tendency to feel obligated to be constantly engaged in productive activity. We attend to our sensory impressions mainly as cues to expend effort. We must get things done, save time, plan ahead. The here and now is always kept subservient to the forbidding demands of the future. We are too busy negotiating a restrictive path of becoming that ends in itself to give any of our energy to simply being.

A large part of our current experience of reality is made up of sensory stimuli that we leave unattended along with our reactions to them. We exclude from our field of perception much of what is available to our kinesthetic sense and to our sight, hearing, taste, and smell. Exercise 3-1 offers practical suggestions for getting in touch with our field of sensory awareness and enlarging its scope. It requires us to temporarily discard our incessant, largely unconscious preoccupation with *expression* and consciously open ourselves to the wealth of *impressions* that await our attention. Instead of laboring under the stress of constantly emitting—giving forth—it encourages us to engage in the appreciation and contentment that can be derived from simply receiving sensations.

Exercise 3-1: Receiving Sensory Impressions

Directions: Use initially as an individual or a group exercise, allotting five to ten minutes to each part and scheduling when convenient. To have significant impact on becoming, the essentials of the exercise should be gradually incorporated into the tenor of the individual's everyday life. Frequent practice of the exercise is necessary in the beginning, with recording and review of successive experiences.

Part 1

Kinesthetic Sense Sit in a comfortable, upright position, with eyes closed. Progressively relax musculature from the toes to the head. You will find some muscles especially tight, for example, those of the hands, shoulders, neck, face, and forehead. Pause to ease these specifically.

When completely relaxed, lazily and silently name and enjoy the sensations the exercise produces: pleasurable warmth or coolness, relief of tension in posture and breathing, release of pressure in particularly tense areas, free flow of feelings throughout the body, or comfort in the thought that such complete relaxation is possible.

Part 2

Hearing Take a few minutes to relax as in Part 1.

Avoid further muscle tension, and listen gently until a specific sound comes to your attention. If you recognize it, name it. Whether or not you recognize it, continue to listen passively until it is superseded by another sound.

With each sound that is attended, recognize and enjoy the sensation it produces. Especially enjoy the sensations that accompany sounds you heretofore labeled annoying. This exercise can be used to entice sleep amid noise that you would otherwise meet with resentment and self-pity. It can also be focused to enhance one's appreciation of music.

Part 3

Seeing If possible, select a place for this exercise within sight of a pleasant prospect (for example, a beautiful landscape or picture, a familiar face, a vase of flowers, a single flower, a tree). Relax as in Part 1.

First, give your full attention to the totality of what you have selected to view. Without making any effort, receive, rather than seek, visual sensations from the object you see. Become its subject instead of making it yours.

After a few moments or minutes, as one aspect of what you are viewing becomes dominant (for example, color, shape, light, and so forth), effortlessly shift your attention to it, and remain with it until it is superseded. Do not attempt to name what is seen. Simply enjoy it.

This exercise can be used even in relatively unpleasant surroundings. A class group, for instance, may actually see a barren classroom and the view from its windows for the first time.

Part 4

Smelling and Tasting This exercise may be adapted to home assignment, or a group may identify and enjoy sensations of smell in a familiar classroom or sensations of taste and smell over a shared snack.

a. *Smelling* With eyes closed and body relaxed, attend to your breathing so as to gently exercise the sense of smell. If a room is the subject, the exercise is best done immediately on entering; with a snack or a meal, when preparing or sitting down to it. Names or gradations of pleasure may be attached to odors (for example: with eyes closed, name items of a meal that someone else has prepared, or simply receive impressions and savor or appreciate the differences).

b. *Tasting* While eating a meal or snack, note and savor each of the varieties of taste discovered in the food.

For added sensory enjoyment, note the varied food colors; the different textures of food items in the mouth; or the diverse sensations of salivating, chewing, and swallowing.

Recognizing emotional states Consciousness-raising experiences currently enable some people to recognize the influence of acculturated attitudes in shaping the emotional life of the individual in modern Western society. The communications media draw public attention to our reluctance to move outside expected racial, social, and sex roles and to our nonacceptance of certain areas of feeling as legitimate in certain roles.

There are other conceptions of social roles that stand in the way of experiencing and expressing emotion. They include such regularly associated role pairs as parent-child, teacher-student, nurse-patient, employer-employee, and counselor-client. Many other pairs could be added. Roles, with their complements of identifiable functions, are necessary to give coherence and structure to a society. But when a role becomes a straitjacket, it alters the reality of the person within it and one is required to behave according to a socially or culturally determined life script. Role playing or game playing in a relationship stands at the opposite end of the scale from the authenticity of an I-thou encounter.

If we are to experience and allow others to experience a full emotional life, we must find a way to enfranchise the profusion of feeling that lies within each of us. As suggested in Chapter 1, there is an abundant store of unapprehended emotions pressing for release from the id. To be whole as a human being is to experience the totality of what it means to be human. Of this totality, permitting oneself to feel and knowing what one feels are aspects of paramount significance.

As an aspect of achieving fullness of function, self-actualization, and integrity, this is the work of a lifetime. By the same token, it is never too early to begin. But because we never completely lose our capacity for becoming it is never too late to begin. Parenthetically, it may be noted that the very young and the very old, as well as those in between, benefit from a counseling approach that sets a high value on their individuality. Valuing comes through as their feelings, both negative and positive, are made the subject of a discussion that accepts one as fully as the other. As persons grow in their ability to claim incremental dimensions of their feeling life, they move toward becoming more fully individual and more fully human.

Exercise 3-2 offers a planned opportunity for expanding awareness of positive and negative emotions. It concerns the present and near present rather than the past. Although it is often easier to recall how we felt in the past, it is less likely to further our becoming than identifying our current emotional states. When we know fairly accurately how we feel, we find ourselves in a good position to deal with present reality as such: to *be*, in the fullness of functioning, and from there to move into becoming.

Exercise 3-2: Centering on Feelings

Directions: Use as an individual home assignment, not for examination by another, but to be kept for private use later. With each item, take enough time to explore your feelings until you come to terms, as accurately and completely as possible, with *your* current emotional reality. When you have come up with the names of your feelings, ask yourself, *What more is there in me* (not in the item!) *that brings these feelings into my response?* Complete each item as extensively as is helpful to exploring and expressing your feelings:

1. My dominant mood(s) for the past two weeks may be described as . . .
2. When I became involved in the first exercise in this chapter, I felt . . .
3. When I read and thought about doing this exercise, I felt . . .
4. When I start a new, long-term venture, I feel . . .
5. When I have a bad cold (severe headache, or other acute physical discomfort), I feel . . .
6. When I fail in something that is important to me at the time, I feel . . .
7. When I am with (someone seen as an authority), I feel . . .
8. After I have had a serious disagreement with anyone, I feel . . .
9. When I go into a room to take an examination (to be interviewed for employment, to meet a person who is important and strange to me), I feel . . .
10. When I have to start a social conversation with a stranger, I feel . . .
11. When I think of the possibility of losing (a much loved person), I feel . . .
12. When I am belittled by someone in the presence of others, I feel . . .
13. When I am alone with a good friend who is crying, I feel . . .
14. When I am alone with a comparative stranger who is crying, I feel . . .
15. When I think of (a much desired, impending event), I feel . . .
16. When someone prevents me from doing something I should do, I feel . . .
17. In a social group made up mostly of strangers, I feel . . .

Points for Reflection

1. How many different feelings or moods did you identify?

2. Do emotions usually occur apart from thoughts? Are positive and negative feelings sometimes mixed? Elaborate from your own responses to the exercise.

3. Did some of the feelings that you credited to yourself come as a surprise to you? Elaborate.

4. Which items were particularly easy for you to answer? Which were particularly difficult?

5. Are there any patterns among the feelings that you identified in your responses? What do your responses tell you about yourself? For example: What do I feel about myself? What do I think others feel about me? What do I feel about others? About life in general? When am I likely to feel angry? Challenged? Afraid? Relieved? Ashamed? Depressed? Happy, optimistic, self-confident, and so forth?

Owning Feelings

Exercises 3-1 and 3-2, if carefully and honestly studied, enable us to objectively examine a small slice of the physical and emotional sectors of our physical and emotional feeling repertory. Bear in mind that because the examination is in the nature of a laboratory experiment, it suffers all the limitations of that type of inquiry. Identifying our feelings in the protected atmosphere of a classroom or place of study is like watching a police or hospital emergency on television. It is a spectator rather than a participant activity.

For example, one response may be, *I was infuriated.* Using the passive voice postulates a hypothetical source outside of the self. We bring language to our defense in other ways. When language does not automatically protect us from having to acknowledge an undesirable emotion as our own, we contrive to protect ourselves linguistically by saying, *He (she, it) made me angry.* We reject many unpleasant feelings as part of the present self-concept by placing the instigating agent outside it. Blind emotion is feeling that is completely incapable of seeing itself for what it is. By disowning unwanted emotions and armoring itself against them, the self-concept renders itself increasingly impervious to experience, and becoming is impaired.

In continually preparing to work with clients, helpers must strive to remedy the lack of inner vision that obstructs their own acknowledgment of unwanted emotion. A course of study with exercises is only somewhat more helpful than a purely academic inquiry. Investigating the phenomenon of anxiety is a further aid (Chapter 6). But the real work remains to be done in real situations. As we gradually learn to recognize and own our physical and emotional states, we penetrate their cover and increase our recognition and honest acknowledgment of the individualized defensive patterns that we use against them.

Recognizing and Owning Values

We have seen that realistic self-awareness is a significant aspect in growth toward personhood. The fully functioning person is one who inwardly accepts a wide range of feelings. The emotions and physical sensations thus owned extend from the most pleasurable at one extreme to the least pleasurable at the other. Acknowledging them as part of the self constitutes an important step in the direction of total self-acceptance and realistic self-esteem. Affirmation of the self as one is and has been is a basic necessity to becoming all that one is capable of being. It is therefore a vital objective in counseling.

Equally desirable for both helper and client is a recognition, however limited, of their own personal values, those meanings to which they attach merit or approval. We found earlier in this chapter that feelings are difficult to grasp and examine, especially while they are operating. In the case of values, the difficulty is even greater. However, when one is able to get close to one's feelings, they can serve as an immediate clue to one's values. The things, events, actions, and people that we feel completely and consistently right, or OK, about are in keeping with our values. Those that we feel definitely not OK about, we may be sure, contradict our values in some sense.

Rogers (1964) observes that as the individual moves toward increased self-acceptance, he or she has a corresponding tendency to gain confidence in this intuitive source of valuing. To the extent that we are motivated by standards that we hold to without question, intention gives way to blind, servile conformity. And to those who inflexibly refuse to examine the standards that keep them constantly out of step with their immediate social group, nonconformity becomes a blind end in itself. The humanist's moral values are the many-faceted products of creative interaction between the individual's external reality and his or her private world of meanings. They are a dynamically systematized part of being-in-the-world (Chapter 1).

Existential philosophy hypothesizes that each of us, whether consciously or unconsciously, holds one specific value or value category that is central to our existence. This view corresponds to another expressed in quite different terms in transactional analysis (Chapter 1). Here the individual's life script represents the pivotal value. With poetic but insistent expression, the novelist Saul Bellow (1956) gives literary recognition to the same philosophic-psychologic notion in *Seize the Day.*

> *On Broadway it was still bright afternoon and the gassy air was almost motionless under the leaden spokes of sunlight, and sawdust footprints lay about the doorways of butcher shops and fruit stores. And the great, great crowd, the inexhaustible current of millions of every race and kind pouring out, pressing round, of every age, of every genius, possessors of every human secret, antique and future, in every face the refinement of one particular motive or essence–*I labor, I spend, I strive, I design, I love, I cling, I uphold, I give away, I envy, I long, I scorn, I die, I hide, I want. *Faster, much faster than any man could make the tally.*

Humanistic helpers investigate their own motivating values as a significant aspect of heightened self-awareness. The concept of life scripts as advanced in transactional analysis offers one model for exploration. Humanistic helpers try to disentangle themselves from the control of any one script and to meet each new experience with authenticity and openness. But to the extent that they are labeled by other people, they hope to merit "Courteous Toward All" rather than being scripted for life as "Exploiting Others."

Kohlberg's formulations (Chapter 1) offer the helper reference points from which to assess both the helper's and the client's personal mode of valuing. Before using them, each step of Kohlberg's classification must be thought through with realistic applications. The limitations of a theoretic review of a human value system is obvious. In many respects the exercise parallels developing a nomenclature for emotions and moods.

It cannot be overemphasized that to the extent that a person becomes increasingly human, the self is a unity. Except for purposes of cognitive identification, the elements of the physical and emotional life are not separable. This applies equally to compartmentalizing that might be attempted between cognition and feeling and between either of these and valuing. All are processes rather than entities, and they interact unceasingly. Together they compose the major dynamisms of one's inner existence. They initiate the judgments that determine choices and behavior and personal goals and interpersonal relationships.

Values predominate among a myriad of inner, interacting influences. Unfortunately, they do not always function smoothly. It is possible for a person to hold values that are so contradictory that there is frequent warfare within. When this is the case, emotions conflict and thought is confused. As the person moves toward self-actualization this happens less often. With increasing authenticity, judgment is based on well-established principles. The continuance of such authenticity is not assured, however. One's beliefs and values must be reassessed frequently. In an examined life, each of the acute crises that inevitably occur tends to enforce reexamination. Quite apart from this, note that the great thinkers of the world have found it necessary to set aside periods of quiet solitude for just such an exercise.

SELF-DISCLOSURE AND COUNSELING

As a means of heightening our self-awareness, self-study is a useful, but decidedly limited, process. Jourard (1971) and his co-workers fully investigated the relationship between well-being and self-disclosure: talking freely and frankly about oneself with another person or persons. Jourard (1973) suggests that people who require the ministrations of professional counselors or therapists may need them because they have not developed the capacity to reveal themselves to others. In failing to communicate with others about themselves, they lose touch with their own feeling life. They lack the quality of transparency to self and others that is essential to the fullness of human functioning. They freeze themselves into a set of roles and personifications, each with its compendium of conventional modes of communication. Denied the joys and satisfactions of being themselves, of continual growth in becoming fully human, they seek therapeutic help in extricating themselves from their sterile, static conditions.

An important, and often most difficult, task faced by the humanistic helper is to free the client from the fear of self-disclosure. The successful practitioner can form a relationship with a client in which it is safe for both of them to find satisfying ways of being authentically, transparently themselves. The degree to which counselors express their own feelings to clients varies according to the particular philosophic approach he or she adheres to. This point is further discussed in the chapters devoted to the major counseling modalities.

Regardless of the extent to which the counselor believes it necessary to reciprocate in the process of self-disclosure, the art of expressing feelings in an open, genuine, and nonthreatening manner remains an essential counselor competency. The client looks to the helper as a model of behavior that brings support and satisfaction to interpersonal relations. With practice, in the safety of the helping situation, the openness learned can then be transferred by the client to the more hazardous milieu of everyday life.

There are many ways that people express their feelings to each other: vocally, through the positions they choose vis-a-vis each other, through posture, facial expressions, gestures, and touch (Chapter 6). The art of communicating positive feeling lies mainly in the choice of timing and mode of expression. The humanistic helper cultivates sensitivity to the varying states of receptiveness recognized in each client. For the client who experiences the unaccustomed fulfillment of an I-thou relationship with the counselor, the counselor's positive attitudes and responses make a model to pattern other relationships on.

The expression of negative feelings, an inevitable occurrence in any relationship, may present greater difficulty. The art in this instance stems from the capacity to recognize and own the feelings to the extent that one authentically reports them as belonging to oneself. To achieve this mastery, one must develop an ability to forego the almost universal tendency to subjectively displace, rather than objectively own, what one feels. We normally react defensively to a display of anger, for instance, by projecting or displacing a reactive countervaluation. Our immediate response to an accusation is likely to be a counteraccusation or another similar defensive reaction. For example:

Speaker 1: *Leave me alone. You always have to be right!*
Speaker 2: *You don't have to throw a fit about it.*

or

I'm always wrong as far as you're concerned.

In contrast, a nonevaluative report of the immediate feeling state of the second speaker may clarify the situation. For example:

When I think you are angry with me, I feel hurt and defensive.

An initial report rather than a display of anger by the first speaker would probably have averted the altercation entirely.

The student or practitioner who decides that reporting of feelings should be adopted as part of the counseling role may, like the client, find the task difficult in the beginning. If either client or counselor has followed a lifelong pattern of having role relationships only, the breakthrough to any expression of real feeling is a significant accomplishment. Repeated, planned rehearsals may be needed within the counseling situation for the client and outside it for the counselor. Still, it will not be easy to make a transfer within the realities of relationships that have long existed on a defensive-accusatory footing.

The process of helping requires a climate in which clients can reveal themselves without reservation. Many have lost the capacity not only to articulate their feelings in genuine communication with others, but even to bring their feelings to the surface of consciousness. The self-concept has become hemmed in by defenses against the possibility of being hurt by confronting a bruising reality. In the unaccustomed protectiveness of the humanistic counseling situation, a narrow, defensive self-concept finds itself free to expand and grow. Self-disclosure is the primary means to this end.

Whenever we hear ourselves telling our thoughts and feelings in an atmosphere of uncritical acceptance, we hold them up for open scrutiny, not only to our listener, but to ourselves as well. We are then likely to reevaluate them and, sometimes, to see them in an entirely new light. We come to know ourselves, perhaps for the first time. In recognizing previously unknown aspects of self, we begin to assent to the whole and to clear the paths of becoming. Affirming the self brings with it a degree of assent to others in their entirety and eventually brings us to more gracefully accept the "givens" of life itself. The path to integrity, self-actualization, fullness of functioning, and becoming a real person is unveiled before us.

Exercise 3-3, adapted from Jourard's *Disclosing Man to Himself* (1968), provides a way to try out one's willingness to exchange information about oneself with another person under confidential conditions. If participants know each other well, the exercise may be more or less difficult as a result. It is sometimes easier to confide in a stranger than in someone with whom we have previously played a different role. Besides estimating our capacity for self-disclosure, this exercise allows us to consider the changes in feeling that self-disclosure brings about and the new insights that it engenders.

Exercise 3-3: Self-Disclosure

Directions: You and your partner ask each other questions from the list that follows. Read all the questions together before answering them. The questions vary in intimacy, so you may wish to begin with relatively less intimate ones. You may take turns asking the questions. Follow the rules below:

- Agree with your partner that all communication between you will be confidential.
- You must be willing to answer any question that you ask your partner.
- You may decline to answer any question your partner asks.

1. How successful are you in your work (studies)?
2. How do you react when someone in authority criticizes you?
3. To what extent do you feel indebted to your parents?
4. How often do you resort to lying to get out of something unpleasant?
5. Are you ever fearful of losing (never getting) a permanent love partner?
6. Do you enjoy manipulating or directing other people? Why or why not?
7. How do you retaliate when other people threaten or frustrate you?
8. Have you ever seriously considered committing suicide?
9. Do other people's sexist or racist attitudes anger you?
10. How do you react to compliments?
11. What does it take to make you break down and cry?
12. Is there anyone you think you should love but really despise?
13. How often do you express genuine love toward your spouse (the person closest to you)?
14. Approximately what is your (your family's) annual income?

15. How do you feel about returning unwanted purchases?

16. Do you still hold resentment against either of your parents for the way they treated you as a child?

17. How important is religion in your life?

18. Which aspects of your appearance are most embarrassing to you? Most pleasing to you?

19. Would you stand up in a public meeting to voice a protest?

20. Which aspects of your personality are most pleasing to you? Which would you like to change?

21. Which actions in your past are you ashamed to look back on?

22. Have you ever considered seeing a psychologist or a psychiatrist about yourself?

23. Is there anything or anyone that you value enough to die for?

24. Have you ever used any psychoactive substance to become intoxicated? Why or why not? If yes, were there any outstanding consequences?

25. What are your favorite TV programs? What kind of music do you prefer?

Points for Reflection

1. Which items did I feel comfortable in answering? Why? Which items did I avoid asking or answering? Why?

2. What difference did my previous acquaintance (or lack of it) with my partner make?

3. What did I learn from my partner's responses about him or her as a person? About people in general? About myself?

4. What did I learn about my partner that I would prefer not to know? Why?

5. What did I tell my partner that I wish I had kept to myself? Why?

6. Is the net effect of this exercise likely to increase the possibility of closeness between myself and my partner? Why?

7. To what extent was I able to be honest and open?

8. What about myself became clearer to me as a result of this exercise? What new insights did I gain about myself?

The main focus in this chapter has been our inner states and how we can increasingly bring them, through practice in self-awareness and self-disclosure, into our cognitive field of perception.

We must remind ourselves that only by analogy can we transfer conclusions about our own feelings and our reactions to them to the unique qualities and circumstances of our clients. But some real similarities can still be expected. To a degree, the process of becoming is the same for all, as are its incentives and impediments. In addition, the skills that we learn to use in self-observation serve us well in observing others.

The humanistic helper uses this knowledge in understanding clients' observed and reported behavior and he or she attempts to help them achieve self-understanding. With enhanced receptivity, they can appreciate and enjoy the unique richness of feeling they find in themselves and anticipate with genuine respect the singularity and inner richness of others. Between persons who are realistically in touch with their own feelings and values, authentic, intimate relationships are possible.

References

Allport, G. W. 1970. *Pattern and growth in personality.* New York: Holt, Rinehart and Winston.

Bellow, S. 1956. *Seize the day.* New York: Viking.

Jourard, S. M. 1964. *The transparent self.* Princeton, N. J.: Van Nostrand.

——. 1968. *Disclosing man to himself.* Princeton, N. J.: Van Nostrand Reinhold.

——. 1971. *Self disclosure: An experimental analysis of the transparent self.* New York: Wiley.

——. 1973. Healthy personality and self-disclosure. *Interpersonal dynamics: Essays and readings on human interaction.* Warren G. Bennis et al., editors. Homewood, Ill.: Dorsey, pp. 538–546.

Kohlberg, L. 1973. The claim to moral adequacy of a highest stage of moral judgment. *J. Philos.* 70:630–646.

Maslow, A. H. 1970. *Motivation and personality.* 2nd ed. New York: Harper & Row.

Rogers, C. R. 1964. Toward a modern approach to values: The valuing process in the mature person. *J. Abnorm. Soc. Psychol.* 68:160–167.

PART II

Helping Individual Clients

CHAPTER 4

The Client-Centered Approach

There are many different ways to categorize the various systems of counseling and psychotherapy. With a view to their adaptability to short-term counseling, three currently standard modalities are presented in Part II. Each is described in detail, with applications of theory and methods to professional helping. The main theoretical constructs used are those of the following systems: **client-centered counseling and therapy**; **the interpersonal, problem-solving approach**; and **behavior modification.** In Part III, additional concepts are drawn from various approaches to group and family counseling.

The methods and techniques of each approach are described with a view to using them in a distinctively humanistic mode of helping. Furthermore, the presentation is eclectic and cumulative. Each approach offers a distinct contribution to the counseling work of the professional helper. The content of each chapter is therefore constructed on the foundation of concepts and methods explored and exemplified in previous chapters.

A set of premises on which a theoretic framework has been built by its proponents underlies each approach. A selection is made from these assumptions, and the resulting theories are examined with a particular aim in view. Universally applicable concepts are presented to broaden the reader's understanding of people as individual, unique persons. The sine qua non of good counseling is the quality of human perceptiveness and sensitivity that enables the counselor to enter into the private world of the client and to use this privilege for the client's benefit.

Each of the approaches is delineated with a theory base of sufficient scope to substantiate the particular form it takes in practice. The student or practitioner in a helping profession thus receives an intellectual handle for grasping and implementing the techniques presented and for gradually developing the requisite counseling skills. For the humanistic helper, the client-centered approach is basic to all others. It is therefore placed first among the three modalities to be explored.

THE CLIENT-CENTERED RELATIONSHIP

Carl Rogers has held a position of undoubted leadership in clinical and counseling psychology since the publication of *Counseling and Psychotherapy* in 1942. It represented a clear break from other methods in vogue at that time. Whereas other approaches stressed the role of the counselor-therapist in directing the focus and progress of treatment, Rogers' newly introduced system signaled a complete reversal of client-counselor roles: The counselor role provided conditions under which the client might move toward a change that would be entirely self-determined in aim, pace, and direction.

Rogers' book was published at a time when the thoughtful observer of the world scene agonized over the evils of authoritarianism as exerted by Hitler, Mussolini, and Stalin. In contrast, the right of self-determination was a widely held value. Nonauthoritarian ways of working with people were sought in many fields of endeavor. A therapy that was nondirective and client-centered rather than therapist-centered promised a democratic modus operandi between counselor and client.

The theoretic framework that has since been developed starts from the premise that the individual has inherent growth potential (Chapter 2). Through continued research based on the raw data of recorded interviews, Rogers and his colleagues amply demonstrate that clients seeking help with personal problems are capable of changing in ways that bring their own self-chosen aims to fruition. The data also show that this change is proportionately fostered as the climate created by the counselor is less authoritative and more productive of the freedom conferred by a sense of being unreservedly accepted as one presently is (Wexler, 1974). The client's inner drive toward self-actualization continues to be the moving force of the effort, in contradistinction to any presumably superior wisdom of the counselor.

Each of the numerous philosophic approaches to counseling has its own implicit objectives. Increasing the self-actualization of the client is the central aim of every helping endeavor in client-centered counseling. A fully functioning person represents its humanistic ideal. Although circumstances may dictate that the helping professional's relationship with a client be short-term, it is designed to promote the client's fullness of functioning within his or her personal and environmental situation.

The qualities of the fully functioning person are described in detail by Rogers. They have much in common with those of the self-actualized person in Maslow's scheme (Chapter 2). Condensed into a set of succinct aims, they may be stated as follows:

1. Realistic awareness of and openness to experience
2. Acceptance of self and others
3. Independence of judgment and decision making

In whatever terms they may be expressed, the preceding counselor aims are implicit in the client-centered approach. Obviously they can only be applied to an individual client in an individualized way. Rather than being held up to a client as goals to strive for, they are made into a living experience for the client as the counselor functions in the relationship.

In the client-centered relationship, the client is given responsibility for the direction and pace of interaction and for choosing the content to be worked with, in single interviews as well as in a series of counseling sessions. The counselor assumes the major responsibility for creating a climate that provides warmth and acceptance. When relieved of the need for defensiveness or duplicity, clients freely express the full range of their feelings and attitudes.

As humanistic helpers, we can safely adapt this framework to any helping relationship. We try from the beginning to understand our clients as fully as possible. The helper's effort is directed toward perceiving the client's feelings as the client experiences them and toward judging a situation at any given moment as the client judges it. This effort is not always successful, but even so, the client sees and appreciates the helper's desire to comprehend. The effort itself counts for more than its success or failure. The client responds to the helper's sincere desire to understand.

Equally vital to the relationship is the helper's attitude of unqualified acceptance. Successful counselors like people. They are not inclined to judge anyone else by standards they hold for themselves. Neither do they base their estimation of an individual on his or her past performance or on a second-hand report of that performance. Their way is to let be: to respect each person's right to be whatever he or she has to be at the present moment, with confidence in the capacity of every person for further becoming.

Throughout every interview, the helper tries to be completely present to the client. This is a new and rare experience for many clients. To the extent that they are able to enter into a relationship of mutual trust, they find themselves receptive to the warming, relaxing effect of the helper's complete, unconditional regard for them. Clients who are habitually mistrustful of others may need to repeatedly test the authenticity of the helper or of a series of helpers before they can experience this effect.

Those who are receptive are able to respond with unaccustomed openness. The self-disclosure that results brings to the surface ideas, feelings, and meanings that may have previously existed only at the murky level of the preconscious. Emerging into the light and welcome of the counselor attitudes of understanding and affirmation, such inner experiences come clear for the first time to the client, and accepting and owning them becomes possible. Increasingly, such clients are able to rely on the validity of their own feelings and judgments. They depend less on approval from outside or on introjected dictates they previously subscribed to without question.

Because the client and not the helper is the locus of evaluation of the client's thinking, feeling, and acting from the beginning, there is little danger that dependence on the helper will develop to complicate the client-centered situation. The freedom of give and take inherent in the helping relationship is an experience that clients are eager to try out in other relationships. As accuracy and accessibility of perception increase, the client establishes self-selected goals for the future, and he or she moves with new freedom into self-directed decision making and action.

SKILLS AND TECHNIQUES OF INTERVENTION

Client-centered counselors, like the practitioners of any art, continuously examine their work to detect areas of successful accomplishment and needed improvement. Whether or not they engage in formal research, they regularly study the content and process of their interchanges with clients. For both incidental evaluation and formal research, recorded interview material is a necessary source of raw data. Tape recording, with the client's permission, is the preferred method in research.

Apart from research, counselors usually depend on written notes made immediately after each interview as a memory aid. Especially for the student of counseling, an accurate recording system is essential. Although tape recording is the most complete and dependable method, it does not provide the needed practice in precise recall of verbal interaction. For this reason, written process recording (keeping a running account of interaction) is preferable.

A written account containing verbatim material gives the student, with supervisory assistance as required, material to use in analyzing every interaction that takes place. The student who finds recall especially difficult in the beginning may wish to jot down reminders during the interview. Most clients expect professionals to make notes for future reference, so permission is scarcely necessary. Casually mentioning the confidentiality of recorded material is usually sufficient.

A classification scheme for analyzing the nature and effects of helper responses is detailed in the remainder of this chapter.

Types of Helper Responses

As used in any of the various counseling approaches, responses may be conveniently grouped as either **continuing** or **leading responses**. The difference between the two types lies in their anticipated effect on the client. Continuing responses are intended mainly to encourage the client to lead the interaction. In answering, the client chooses to further the topic already under discussion or to move into a different subject area. When using a leading response, the counselor takes the initiative. He or she may intend to push the topic further, to obtain or give information, or to reassure or advise the client.

Chapter 6 describes leading questions that may be used as openers in any type of helping under "Questions." Applications to the client-centered approach can be found in that section. Apart from a few such exceptions, continuing responses are employed almost exclusively in a client-centered approach.

The client-centered helper draws on a small range of techniques and prefers that the client's expressed or evident concerns remain central throughout the interaction. The helper directs his or her effort mainly toward being as genuine and open as possible and tries to be *for the client* rather than for self, professionally or personally—to be a partner in the troubled client's gropings for self-understanding, self-acceptance, and self-motivation. The following sections attempt to classify and describe the various continuing responses the helper can use in client-centered communication. The first two responses are arbitrarily designated as **skills**, the remaining as **techniques.**

Creative Listening

In this context, listening is regarded as the basic skill, not only of the client-centered approach, but of the art of counseling itself. It is the main instrument through which the helper attains and maintains authentic communication with the client. For the helper, listening is an energy-consuming activity. It is not passive in any sense of the word. The helper must depend on it to activate all the inner qualities and attitudes he or she needs to draw on on behalf of the client: authenticity, unconditional acceptance, and a compelling desire to understand.

At any part of the interview, the listening helper tries to remain present to the client as he or she is or appears to be. The client's past is not allowed to unduly obscure the situation. The client is moving, growing, becoming, from this moment to the next. The counselor attempts to move with the client, from the inside, as it were, seeing the client's inner and outer world as it appears to the client. The self is deliberately forgotten. If this were not so, the helper's self-consciousness would crowd out the empathy needed to experience every thought and feeling as the client experiences it.

Being completely *for* the client requires the counselor to put aside many aspects of the self: preoccupations, desires, biases, and prejudices and to disregard inner and outer distractions. This is listening of a very different sort than we are ordinarily accustomed to. In a typical social situation, only a fraction of my attention is likely to focus on the person with whom I am in dialogue. Instead of being really present while the other is talking, I am busy preparing my responses. The chances are great that my answer will satisfy my own ego, with little regard for the speaker as a person. My response matches what the other has said—or tops it or gives advice about it or changes the subject to one I am waiting to talk about. For example:

Speaker 1: *I didn't sleep well last night.*
Speaker 2: *I never have any trouble sleeping. You should try jogging. It keeps me in A-1 condition.*

or

I had such a good time last night that I wouldn't have cared whether I slept or not.

Satir (1969) characterizes two levels of communication: **denotative** (report) and **metacommunicative** (command). The denotative level conveys a literal message such as is obtained on first reading the above examples. Metacommunication is "a message about a message"—a hidden affective demand or request made of the hearer. In the first speaker's remark, one can find metacommunications such as: *Sympathize with me. Notice me. Listen to me.* The second speaker's hidden messages seem to be: *Envy me. Admire me. Do as I say. Listen to me.* Because metacommunication is usually both given and received at a level below complete consciousness, it carries a message about what the sender is, not necessarily about what he or she wishes to put into words.

Listening to demonstrate that one is really present to the speaker is also metacommunication. Although certain nonverbal signs of listening can be identified (Chapter 6), they do not add up to its totality. The client-centered helper assiduously tries to comprehend the total content of each verbal message received from the client. Its denotative, and, more especially, metacommunicative contents are given meticulous attention. The helper listens for the latent emotion in the metacommunication in order to respond to feelings rather than factual content. Reflecting feelings is discussed as a separate skill in the section with that title below. It is a counselor response that depends entirely on listening creatively to metacommunication.

Using Silence

A second type of continuing response is the counselor's use of silence. Using silence effectively requires considerable skill. Like listening, this skill is not usually used in ordinary social interaction, where silence is likely to be regarded as a vacuum that must be filled with conversation. Except between people whose relationship is long-standing and comfortably intimate, silence tends to engender anxiety. In the helping interview the novice counselor and thus the client may be quite uneasy with prolonged silence. There may be an urge to keep things moving, to *do something,* to ensure success in helping the client. Actually, silence may be what the client needs most at that particular moment in the interaction.

A client's silence may have one of several meanings. It is possible that the client does not feel able to take the initiative in resuming the interaction immediately. A certain lassitude may follow an intense emotional outburst or a blocking of communication may precede or follow an expression of feelings that are particularly painful. Silence may indicate the client's uncertainty or embarrassment, fatigue, or even boredom. In these instances, the helper's continued silence may give the client time to rest momentarily and to gather the resources needed to go on.

A client's silence may also convey strong feelings that are as apparent as if they were spoken: a reddened face with firmly pursed lips is a likely indication of stubborn anger; trembling lips and eyes blinking to hold back tears are obvious signs of grief. Whether spoken or silent, emotion requires a response that reflects the feeling and acknowledges its validity in the client's current experiencing. Blocking that occurs when an area of emotional conflict is touched may be gently reflected as a sign of difficulty in disentangling mixed emotions.

Anxiety that continues at an acute level may make communication impossible. As soon as the helper suspects that a client's silence results from anxiety or that the helper's silence is causing anxiety, he or she intervenes to offer understanding and support.

Regardless of his or her persuasion, a counselor may intentionally use silence to encourage the client to move from trivialities to serious discussion or from theorizing to considering the real here-and-now situation. Experienced counselors recognize that silence has positive values for themselves as well as for the client. The counselor, too, may need time to relax momentarily and to think through what has been said and its meanings. Sometimes the helper can clearly see that silence is preferable to any other response. When we do not know what to say, our best choice is to say nothing. This is as true outside the counseling situation as inside it. Socially, we often hasten to fill silences, yet we admire people who can endure them. From a professional standpoint, silence is a necessary adjunct to all the other counseling skills.

Verbal and Nonverbal Cues

Client-centered counseling makes frequent use of *mhm* and *uhhuh.* These responses are not to be employed indiscriminately because *mhm* and *uhhuh* offer an easy means to fill embarrassing silences. The effective counselor uses either expression as a response to fulfill a definite counseling purpose. The meanings conveyed by these cues are variations of the themes: *I'm listening. Go on. Continue talking about the things that have meaning for you. You may safely express whatever you feel. I think I understand. I accept you just as you are.*

The specific cues that a helper uses in counseling are those that come most naturally. If a response is forced or used as a deception, its unauthentic nature comes through as metacommunication to the client. When it is a genuine response denoting unqualified acceptance, its metacommunicative and denotative aspects coincide. It is authentic.

Mhm and *uhhuh* may be classed as either verbal or nonverbal. They are nonevaluative: they do not signal agreement or approval of what the client has said. They should therefore be pronounced tentatively, with a slightly questioning, upward inflection. I use the word *slightly* advisedly. A *distinctly* questioning inflection implies doubt or disapproval of the client's statement; a distinctly positive inflection implies agreement or approval. The reader is advised to try out various ways of articulating the two sounds.

Some verbal cues are listed here because they are variations of the acceptance denoted by *mhm* and are cues rather than statements with more specific content. They include: *Yes... Yes. Go on... I see... I think I understand.*

These simple continuing responses are likely to be used frequently by the client-centered helper. The ellipses are employed here to indicate tentativeness. As with *mhm,* upward inflection should be used at the end of each cue. To say *Yes* or *I see* in a distinctly positive tone again implies agreement or approval. These are likely to be pronounced in a slightly protracted tone, as well as with a slightly questioning inflection. In employing any of these cues, it is important that helpers use expressions that are genuine for them, but not because they don't know what else to say or because the expressions are used by other counselors.

There are many nonverbal cues, used with or instead of vocal cues, that also express the helper's unconditional acceptance of the client and the client's communications. Our feelings and attitudes are conveyed through facial expressions gestures, posture, and even through dress and grooming. The meanings associated with nonverbal communication are explored in Chapter 6.

Reflecting Feelings

Reflection of feeling was for some years a distinctive skill only of client-centered counseling. Now it is advocated in most approaches and used by almost every professional counselor. It is also recognized as a healthy component of communication in family life, in schools, in hospitals, in industry, and in self-help organizations of all types. It is, as its name implies, an attempt to mirror the metacommunication or affective message in what an individual has said. The content of the reflection provides the speaker with a completely nonevaluative type of feedback, having neither a positive nor a negative connotation. The response represents a tentative effort to verbalize the unexpressed, almost visceral, meanings beneath the factual content of the speaker's words. Its immediate effect is to broaden the radius of accessible information as a focus of the client's attention and evaluation. Repeated reflection provides the client with cumulative learning opportunities in attending to new dimensions of the data of experience.

An everyday family example might occur when either husband or wife comes home from work:

> Speaker 1: *Well, I'm glad that day's over!*
> Speaker 2: (voicing concern) *You've had a rough day.*

Although the second speaker's response does not name a specific feeling, it brings out the underlying affective meaning of what the first speaker said. It is a continuing response that keeps an open channel of expression for the other, acknowledging that person's right to have and to discuss feelings.

An example of more direct naming of feeling is found in the following exchange:

Ten-year-old Tom: *If Jim comes in our yard again, I'll kill him!*
Mother: *Well, you're good and mad at Jim right now.*

Note that the recognized content of the first speaker's statement is not directly alluded to in either example. The counseling purpose of reflecting is to help others bring to the surface and openly express their feelings and/or underlying attitudes and values. In the first example, the first speaker is fully aware of inner disturbance. At that point he or she needs only to be assured that further revelations will be met with attention and empathy. Tom, however, is only partly aware of the nature of his own feelings and is intent on placing them on an enemy where they can be physically attacked. His awareness will be sharpened by hearing the feeling put explicitly into words and he will move in the direction of claiming the feeling as an element of his, rather than Jim's, inner experience.

In reflecting feeling, the helping person very often uses the pronoun *you.* This immediately places responsibility for the feeling where it authentically belongs. Because such responses are voiced in accepting, nonevaluative words and tones, clients are not aroused to defensiveness. Instead, they are given freedom to recognize and accept the identified feelings. They may then be able to acknowledge the feelings as their own. The mother's response to Tom is an example of this aspect of reflection of feeling. Tom's mother does not ask what Jim has done or in any way imply that the source of Tom's feeling lies outside himself. Neither does she upbraid him or otherwise arouse defensiveness by questioning his right to express his anger in extreme terms. When helping persons succeed in reflecting feelings accurately without threat or censure, their helpees can really hear the meanings they themselves convey.

After a feeling is accurately reflected, the client is likely to repeat or restate the reflection slowly and thoughtfully. We recognize from observing our own behavior and that of others that both our ideas and our feelings become real to us only when we give them our serious attention. This is especially true when we succeed in putting the thought they stimulate into our own words. Following a serious interchange with a friend, or even more so with someone currently viewed as an enemy, we tend to have a better verbatim memory of what we said than of the other person's words. Teachers know that when students can be led to make an important point in their own words, they really learn it. But if the teacher makes the same point, it may be lost on many students. Our feelings, too, take on meaning when they become observable to us as actual data of experience. After giving serious attention to our feelings, we begin the process of claiming them as our own.

Skillful helpers catalyze in their clients a process of attending, acknowledging, and accepting an increased range of inner experience. The self-concept is accordingly expanded and enriched. Furthermore, trust engendered in the client-helper relationship can enable a client to carry greater confidence into other relationships and move more freely toward exercising a mature capacity for intimacy.

Reflection usually stimulates the hearer to recognize and begin to own the full import of a statement made under the impetus of emotion. Tom's response to his mother's comment might be *I'm madder than a hornet!* A wise mother remains silently attentive while Tom gets the story of the whole incident off his chest. With the refreshing resilience of childhood, he would probably then be ready to take a less emotional and more rational view of the situation.

Clients often respond to reflections of feeling with a thoughtful *Yes* or *That's right* with a short silence preceding and perhaps a longer one following the comment. In such instances, clients are usually taking time to fully recognize and adopt the feelings as their own. Ways of acknowledging and owning feelings are illustrated in this interchange:

Ms. R: *When he said that, I just hit bottom.*
Counselor (after a pause): *It was as if you had nothing left.*
Ms. R (after a pause): *God–yes!*

or

I never felt so lonely in all my life.

Either response shows that Ms. R recognizes her feeling. The second response, which paraphrases the counselor's comment, may indicate a more definite internalization of the acknowledgment than the first.

At the end of the section on listening, it was pointed out that the counselor's attention is directed toward both the denotative and metacommunicative aspects of the client's conversation. This requires a much greater effort at comprehension than that given to a speaker's message in most other situations. Because our cultural background has accustomed us to directing our attention more to the factual than to the affective elements of communication, the counselor finds it necessary to cultivate a true sensitivity to affect. To reflect feelings within their current context requires that the counselor organize and integrate both factual and metacommunicative material and then respond to the total meaning of the client's communication. The counselor certainly cannot expect to achieve in every response a perfectly phrased mirror image of what the client is feeling in a complex set of circumstances. Because counselor and client are different persons, one can, at best, only approximately duplicate the inner experience of the other. As counselors, we hope to consistently communicate our *present understanding* of the client's here-and-now experience as a being-in-the-world.

There are many nonverbal clues that, taken together with the client's words, round out our perception of what a client is feeling. Spacing and ordering of ideas; gestures; and changes in position, posture, and facial expression all lend special meaning to what is said or left unsaid. A fleeting impression, incompletely grasped at the time, may be left by a movement, a catching of the breath, or a sidelong glance. With practice, we can consciously observe and interpret many of these signs. Chapter 6 discusses this aspect of nonverbal communication. For the client-centered counselor who is also a humanist, they are an inseparable part of one person's experience of another person.

Reik (1972) tells of the elusive nature of the cues that are picked up by *listening with the third ear.* We partly know how others are feeling when we are with them by knowing how we ourselves feel at the time. The counselor realizes that this can be a two-way process between client and counselor and that it is the counselor's responsibility to find ways to becoming thoroughly attuned to it. The student of counseling will find it necessary to begin with a concentrated self-study such as that recommended in Chapter 3. When unhindered by tension, and with all senses open, the helper is free to feel *with* the client, maintaining both closeness and objective distance in the I-thou relationship.

Although it is important to be able to draw on a fund of terms to use in identifying feelings, one need not be fearful of causing harm to the relationship by using words that the client finds inaccurate. In an atmosphere of unconditional regard, the client will simply reject ownership of the feeling or respond by correcting the helper's impression. Maybe the helper has misidentified the feeling or the client is not ready to bring it into full awareness. If the helper tentatively identifies the feeling, the client will appreciate that the helper is not claiming omniscience. The helper recognizes that no one can tell for certain what another is experiencing or extract its meanings with unerring accuracy. A necessary quality in a counselor is the capacity to tolerate ambiguity. An unperturbed acknowledgment of uncertainty is an aspect of counselor self-disclosure that encourages similar openness in the client.

The following interchange illustrates the use of a genuinely tentative counselor response:

Mr. C: *Everything seems to be going wrong. If I plan anything it never works out. The boss was supposed to come in late yesterday afternoon, but she didn't show at all. I waited for her and was late getting home, so I don't know whether Jenny phoned or not. I stewed for hours about whether to call her, and now she'll be mad because she must have expected me to call her.*

Counselor: *I wonder if this is what you are saying: you are afraid of bothering her if you call, but afraid of losing touch with her if you don't?*

Mr. C: *Maybe. Maybe I'm just cautious.*

The counselor now waits to give Mr. C time to continue examining his feelings, return to the narrative, or move to another topic. If Mr. C does not seem inclined to take the lead, the counselor continues with: *You're wary of offending Jenny?* The question here is a continuing response, rather than a leading or investigative type of question (discussed in Chapter 6).

When a client discloses a number of different feelings or attitudes in an unbroken series of statements, the counselor faces a choice as to how much to reflect back. Some counselors maintain that as many feelings as can be identified should be reflected. This might indicate that all of the client's feelings are significant. If the counselor feels that some feelings have been missed in the response, it is wise to say so and to ask the client to help in recalling. In the example above, a counselor might begin the first response with a reference to Mr. C's general discouragement as evidenced in his first remarks and then relate it to Mr. C's attitude toward Jennie. On the other hand, the client's concern about his work might be considered more significant at this particular stage of counseling and be singled out for reflection. Other counselors prefer to avoid the danger of overloading their responses. Accordingly, they reflect only one or two predominant feelings or those expressed toward the end of the client's total statement.

The skill of reflecting feeling has been examined here concentrating on its technical details. These minutiae must not distract attention from the client-centered relationship in which practiced techniques play a relatively small part. To be intent on a meticulous choice of words for every response would be to lose sight of the person who is the focus of every facet of the client-centered encounter. If the helper is generously giving of self, authentically present to the client, and highly sensitive to the client's current experiencing, the meta-communication of each counselor response, no matter what words it contains, will convey genuine concern for the client's feelings.

The client-centered relationship is conducive to growth in the helper as well as the client. As we strive to recognize and articulate the latent attitudes and values in what others say, we gradually become more cognizant of our own attitudes and values. This increasing contact with the inner core of self, this enlarging openness of the self-concept to experiencing, brings richness to our personal lives. Counselor growth toward integrity comes as a byproduct of unreservedly offering oneself to the interests of person after person. With mature integration comes greater wisdom. We do not expect to escape, or even wish to escape, any of the normal vicissitudes of life. We nevertheless remain susceptible to being temporarily overwhelmed and helpless in the face of personal disaster. But we recognize the potential for becoming in all that happens to us, and hope to measure up to it more adequately as we continue to grow.

It is fortunate for our learning that the attitudes and skills of client-centered counseling may appropriately be practiced in any situation of person-to-person interaction. Everyone we encounter, from our close friends and family to the checkout clerk or the waiter, appreciates being responded to as a "thou" rather than an "it." It is a novel experience to meet with real regard, especially for those who wait on us in various public capacities. No one grows out of the need for personal recognition. Many people we contact daily are seen only as anonymous instruments to be used for our practical advantage. A comment or question that acknowledges the person as a person meets with a response that contains that person's own meanings. We may use the offhand *How are you?* many times in the course of a day. When we make it a genuine inquiry about another's well-being, the person's face lights up and his or her response is also likely to be genuine, with feeling that welcomes reflection. To be listened to with attentive caring is such an unusual experience that most people can benefit from it. Likewise with reflection of feeling. One's family and friends can advance in self-knowledge by having their expressions of feeling listened to, comprehended, and, when a need is apparent, accurately and compassionately mirrored back to them.

One can only become by being. Helping persons who are attempting to become more open to the covert meanings in communication can learn by trying out their skills with each other. The following exercise is recommended.

Exercise 4-1: Listening for Feelings

Directions: Work with a partner you do not know very well. Read the total exercise together before beginning. When in dialogue, sit close together but not touching and face one another in speaking-listening postures.

Part 1

Partner 1 talks to Partner 2 for three minutes. Use a clock or timer, or have a third person be a timekeeper.

Partner 1 Speak only about your father or mother or about two other close family members. Tell what you see as most significant about them.

Partner 2 Listen without commenting, questioning, or interrupting. When time is called, tell your partner about all the underlying feelings, attitudes, or values that you identified in what Partner 1 said, and indicate the person toward whom each feeling was directed.

Partners 1 and 2 As each feeling is brought out, discuss the validity of Partner 2's identification.

Part 2

Reverse roles and repeat.

Points for Discussion (in dyad or larger group)

1. How did you feel when you were the first speaker? How were you affected by the fact that the other was *really* listening?

2. What did you notice about the other person's nonverbal behavior?

3. Which role did you prefer, speaker or listener? Why? Which was more difficult? In what way?

4. How well did your partner zero in on your feelings? Were you surprised by what your partner thought you were feeling? Explain.

5. How would listening of this type affect a relationship between two people such as: Employer-employee? Teacher-student? Intimate friends? Lovers?

Exercise 4-2 offers a structured opportunity to try out the technique of reflecting feelings. Note that such fragmented responses must be artificial at best. The openings are almost devoid of background information. They do not specify the nature of the interpersonal relationships that exist, if any. They do have the advantage of representing many encounters in which reflecting feelings may be used to the immediate benefit of the individuals concerned.

Bear in mind the philosophy behind the use of reflection of feeling. The individual in need of help, regardless of class or condition, is a person—a thou. This unique person has the potential to become fully human: secure, autonomous, self-aware, and self-actualizing. Any person's problems are his or her own. If they can be accurately conceptualized in relation to reality and acknowledged as one's own, a solution that is one's own can be sought; or perhaps an altogether different approach can be taken to defuse the original problem. As the helping person, you must therefore resist the impulse to cover up the problem, to lead in exploring it, or to advocate solutions or resources. You simply reflect the feelings that seem to be implied in the statement as the speaker experiences them.

At the same time, remain emotionally separate from the speaker. Maintain your own integrity. Reflect what the speaker feels, and name it as the speaker's present feeling. Do not foretell future feelings. Do not take the side of the speaker against an envisioned opponent, or vice versa. Each person involved in a reported situation, whether present or absent, is worthy of your unconditional acceptance and regard.

Exercise 4-2: Reflecting Feelings

Directions: With a partner, roleplay a conversation beginning with each numbered statement. Continue with four or five interchanges. The second speaker attempts to reflect the first speaker's feelings after each statement. Take turns being first and second speaker. For example, Partner A is first speaker with numbers 1, 3, and 5; Partner B is first with 2, 4, and 6.

Discuss each situation enough to establish fictional identities before starting to roleplay them. The second speaker must be able to depend on the first to play the role with real feeling. Both must genuinely try to *be* the persons they are portraying.

1. High school senior to older person:
I never get anywhere with my parents. They never even hear what I'm saying. Every time I start to tell them something they start telling me what I ought to do before I even get a chance to explain what it's all about.

2. Child of seven to parent:
I don't want to go back to that school anymore!

3. Twenty-eight-year-old mother of three to visiting helper:
Six months ago, when I came home after Jason was born, I was so happy that it was all over that I felt I could go ahead and have another. But now . . .

4. Forty-five-year-old shipping clerk to friend and co-worker:
The boss is getting worse every day. I had to tell him about a rip-off in a shipment today and he came down on me as if I had taken the stuff myself. If anybody had talked to me that way ten years ago, I would have quit right there. But what the hell can I do now but just take it?

5. Seventy-five-year-old man to nurse in extended care facility:
There's nothing for me to live for any more. My wife's dead. My kids don't need me. I'm too old to get any kind of job. I'm just a nuisance to everybody.

6. Thirty-year-old man whose wife was recently killed in a car accident to industrial health nurse:
My head is going around in circles. I need something to calm me down. I get started on something and before I know it I've made a mistake because I'm back where it happened. I can't work right, but I can't face staying home from work.

Points for Discussion

1. How did you *feel* in each of the roles that you portrayed? Go down the list and relive your feelings aloud in each of the parts (helper or helpee) that you played.

2. As the second speaker in 1, 2, and 4, was it difficult to identify as much with the parents, teachers, and boss as with the first speaker in each instance? Why or why not?

3. Which was the most difficult role for you to take? Why? What does your answer tell you about yourself?

4. As second speaker in 5 or 6, did you succumb to the impulse to reassure the client (sweep the problem under the rug) with a type of response such as *Everything's going to be all right?* If you did, whose need were you meeting? What does the first speaker need at this point instead of a placebo?

Clarifying Feelings and Attitudes

The term **clarification** is often used to refer to a listener's need to understand the factual details of any situation that has significance to the speaker. When a client presents information that is not clear, the counselor must ask for an explanation. As may be expected in any type of interpersonal encounter, the request may be phrased as either a question or a tentative statement. This feedback is used interchangeably between two individuals or between an individual and a group; a client may ask the counselor for similar clarification at any time.

As a counseling technique, clarification may relate to information, as above, or to feelings and attitudes. The use of clarification of feeling as a technical term originated with nondirective counseling. Because it is a leading rather than a continuing response, it is used sparingly in client-centered counseling at its present state of development. By using it, the counselor takes the initiative by calling the client's attention to an implicit message conveyed in his or her last statement. In reflection of feeling or attitude, the counselor *identifies* a metacommunication revealed by the client; in clarification, the counselor goes further than the client has gone, and *decodes* the metacommunication. The *command* implicit in the original message is translated into plain language to confront the speaker.

Tom's interaction with his mother can be used to point out the difference between reflection and clarification of feeling. In Tom's message to his mother, what command is implied as a metacommunication? What request is Tom making of his mother? She might interpret it as: *Jim is my enemy. I want you on my side!* To clarify the attitude, the mother might respond with a statement or a question put forward tentatively to avoid arousing defensiveness. She might reply: *Is Jim really all that bad?* or *You seem to be saying that you and Jim aren't good friends anymore.*

With Mr. C, the counselor found the client reluctant to accept the identification of feeling afraid. Clarification, because it goes deeper into motivation, would have been even less acceptable than reflection. If Mr. C's counseling had progressed to the point where he could usually acknowledge his feelings, the counselor might have chosen to clarify the underlying attitude by saying: *Is it because your relationship with Jenny is rather shaky?* or *Perhaps your worry comes from being uncertain about the stability of your relationship with Jenny.*

Either remark could help the client who is ready to face the evident significance in what he is saying. At the present stage of development of client-centered counseling, it is usually considered more sound to leave such self-revelations entirely to the client. Once recognition of motivations comes to the surface in one's own spontaneous verbalization, they are likely to be fully owned and available for one's control and channeling. When clients progress and are capable of identifying and acknowledging feelings as their own, they often reply to an astute reflection of feeling by clarifying and placing the feeling in the larger inner context. Under such circumstances, Mr. C might have paused after the counselor's first response and replied with: *I keep coming to you with stories like this. Let's face it. Jenny and I are just about washed up.*

In the ordinary sense of all three terms, clarification is a synonym for both interpretation and validation, but each of the three has a technical, psychologic meaning that distinguishes it from the other two. Clarification, as we have seen, originated in nondirective or client-centered counseling. **Interpretation** is a psychoanalytic term. **Consensual validation** was first used in a technical sense by Harry Stack Sullivan. It is illustrated in Chapter 6 in connection with problem-solving counseling. Both interpretation and consensual validation are decoding techniques in which the therapist presents an inferential assessment of the unconscious mechanisms and motivations underlying the client's words, actions, or life patterns and choices. In contrast, clarification verbalizes the almost unconscious affective assumption underlying a statement made by the client. Another important difference is a philosophic one. In clarification, as in reflection, the client and not the counselor is the locus of evaluation. It is important that the helping professional recognize that reflection of feeling is one technique and clarification of attitudes that underlie the feeling is another. Because the latter goes deeper into the dynamics of the client's motivation, it has the potential of stirring up emotions that the client will have difficulty in handling. Reflection of feeling, in contrast, deals with emotions that are already surfacing and can therefore be safely called to the client's attention. Through instruction, record keeping, and expert supervision, the student of counseling learns to assess the degree of trust in both self and helper that the client has attained. A certain degree of autonomy, or ego strength, is necessary before self-awareness and self-disclosure of any depth of emotion can be tolerated.

This chapter has explored the nature of the client-centered relationship. It has also attempted a breakdown of the interaction that takes place between client and helper in the relationship by naming and defining the various skills and techniques used by the helper in a sensitively humanistic approach to intervention.

Although this mode of intervention may safely be used with clients within a wide range of circumstances, its effectiveness in fostering self-awareness and self-acceptance will vary from client to client. In Chapter 5, the conditions and probabilities of effective client-centered helping are examined.

References

Avila, D. L., et al. 1977. *The helping relationship sourcebook.* 2nd ed. Boston: Allyn and Bacon.

Benjamin, A. 1974. *The helping interview.* 2nd ed. Boston: Houghton Mifflin.

Carkhuff, R. R. et al. 1977. *The skills of teaching: Interpersonal skills.* Amherst, Mass.: Human Resources Development Press.

——. 1979. *The art of helping.* 4th ed. Amherst, Mass.: Human Resources Development Press.

——. 1979. *The skills of helping: An introduction to counseling.* Amherst, Mass.: Human Resources Development Press.

Combs, A. W.; Avila, D. L.; and Purkey, W. W. 1978. *Helping relationships: Basic concepts for the helping professions.* Boston: Allyn and Bacon.

Hart, J. T., and Tomlinson, T. M., editors. 1970. *New directions in client-centered therapy.* Boston: Houghton Mifflin.

Reik, T. 1972. *Listening with the third ear.* New York: Arena Books.

Rogers, C. R. 1959. A theory of therapy, personality, and interpersonal relations as developed in the client-centered framework. *Psychology: A study of a science,* vol. 3. S. Koch, editor. New York: McGraw-Hill.

——. 1961. *On becoming a person.* Boston: Houghton Mifflin.

——. 1980. *A way of being.* Boston: Houghton Mifflin.

Satir, V. 1968. *Conjoint family therapy.* Palo Alto, California: Science and Behavior Books.

Sullivan, H. S. 1954. *The psychiatric interview.* New York: Norton.

Watkins, J. G. 1978. *The therapeutic self.* New York: Human Sciences.

Wexler, D. A., and Rice, L. N. editors. 1974. *Innovations in client-centered therapy.* New York: Wiley.

CHAPTER 5

The Process of Client-Centered Intervention

With the aim of optimum self-actualization for the client, the principles and techniques of client-centered counseling are appropriate to use in almost any helping situation with the exception of a few emergency situations requiring a more direct form of intervention (Chapter 6). But to feel free to be fully oneself, even briefly, is a growth experience. At the moment when I become more acutely aware of the person I am, with feelings, attitudes, and values I can openly acknowledge and appreciate, I move to becoming more a person than I was the moment before. An aspect of myself that was closed to me is now available to be claimed as my own. When I possess more of myself, I become more secure in my own person. I value myself more and, accordingly, see others in a new light. Reality is more a part of me and I am more a part of reality.

As in any approach to counseling, the degree to which the aims of client-centered counseling are fulfilled depends on several interacting conditions, including the attributes of the helper, the potentiality for change in the client, and the circumstances under which the help is offered. The process can be counted on to humanize a single interview or interaction, and, for the trained therapist, can be the therapy of choice in the long-term treatment of a severe personality problem. As used by the practitioner in any of the helping professions, a client-centered approach enriches either a short-term or long-term relationship. The helper's acceptance and willingness to understand can be supportive and reassuring to an individual in any age group or in any state of physical or mental health, as long as some kind of communication is possible. The discussions of successive methodologies in later chapters will indicate that the desirable establishment of a helping relationship under the rubric of any helping modality requires at the minimum that the helper: (a) genuinely like people and (b) have some ability in the use of the continuing responses discussed in Chapter 4.

THE CONTEXT

Every approach to counseling tends to develop a characteristic preference for the ideal environment in which to use it. With a completely egalitarian view of the desirable relationship, the client-centered practitioner opts for comfortably informal surroundings. A degree of privacy is essential. A face-to-face, easy chair encounter is preferred, without the physical and psychologic barrier of a desk or table. If this arrangement is patently unacceptable to the client, his or her choice is respected. Some people find it unbearably difficult to face a stranger directly. Until a relationship of trust is established, it is not unusual for a client to select the chair farthest from the helping person or to sit sideways to avoid as much eye contact as possible. A child or a psychotic patient may at first refuse to face the practitioner, to sit down, or even to stay in a room with the practitioner for any length of time. Fortunately, a client-centered encounter may occur anywhere or at any time that there is a helper and a person to be helped.

From the beginning, the helping person assumes as relaxed and natural a listening posture as possible. The helper's regard is directed solely to the client, who is always central to the total situation. When with a child, the helper is likely to take a place on the child's level. When clients meet in a group, the helper faces each speaker directly, hears each one individually, and responds with undivided attention. This is an attitude as well as a posture, and as such is likely to be imitated. As clients begin to relate positively to the helper, they tend to do so with each other and to carry this attitude into their outside contacts.

In the various approaches to counseling, different views are held as to the amount of structuring that should be used. **Structuring** is orienting the client regarding expectations of the counseling experience and its outcomes. Formal, verbal structuring is considered an important first step in some methodologies. It is seen as providing a psychologic context that is as important as the physical context. In client-centered counseling, formal structuring is minimal. Agreement is reached early on routine items such as time and place of interviews. If there are any factors that may affect the duration of the relationship—the end of a school year, for instance—they are also made the subject of early consideration.

The client is left free to take the lead on other questions that arise as part of the total counseling experience. When a request for such information is made by the client, the helper is comfortable in sharing with the client a personal version of the values underlying client-centered counseling. Those values, which are manifest in the person of the counselor, are its indispensable climate and context. If and when they are germane to ongoing discussion, they are imparted in terms that are understandable and believable to the client. Taking care not to go beyond what the client is asking, the helper expresses such beliefs as: each person is unique; differences among people are prized; each strives to maintain and enhance, according to one's own ideas of "the good," one's concept of self; to be human is to have feelings about oneself, other people, and one's inner and outer experiences; to vividly experience a full range of feelings from ecstacy to pain is conducive to becoming more fully human; the appropriate disclosure of feelings is a vehicle of self-understanding and growth toward integrity and wholeness; the person who is growing to fullness of functioning becomes more open to both inner and outer reality, more accepting of self and others and more able to make realistic judgments and decisions.

It is unlikely that the helper will be called on to verbalize many of the values specified. All are implicit in the counselor's work on behalf of the client and form the metacommunication latent in the counselor's words and actions.

Together, the helper's values add up to the main contribution brought to the relationship. Techniques are secondary. To the extent that professional helpers make these values focal to their work and to their personal lives, they will be successful in forming short-term or long-term helping relationships with clients.

THE GROWTH CONTINUUM

In relationships of short duration or in a single interview, the helping person does not experience the satisfaction of witnessing gradual growth in clients. Gratification is felt, however, as a client breaks through frustration and defensiveness into open expression of feelings, recognizes and accepts a feeling, becomes more open to either the pain or promise that reality offers, or reveals an unexpected capacity to integrate new experiences into an already fairly mature self-concept. Most of the people who seek professional counseling or psychotherapy do so because of inadequacies in their capacity to function in interpersonal or occupational situations. In other types of service such as the fields of general health, education, social service, or ministry, the helper's clients may be in either greater or less need of psychotherapy than those who actually seek it.

A client may be at any point on the continuum along which we all move toward fullness of functioning. One may be barricaded behind a wall of defenses; another may have progressed far into the freedom of affiliation, integrity, and universality of outlook. We sometimes encounter clients who are functioning fully enough that they give more than they receive in our relationships with them.

Rogers (1961) attributes progress in therapy to a circumstance that he terms the **basic condition of growth**. Using the metaphor of a plant's need for constant conditions of temperature, light, and moisture, he refers to the climate produced by the practitioner (described in Chapter 4). Summed up into one basic condition, the climate must be such that *the client experiences self as being fully received.* Rogers (1961) explains:

> *By this I mean that whatever his feelings–fear, despair, insecurity, anger; whatever his mode of expression–silence, gestures, tears, or words; whatever he finds himself being in this moment, he senses that he is psychologically* received, *just as he is, by the therapist. There is implied in this term the concept of being understood, empathically, and the concept of acceptance. It is also well to point out that it is the client's experience of this condition which makes it optimal, not merely the fact of its existence in the therapist.*

The client is not passive in the relationship. Progress depends on the client's **experiencing** the self as being fully received. In other words, the client must be able to reach the state of openness to experience that permits awareness of the acceptance and empathy of the helping person. In times of stress, anyone may close out this awareness along with many other aspects of experience. Given a degree of receptivity on the part of the client, an ability of the counselor to **communicate** attitudes of acceptance and empathy is also required. As helpers, we may encounter clients who are chronically hard to reach. However open our attitudes toward them, the establishment of a relationship of trust may be difficult to accomplish.

By analyzing many recordings of his therapy with individual clients, Rogers (1961) was able to identify the affective changes observed in clients in the course of successful counseling. Because they demonstrate human progress from psychologic captivity to unhampered self-determination and altruism, recognizing the areas and types of change is pertinent to our helping function. It provides a means to understand and appreciate the varying needs of clients. It also gives us a measuring rod for evaluating our own progress toward fullness of functioning.

The process recordings made by counseling students who practice under expert supervision provide data for analyzing clients' progress. As practitioners, helping professionals may or may not be in a position to relate to their clients beyond the limits of a few brief contacts. Still, they may hope to contribute, however minimally, to their clients' growth toward self-actualization. Rogers' informal scale of emotional progress enlarges our vision of what may result for others if we are able to receive them unconditionally and use ourselves as persons who are fully present to them, whatever the circumstances.

The following characteristics of emotional growth perceived by Rogers are organized to correspond with four predominant areas of affective functioning:

1. Perception and expression of feelings and attitudes
2. Openness to experience
3. Past-present-future orientation
4. Congruence between feeling-experience and awareness and between feelings and communication of feelings

A brief sketch of the progressive changes that may be expected to occur during the course of effective counseling within each area of functioning is outlined below. Progress is uneven and depends on the climatic conditions already described, together with the client's ability to respond to them.

1. *Expression of Feeling:* Expression of feeling in a client who is at an early stage of growth toward emotional maturity may be largely blocked or may be tentative, embarrassed, and impoverished. Feelings are often disowned and placed apart from the total self. Generalizations are common. These trends are evident in remarks such as: *It's all in my nerves. People always get me*

wrong. Or perhaps *Nobody can get the best of me–I always have the last word.* With progress in counseling, the client's expression of feeling gradually becomes more specific, open, and rich in content. The range widens with experiencing, both inside and outside the counseling relationship, feelings that are new to the client. Unaccustomed heights and depths of feeling may be reached, recognized, and owned and their contrasts savored.

2. *Openness to Experience:* In adults whose emotional growth is underdeveloped, experience is interpreted in narrow, repetitive formulations. The self is regarded as an object propelled into habitual failure or, in the view of some clients, into habitual success by outside forces. There is little communication with the self, and no desire to change. Other people are dichotomized into liked versus disliked, good versus bad, bright versus stupid, and so forth.

With progress, rigid constructions placed on inner and outer experience are loosened. Problems are recognized and acknowledged as part of one's existence, and more realistic meanings are found in events and people. Correspondingly, increased value is discovered in authentic communication with the self and others. Once the self becomes known as having a valid, here-and-now existence and as capable of becoming, genuine self-esteem is increased and constant self-justification is no longer necessary. Others are gradually accepted as having separate existences and as no longer a threat or an indispensable support to the self.

3. *Past-Present-Future Orientation:* Adults in the early stages of emotional growth express feelings oriented to the past, which is a way of disowning them as part of the present self. Responsibility for current experiences is placed on bygone circumstances and people, with parents or other significant persons commonly singled out for blame. Meanings are so static that change in self is deemed undesirable and unnecessary, and changes in others seem unlikely to occur. With forward progress, interpretations are gradually loosened and related to present realities rather than past fantasies. Experiences are viewed as new and therefore as having present significance. A future way of life is conceived that can be guided by cognitive choice instead of compelling determinants lying in the past.

4. *Congruence:* In the early stages, feelings that are unacceptable to the self-concept are denied awareness. Responsibility for feelings is ignored or externalized. With beginning self-awareness comes some recognition, but little acceptance at first. Instead, feelings are labeled bad or abnormal or are described as something that should not be felt. As acceptable meanings are found in the currently existing self and in immediate experience, feelings and attitudes are gradually owned. Communication of feelings is less difficult, even if phrased in semiarticulate terms. Once free of constricting defenses,

the self enjoys communicating the gamut of new feelings that freedom engenders in new relationships.

We may find a client at any point of the growth spectrum in each of the four categories. The important function of the helping professional is not to diagnose the client's position, but to understand and receive the client without conditions related to growth or to any other quality. In its complete form, Rogers' model of adult progression in emotional growth (1961) offers a refinement of the affective aspect of Erikson's crises of psychosocial development (1963). These and other such perceptive sources combine to furnish the knowledge base from which our understanding of people as persons can grow.

Case Example: Mrs. Gregory and the Community Health Nurse

A community health nurse is making her last postnatal visit to the middle-class home where Elaine Gregory, a sixteen-year-old unmarried mother, and her month-old baby live with Elaine's parents and a younger brother and sister. The nurse discovers that Elaine has returned to school that day for the first time. Mrs. Gregory is taking care of the baby, whom the nurse finds to be in excellent condition. She compliments Mrs. Gregory on the care the baby is receiving.

1. Mrs. G: *He's fine. I wish I could say the same for the rest of us.*
   Nurse: *Oh?* (sits down, pulling her chair around to face Mrs. Gregory)
2. Mrs. G: *Elaine was as nervous as a cat this morning and so was I. We snapped at each other till she got some breakfast and left. I guess she didn't know which would be worse, going to school or staying home with me.*
   Nurse: (leans forward, touches Mrs. G's hand momentarily, and continues to lean slightly toward her) *You're both going through a rough time.*
3. Mrs. G: (tearfully) *Our whole family life has been changed.*

She continues at some length about the changes that she has noted in each member of the family. The nurse does not comment, but nods slightly from time to time and says *Mhm* at intervals. Mrs. G finishes with:

Our life isn't the same ever since Elaine got pregnant. It's almost more than I can stand!
Nurse: *You're hurting a lot over what you have all been through.*

4. Mrs. G: *Yes. I guess we're all ashamed of Elaine and the baby. He's so sweet. It isn't his fault, but I think we all hate*

him as well as love him. And Elaine—well, I just feel as if I don't know her any more.

Nurse: *Mhm.* (pause)

5. Mrs. G: *She doesn't come near me unless she has to. She doesn't even want me to teach her how to take care of the baby.* (weeps a little)

Nurse: (waits until Mrs. G wipes her eyes and looks up) *You have some mixed feelings, is that it? About both the baby and about Elaine. You want to help Elaine but you're ashamed of her, too. And you love the baby, but he's part of the shame.*

6. Mrs. G: (after a long pause) *I'm mixed—all mixed up. I just can't resist this baby any more than I could one of my own when they were that small. My husband loves him too, and he says I shouldn't care what other people think. And it isn't that so much, really . . .*

Nurse: *It's that and something more.*

7. Mrs. G: *Yes—s. I guess I feel somehow that it was my fault. Maybe if I could have kept Elaine close to me the way she used to be—maybe none of this would have happened.*

Nurse: *If you and she could have stayed the way you were when she was younger . . .*

8. Mrs. G: *Well, that doesn't make sense. But we used to be so close. And now we don't know what to say to one another.*

Nurse: *You're wishing you and Elaine could talk freely together again.*

9. Mrs. G: *Yes. That's it.* (long pause) *I wonder how she'll get through today. The first day—having to face her classmates and teachers. And all she's been getting at home is the hate and the shame . . .*

Nurse: *Your sympathy is with Elaine today especially.*

10. Mrs. G: *Oh—yes. The poor kid. It's bad enough for the rest of us, but it must be awful for her.* (pause) *Well, I've taken up a lot of your time. Thanks for listening. It's our problem, and we'll work it out eventually, I guess.*

Mrs. G then changes the subject back to the baby's progress.

The interchange between Mrs. Gregory and the nurse illustrates the progress that can be made in a single client-centered interview between a skillful helper and a troubled client who is nevertheless well on the way toward fullness of functioning. The nurse's first response is crucial to all that follows. She does not assume that Mrs. Gregory is referring to physical ailments as a problem, but instead shows her interest and concern nonverbally and leaves the client free to move in any direction that she chooses.

An opportunity for this type of response might have been presented by Mrs. Gregory to any number of people in the helping professions: a teacher or guidance counselor at Elaine's school, a clergyman, or the social worker at the hospital who had talked with her and Elaine before and after the baby's birth. Under the circumstances, Mrs. G expressed her feelings quite openly to the nurse as soon as the latter demonstrated her own openness to the need for listening and understanding.

In her second response, the nurse's tone and touch, as well as her words, convey empathy and acceptance. Mrs. G (3) follows this by ventilating feelings about the family situation that have obviously been building up over a period of months. Wisely, the nurse encourages this flow without any interrupting verbalization. When a specific feeling is finally identified and implicitly owned, the nurse's third response reflects it in a way that sums up the present situation. Mrs. Gregory then reverts to scattering and generalizing, which the nurse merely acknowledges (4).

The nurse's fifth response reflects Mrs. Gregory's currently ambivalent state of mind, and Mrs. Gregory (6) replies in insightful terms that carry her a step farther into self-awareness. This is demonstrated by her oblique reference to another troubled feeling. When the nurse (6) makes her reference more specific, Mrs. Gregory (7) is able to identify her sense of guilt, although she nostalgically attaches it to the past rather than to the present. When the nurse reflects this orientation (7), Mrs. Gregory (8) recognizes its implausible aspect and locates the feeling in a more accurate time relationship, which the nurse reflects in turn (8). In her ninth statement, Mrs. Gregory moves to a new and positive attitude toward Elaine, which brings her up against immediate reality. When this new attitude is reflected (9), Mrs. Gregory responds by amplifying her new feelings in a way that portends new action to follow.

Mrs. Gregory's responses show elements that correspond to those of the process of counseling effectiveness described above. It is evident that Mrs. Gregory is starting from a point well along the continuum. She is able to perceive her feelings and attitudes fairly accurately and express them openly. As she becomes aware of her ambivalence toward the baby and her temporary rejection of Elaine, she is close to recognizing that she has projected her negative feelings to the two individuals she views as representing a problem. Only gradually does she move away from generalizing and projecting her feelings and from looking toward the past for a solution. By degrees she becomes able to place her problem less in the family as a whole and more within herself. Toward the end of the interview, her feelings, which at first were negative and defeatist in nature, take on a more positive cast. One may conclude that she is beginning to think in terms of constructive, independent action.

A change from attitudes that are largely negative to those that have a more positive and action-oriented coloration typically results from the helping process. Although it may take more than the span of a single interview and run a very uneven course, the change tends to move from negative to positive. When open expression of feelings begins, the trend of both the client's general attitude and the feelings that are identified is unhappy, rejecting, blaming, and later, self-blaming. We may note a similar direction in our own thinking patterns. After a prolonged period of indulging, either in words or in thought, in feelings that are essentially destructive, we find that we need to achieve a measure of balance in the situation, whatever it might be. At this point we begin to look for something constructive to fix our attention on. As would probably be the case with Mrs. Gregory, the change is not sudden and complete. After any major trauma, we all tend to slip back repeatedly into despondency and negativism before we eventually settle into a fairly even tenor of comfortable and responsible participation with people and events.

Helping the Hard-to-Reach Client

The case example that follows introduces a client who is at a very early stage of the growth continuum. As helping professionals, we may encounter a client at any point whose self-concept is so constricted that accurate perception of feelings is minimal. Expression of feelings is either blocked or lacks normal controls. Large areas of experience are denied admission to consciousness. Events that are considered of causative significance have occurred in the past and blame for them can be fixed on an outside agent. As a result, neither of the two areas of congruence is evident.

Such persons may settle for being themselves in ways that are destructive rather than constructive to self and others. They may long ago have made a blind compromise with their condition, and seek no other. The feelings they admit to awareness are only those that are supportive of the status quo of the self-concept. Expressions of feeling are likely to be significantly skewed in one direction: all pleasant or all unpleasant. This occurs because inner and outer experiences are unrealistically symbolized as either threatening or vindicating the self.

In helping a person enclosed within a self-concept of this mold, we enter into the relationship with a genuine belief in the potential for growth in this person, as in all others. We are fully present to such individuals, and we are for them, not against or above them. We try to avoid categorizing them in any way in our thoughts other than as persons who have an appeal for us because they simply are. We proceed from the premise that, for them, expression of feeling *in a climate of unconditional acceptance* cannot obstruct growth and may well foster it in the direction of more adequate functioning.

Case Example: Rosalyn and Dick

Rosalyn is a fourteen-year-old high school student who lives in a residential setting for disturbed adolescent girls. Within the past week she has twice stayed out all night and has been absent for a day from school and home. When asked about the escapades by the group parents, Dick and Miriam, she responds defiantly that her behavior is her own concern. She threatens to run away if they make things unpleasant for her.

Because Rosalyn has previously related more positively to Dick than to Miriam, the group parents have agreed that he will try to talk with her. He takes advantage of an opportunity when Rosalyn stays indoors while his wife and the other residents are preparing a barbecue:

Dick: *I'm glad we are here alone, Rosalyn. I have been looking for a chance to talk with you.*

Rosalyn: *Well if you're going to lecture me the way Miriam does, I don't want to.*

Dick: *You don't like the way we show it, but Miriam and I have been worried about you.*

Rosalyn: *You don't need to be. I can look after myself. I've always had to anyway.*

Dick: *When we show how concerned we are, it seems to you that we're interfering.*

Rosalyn: *People are always sticking their noses where they're not wanted.*

Dick: *You've had about enough of other people getting into your affairs.*

Rosalyn: *Other people just make things worse for you. I can't wait till I'm eighteen and nobody can tell me what to do or what I can't do.*

Dick: (slowly) *Mhm . . .*

Rosalyn: *You just think I can't take care of myself. Nobody's ever really taken care of me. With drunks for parents, how do you think I ever got this far?*

Dick: *It seems to you you've always had it hard. Your parents weren't able to help you.*

Rosalyn: *They didn't want to. But I can take it. And I don't need any Dick or Miriam to order me around.*

Dick: *You're not very happy about grown-ups, whether they're concerned about you or not.*

As Dick reflected back to her in her last response, Rosalyn is bitter and somewhat ambivalent about roles taken by adults in her life. This is no wonder considering the nature of her experiences with them. That she does not trust Dick is evident in her repeated testing of his acceptance of her. She attempts to relive a relationship of antagonism that is as familiar to her as kindness is strange. Because of its strangeness, kindness is as threatening as its opposite. Dick withstands her hostility with consistent gentleness, and he keeps the focus on her feelings. He offers no evaluation of her attitudes toward herself, her natural parents, or her group parents.

Although our information about Rosalyn is meager, she seems to represent the early pretreatment stage in each of the four categories of the growth continuum. Her own feelings and attitudes are not freely accessible to her—she projects her hostility to her natural and foster parents. In this way she bolsters the defenses of her self-concept against the possibility of allowing entrance to a new experiential relationship with an adult. Her symbolization of her here-and-now experience and feelings is distorted to conform to her view of a past rather than a present reality.

Case Example: Rosalyn and Dick (continued)

It is unlikely that Rosalyn can move quickly into a realistic evaluation of her own feelings and attitudes. Miriam and Dick recognize this and they resist any tendency to respond to her in terms of a category. They attempt to remain open, consistently accepting, and trustworthy, thus providing a way for her to authentically relate with adults. Additional models are provided for her by the relationships the foster parents have developed with other, more pliable residents. It may be that a particular resident will pave the way by relating to Rosalyn in a peer climate of mutual confidence.

If long-term, professional group counseling were made available, Rosalyn might succumb to peer pressure to the extent of genuinely participating in the endeavor. Rosalyn and other residents might be helped to help each other move along the continuum in the direction of relative fullness of functioning. A behavioral approach is sometimes found to be effective with such groups.

Helping persons who work with delinquent or emotionally disturbed clients will encounter attitudes similar to Rosalyn's on many occasions. Seemingly impermeable defensiveness may also be met at times of acute or prolonged stress in individuals who ordinarily function quite adequately. Whatever the circumstances, the helper operates from a belief in the universal human potential for progress toward becoming more fully human. The person in need of help is accepted without conditions, and the helper responds to feeling with a genuine attempt to reflect the person's meanings.

To combine the social role of disciplinarian with these attitudes is difficult. Children and adults who have had the opportunity to develop relationships of mutual trust with others have a sense of their need for reasonable controls. With those in whom confidence in self and others is severely limited, the disciplinary function is liable to be the focus of excessive mistrust. The helping person must accordingly have an extraordinary capacity to both trust and be trusted in relating with clients whose need is so great.

INTERVENTION AND GROWTH

The cause-effect relationship between client-centered helping and the changes that occur in clients is an open question. Gendlin (1970), who calls his adaptation of the client-centered approach **experiential psychotherapy**, suggests that each step of successful therapy brings about a *carrying forward* of the client's experiencing.

We might explore this idea by transferring it first into a more ordinary milieu than that of therapy. Throughout our lives, experiencing is carried forward by thinking, feeling, acting and being acted upon and by relating to persons, words, things, and events. All of these experiences move us along in the process of becoming. For the most part, the carrying forward occurs through our real or vicarious involvement in interpersonal relationships. The meanings that we find in our experiences are largely adopted by us from meanings that others have found in similar experiences. Chiefly through our interactions with others, we become the persons that we are. We learn to value or devalue aspects of ourselves and our experiences mainly from the others' reactions to us.

Particularly in our feeling life, aspects of our experience may become devalued to the extent that we refuse them access to the light of our rational examination. They are so anxiety laden that we habitually relegate them to a "not me" category. Relationships that would bring this type of information to the surface are avoided, or else the data itself is selectively ignored. Because it is never integrated into our ongoing processing of information, the data is not available to serve as a basis for choices that would lead to growth toward fullness of functioning (Wexler, 1974).

The client-centered relationship offers a climate especially adapted to carrying forward the client's experiencing. The consistently warm and accepting attitude of the helping person carries this message to the client: *In this relationship you are valued as a person, just as you are. You may change in any way you choose and still be valued.* The helper's creative listening, use of silence, and continuing cues all say: *Everything that you say about yourself is worthy of attention. You alone are capable of evaluating your experiences and making choices about what you say and do. You alone are capable of becoming fully yourself.*

Reflection of feeling is particularly adapted to the carrying-forward process. Even before the helper responds, the client's expression of feeling may serve as an impetus toward examining and owning a specific feeling. Accurate reflection provides the client with a slightly different view of the feeling and, at the same time, carries the message: *It's OK to feel this way. This feeling is a totally acceptable part of you, and you yourself are equally acceptable.* If the client is open enough to receive and assimilate this message, the carrying forward has proceeded through a significant unit of change. Growth in self-awareness has occurred, and self-acceptance has expanded to include one further aspect of the self. The self-concept has opened itself to a new experience and has been expanded and enriched as a result.

Client-centered counseling, however its success may be explained, offers the helping professions one of several modes of effective intervention. With some clients, as in the example of Mrs. Gregory, it amply suffices to foster the insights needed by a client at a frustrating plateau of becoming. In Rosalyn's case, it serves the important function of keeping communication open in a helping relationship with a client whose early growth has been distressingly stunted.

The reason for placing the client-centered approach first among the several modalities explored in this book is explained in the next chapter. For the humanistic helper, the client-centered method is basic to all others.

References

Avila, D., et al. 1977. *The helping relationship sourcebook.* 2nd ed. Boston: Allyn and Bacon.

Boy, A. V., and Pine, G. J. 1963. *Client-centered counseling in the secondary school.* Boston: Houghton Mifflin.

Carkhuff, R. R., et al. 1977. *The skills of teaching: Interpersonal skills.* Amherst, Mass.: Human Resources Development Press.

Erikson, E. 1963. *Childhood and society.* 2nd ed. New York: Norton.

Gazda, G. M., et al. 1974. *Human relations development.* Boston: Allyn and Bacon.

Gendlin, E. T. 1970. A short summary and some long predictions. *New directions in client-centered therapy.* J. T. Hart and T. M. Tomlinson, editors. Boston: Houghton Mifflin.

Okun, B. 1976. *Effective helping.* Belmont, Calif.: Duxbury.

Rogers, C. R. 1958. The characteristics of a helping relationship. *Person. Guid. J.* 37:6–15.

——. 1961. *On becoming a person.* Boston: Houghton Mifflin.

——. 1980. *A way of being.* Boston: Houghton Mifflin.

Wexler, D. A., and Rice, L. N., editors. 1974. *Innovations in client-centered therapy.* New York: Wiley.

CHAPTER 6

Problem-Solving Counseling and Interviewing in the Helping Professions

This approach to psychologic helping has as its prototype the interpersonal model of Harry Stack Sullivan (1954). He describes the progress of the therapeutic relationship in a series of stages corresponding to those of the scientific, or problem-solving, method. In social casework and nursing, the two most populous of the helping professions, it has been customary to employ a theoretic framework for the interview or relationship with the client that shows it divided into similar stages. Works that classify methods of counseling and psychotherapy often categorize the client-centered approach as interpersonal. That Sullivan's concept of the client-counselor relationship differs from Rogers' is evident in the fact that the former used the term **expert-client** to characterize it. Here, the problem-solving aspects of counseling are emphasized, not to the exclusion of the client-centered aspect of the counseling relationship, but as an extension of it.

The title of Sullivan's publication *The Psychiatric Interview* (1954) is noteworthy for our purposes. Sullivan used the term interview to refer to both a single encounter with a client and a prolonged, deep relationship, or "interview," which is the vehicle of intensive psychotherapy. He saw his principles of interviewing as applicable in any of a number of fields, and he gave social work and personnel management as examples. Like client-centered counseling, the problem-solving approach is highly adaptable to the needs of many different professional helpers and the clients they serve.

For the eclectic, humanistic approach advocated in the present work, each of the three systems that are dealt with in detail makes a different contribution. This and the chapters that follow show how the three may be combined in various ways in helping not only individual clients, but family and other groups with whom professional helpers work. Client-centered counseling and interviewing, described as basic to all other approaches, is first in a logical sequence. Elements of the climate, skills, and techniques usually classed as client-centered are indispensable to forming any helping relationship. Interpersonal relations, to use Sullivan's term, are the only medium within which direct psychologic helping can occur. In behavior modification, the third counseling approach discussed here, the client can be guided effectively by the behaviorist only if a relationship of trust has been established between them.

THE PROBLEM-SOLVING RELATIONSHIP

Although feelings are not disregarded, the problem-solving activity in counseling is viewed as a learning experience for the client that is largely cognitive in nature. The learning problems to be solved are all looked on as difficulties in daily living. Because daily living occurs in an interpersonal context, its difficulties are always found to have interpersonal bonds. To be effective, the Sullivanian practitioner expects to take on two specific roles: those of **interpersonal expert** and **participant-observer**. Equipped by training and experience as an expert in interpersonal relations, the practitioner helps the client to define the difficulties to be worked with and the learning and action objectives to be reached. Since they offer a means of ordering the helping-learning process into problem-solving stages, the interpersonal process presupposes a built-in set of goals and both periodic and terminal evaluation of their attainment.

The expert-client relationship does not rule out the need for those counselor characteristics that are essential to the client-centered approach. Instead, the quality of expertness must be added to those of authenticity, acceptance, and understanding. Sullivan saw the psychiatrist's role of expert as culturally determined. This accords with the medical model still relied on in his profession and with the expectations of the majority of the patients served.

In every helping profession, there is a cultural expectation that the worker will be proficient. Whether or not practitioners intend to appear to be expert in the sense of playing a role, they will usually be cast in that role by clients. In addition, few would deny their own need to be as fully expert as possible in their own field. There is, unfortunately, a small, incompetent minority in any profession. But to the extent that counseling and interviewing form a part of their professional function, a majority will strive to be competent in the skills of those areas. One essential skill is that of the participant-observer function.

Implied in the cultural presumption of expertness are complementary expectations of the client. Expertness as a professional role suggests automatic trust and docility on the part of its subject. In addition, both expertness and participant observation seem to carry the expectation of an unhesitating completeness of self-disclosure. A sophisticated sector of the public is beginning to expect less direction and intrusion from professionals. These people demand a more decisive voice for themselves in whatever concerns them.

This attitude is becoming increasingly prevalent in ways that affect teachers, social workers, the clergy, and all types of professionals in the health fields. Through study and application of the client-centered relationship and approach to counseling, we have the means to equip ourselves to meet the current requirement. Helping professionals can lend expertise to relationships in ways that benefit, but never demean, clients. The client is always deferred to as the only expert in the ordering of his or her own life.

Participant observation is a needed responsibility that can be shared between helper and client. Some ways to implement this in humanistically oriented problem solving are featured in the sections that follow. This second role is a functional one. The counselor observes every nuance of the interaction that takes place in every interview. Every client response is carefully noted, as well as every counselor response. The full significance of each is explored. The client's meanings are clarified by dialogue, and their implications for the client's problem situation are investigated to the extent that the client's anxiety level permits. The meanings of the counselor's responses are pondered retrospectively; the results are used to improve subsequent interactions.

Because of the central position given to anxiety in the interpersonal problem-solving approach, the concept is given prominence in this chapter. It will be evident from the following discussion that anxiety is a salient factor to consider in any method of psychologic helping.

THE CONCEPT OF ANXIETY

Since the publication of W. H. Auden's satirical poem "The Age of Anxiety" (1947) following World War II, the term has come into literary use to characterize our Western culture at the present time. Anxiety is so universal that, for most of us, not a day passes without our being touched by it. The term as used here does not denote a single feeling. It refers instead to a diffuse and intricate complex of feelings and to the responses they evoke in the individual.

Although the experience of anxiety is mainly unpleasant, there is sometimes an admixture of a welcome sense of challenge. This happens, for instance, when students are taking a test for which they are well prepared. Occasionally, anxiety has an aspect of anticipation that is completely pleasurable except for a tinge of apprehension, as is the case immediately before the visit of a lover. A storm of anxiety may accompany an artist's most creative work. Even in these partial exceptions, anxiety always accompanies a perception of threat to some aspect of the self.

Every outstanding theorist on the subject, including Freud (1936), defines anxiety with a slightly different emphasis. The following is a composite of a number of definitions: *Anxiety is the human response to a perceived threat to the self-concept.* Sullivan (1954) specifies the nature of the threat as a lowering of self-esteem, and he uses the term **self-image** in place of self-concept. Others have identified the threat as a loss of some kind, recognizing that anxiety always contains a sense of either impending or actual deficit, defeat, or failure.

In most situations of anxiety, the average person's immediate reaction is likely to be less than constructive. Before we can begin to give thought to constructively resolving the anxiety-provoking problem situation, we usually have a compelling need to share our troubled feelings with a sympathetic listener. This alone may clear the way for rational planning and action. On the other hand, we may begin by using our individual version of some of the more socialized forms of aggression and regression. In addition, we are likely to make use of one or more of the relief-giving devices that have been given specific names under the general designations of the mechanisms, or mental mechanisms, of defense.

Defense mechanisms are socialized responses that we put into service, largely on an unconscious level, as a means of evading the responsibilities signaled by anxiety. Anxiety is a warning that we judge something to be amiss or threatening to become so. It calls for a rational assessment of the situation. If we substitute the use of one of the defense mechanisms, we postpone problem solving in favor of the irrational maneuver of avoidance.

When I place blame for my real or anticipated inadequacies on someone else or on some circumstance outside myself, I use the mechanism of projection to temporarily assuage my anxiety with the false assurance that all remains secure within my self-concept. This response provides me with a briefly serviceable, brittle armor against hurt or loss. At the same time, it cuts me off from an opportunity to own both the pain of anxiety and the heightened awareness that it can bring and then to select from alternative courses of action the one that will serve me best in the interest of learning and becoming. Although each takes on a somewhat different form, reaction formation, denial, displacement, and others serve purposes similar to those of projection.

Like the anxiety that calls them into service, defense mechanisms serve a temporarily adaptive purpose. At times of insecurity, they function to maintain the status quo of the self-concept and keep anxiety within normal bounds. The anxious individual buys time with them to regroup scattered forces to prepare for a more constructive response. But when the mechanisms are used habitually to postpone or replace rational thought and action, they become detrimental to the individual's growth as a person. As we have seen, their continued use rigidifies the borders of the self-concept, rendering it relatively impervious to the perception of new, growth-promoting experiences. As helping professionals, we need to cultivate a heightened awareness of our own patterns of anxiety and defense and a keener recognition of how the mechanisms are used by others.

In the course of socialization, each person develops a system of using defense mechanisms that is part of his or her larger pattern of anxiety and the responses it evokes. Dealing with anxiety and its characteristic patterns is an important part of problem-solving intervention. Before the process of anxiety intervention is delineated, an exercise in anxiety recognition is presented. Our own self-awareness in this area is an essential preliminary to understanding the problems that anxiety gives rise to in our clients. In addition, if we can recognize when we are anxious, we will be in a better position to handle the anxiety that we ourselves experience in counseling. We may then be able to minimize the customary reactions that may disturb the counseling relationship.

Exercise 6-1: Understanding Anxiety

Directions: With a partner, take turns in reliving a significant anxiety experience that you have undergone in the past.

Help each other with pertinent questions and reminders.

Delineate in detail the pattern formed by the anxiety, using the following outline:

1. Type of threat triggering the anxiety; the element of loss involved (dignity, status, loved one, possessions, and so forth)
2. Degree or intensity; changes in intensity; duration
3. Physical changes in body systems; at onset; residuals
4. Negative feelings; at onset; residuals
5. Responses:
   a. sharing
   b. aggression
   c. regression
   d. defense mechanisms
   e. problem solving

CONTROLLING ANXIETY

The following recommendations are applicable to psychologic helping regardless of the worker's methodologic or theoretic counseling preference. In an eclectic approach, skill in dealing with anxiety is an indispensable asset.

At any point in the counseling process, the helper attempts to remain alert to the current feeling states of both participants in the relationship. Special attention is paid to the occurrence of rising anxiety in either helper or client. Many of its outward signs are directly observable both to the sufferer and to others, but at the same time, their connection with the phenomenon of anxiety may not enter into the awareness of the anxious individual. Using observations such as those recommended in Exercise 6-1, helping professionals can gradually learn to recognize the presence of anxiety in themselves, to label the experience accurately, and to exert the control that is necessary to minimize its effect on their moment-to-moment work with clients.

Where the client is concerned, the worker is aware that a mild degree of anxiety is conducive to an increase in both communication and mental concentration. When the state becomes intense enough to interfere with these processes or when other signs of severe anxiety are present, supportive measures are used to reduce its level. The helper attempts to identify and, if possible, anticipate the factors that seem to precipitate the build-up. If it tends to occur toward the close of each of a series of interviews, for instance, preventive reassurance is indicated.

In some counseling situations, the helper finds that the presenting problem cannot be effectively worked with until the client can learn to bring recurring anxiety under control. The worker must then assume a teaching responsibility to help the client toward a cognitive understanding of anxiety and its alleviation. For clients as well as workers, recognizing their own anxiety constitutes a useful first step towards controlling it. Realization may be brought about by a reassuring expression of concern that also reflects the client's feelings. For example: *You are rather anxious about all this,* or, if the helper senses that the anxious label may be disconcerting to the client, *This isn't a very comfortable experience for you,* or *You are feeling quite tense, aren't you?*

If the client is able to acknowledge the feeling under any name, discussion of anxiety per se can be introduced. The worker's acknowledgment of the phenomenon as universal and, therefore, to be expected, will help to consolidate the client's willingness to own the experience. Labeling promotes recognition of attendant feelings as they are discussed and mobilizes the client's ability to think objectively. The client begins to see that the concentrated thought required for recognizing, labeling, and describing feelings as they are experienced leads to a considerable diminution of the tension and physical and emotional discomfort that anxiety brings. Interest can be aroused in the value of knowing what comprises one's own habitual pattern of anxiety.

In a crisis situation, a high level of anxiety may continue over a considerable period of time or recur later at frequent intervals. In such instances, clients benefit from being confronted with the fact that they are undergoing severe anxiety and that relief can be obtained by following explicit instructions. Panic, with the occasional exception of drug panic, tends to be a relatively ephemeral state from which individuals can either talk themselves down or be talked down by a sympathetic person. A persistent state of panic may require the services of a physician.

Whether or not the helper identifies a state as panic, intense anxiety merits the use of interaction with first-aid measures as indicated. If the client has a tendency to hyperventilate, rebreathing the air in a paper bag about a dozen times may afford relief. Hyperventilation, it should be noted, may be accompanied by transient feelings of faintness, palpitation, and spasms in various muscles. The talking aspect of intervention consists of the liberal use of reassurance, ego reinforcement, and other measures described in the next section. Unconditional acceptance of the person and a sincere attempt to understand the suffering involved are essential prerequisites. Ego reinforcement and empathy are combined in responses such as: *It's hard for you to sort out your feelings just now. When you relax a bit, you'll be able to work through them, though.* As soon as the client is able to cooperate, it may be appropriate to suggest a relaxation technique.

Severe anxiety and its accompanying tension may be moderated by the client's use of controlled breathing and generalized relaxation. Instruction in these techniques may, according to circumstances, be given during an attack, between attacks, in person, or over the telephone in an emergency. A simplified method of general relaxation is suggested in Exercise 3-1. A widely used and much more complex technique is Jacobson's therapeutic method of progressive relaxation (1964). Numerous adaptations of the method are currently in use.

Breath control has been used throughout the ages and in a variety of cultures as a means to center the attention, usually before meditation. It promotes the relaxation that promises sleep in insomnia, as well as temporary relief from the pain of anxiety. One begins by relaxing, using a method such as those previously described. An effort is then made to concentrate fully on one's breathing. This can be done by using a system of counting regularly and slowly—from one to four with each inhalation and from one to eight with each exhalation. It is important that each exhalation take approximately twice the time of each inhalation. This prevents the stimulation that results from inhaling excessive amounts of oxygen and prevents the symptoms of hyperventilation. In a case of severe anxiety, the client may not be able to concentrate on the procedure without step-by-step coaching.

When anxiety is less extreme but still produces acute discomfort, it can often be relieved more simply by muscular activity. This uses the effects of the increased secretion of adrenal hormones produced by anxiety or fear. The motorist who has a near accident would be well advised to pull into the next rest stop or side street and jog in place until the physical concomitants of anxiety are diminished. The child client who keeps moving about the room or the adult who paces the floor may not need further help in gaining control of a mild attack of anxiety.

The professional helper is careful to avoid encouraging the client to expect that a way can be found to escape entirely from repeated experiences of anxiety. Because it is an inextricable part of the human condition, a certain amount of anxiety must simply be endured. Healthy individuals tend to discover their own ways of ameliorating the suffering that it brings. Work or exercise offers relief for some, diversion for others. Still others find that if they surrender themselves and enter as deeply as possible into the pain of anxiety, as with intense pain of any origin, the full realization of its necessity gradually carries them into a quiet sphere of existential wholeness.

The control of anxiety has been introduced as a necessary step before adequate problem-solving can be expected to take place. Its use may be indicated at intervals throughout the counseling relationship. The following section deals with skills of communication. Effective communication is basic not only to problem-solving intervention, but to all counseling approaches and to effective interaction in any aspect of human relationships.

SKILLS AND TECHNIQUES OF PROBLEM-SOLVING INTERVENTION

Before the work of cooperative problem-solving can begin, a relationship of trust must be developed. This is the case in all forms of helping, including emergency counseling, when mutual trust must sometimes be attained in a very short span of time. Helper attitudes of acceptance and willingness to listen must then be conveyed by the way in which the necessary leading responses are used. Ordinarily, practitioners communicate these attitudes through listening without passing judgment, remaining silent when silence is needed, and using cues that encourage disclosure of feelings regardless of their nature. The helper's skill in accurately reflecting feeling is an indispensable asset.

From the initiation of the problem-solving process, a number of additional techniques are employed to help the client move through the successive steps of the process and deal with its anxiety. Added to the continuing responses of client-centered counseling are several leading responses that are described later in this section. Informed attention to the nonverbal aspects of the counseling situation represents a skill that is common to all approaches. Although the subject of nonverbal communication is discussed in problem-solving counseling, it has identical applications to client-centered counseling and to the methods discussed in later chapters.

Nonverbal Communication

The interest of counselors in nonverbal communication stems from its unconscious, two-way nature. Variations in voice tone, facial expression, and posture and gesture transmit messages the sender may be quite unaware of. Practitioners strive to be alert to the meanings that may be implicit in their clients' nonverbal behavior and, at the same time, conscious of the interpretations that clients may put on their own.

Sullivan (1954) was among the first to recognize the importance of nonverbal behavior in the therapeutic relationship. In the years since his posthumous 1954 publication, much investigative study has been devoted to the part played by nonverbal communication both in therapy and in day-to-day social life. Mehrabian (1972) reports numerous studies of nonverbal, or implicitly communicative, behaviors. For purposes of classification, he and other theorists use behavioral groupings such as facial and vocal expressions, eye contact, hand gestures, posture and position, and dress and grooming.

Posture has been studied particularly with reference to the body language exchanged when one person is seated in conversation with another. Mehrabian finds that a combination of factors that he terms **immediacy** is interpreted by addressees as liking. Immediacy refers to a combination of the following elements of behavior: physical closeness, touching during conversation, frequent eye contact, and leaning forward with the torso oriented toward the addressee. **Relaxation**, when moderate, is viewed as liking, and when more extreme, as denoting lack of respect. Relaxation involves an asymmetrical placement of the extremities, a sideways or half-reclining torso, and relaxed hands and neck. Subjects in a study using drawings rated according to preference favored moderately open arms over closed or extended arms.

Preferences regarding postural distance, or space between two persons in conversation, varies with ethnicity, prior relationship, available space, and circumstances. Until recently, dress and grooming tended to vary rather predictably with social class, social situation, age, and to some extent, with occupation or profession. The professional helper tends to be moderately informal in posture and dress and to respect obvious preferences of clients as to the physical distance between them.

In observing clients, the practitioner is aware of the fact that no single nonverbal cue carries a specific meaning in and of itself. Each detail of behavior can be interpreted only in combination with many other factors of the counseling situation. When a client seems to be giving specific nonverbal expression to a particular feeling or change of feeling, the practitioner disregards this, reflects it back to the client, or openly discusses it, whichever is appropriate. Practitioners are observant of their own nonverbal behavior, but not in the sense of being self-conscious. They remain regularly alert to the fact that clients may be reading the changes of affect that bring variation into their own nonverbal ways of expressing themselves. This, too, may be made the subject of discussion as a means of furthering the relationship.

The following exercise is recommended to sharpen observation of nonverbal behavior, both in yourself and others.

Exercise 6-2: Nonverbal Communication

Directions: Use as either a small group (triad) or a large group (fishbowl) exercise.

Triad: Take turns in the roles of speaker, listener, and observer. As speaker, converse with the listener for five minutes on one topic: yourself. As listener, participate as a friend or acquaintance in discussion with the speaker. As observer, note and record the nonverbal behavior of both participants in the dyad, using the categories itemized above (facial and vocal expressions, and so forth). Also act as timekeeper. At the end of the five-minute period, provide feedback to the discussants, who also participate at this point.

Fishbowl: Assemble in groups of six or eight. Three or four seat themselves in a conversational grouping; the others sit outside the group, each in a good observational position facing one member of the inner group. Inside the fishbowl, the members hold a ten-minute discussion on a topic of their own selection. At the end of the period, each of the observers provides the whole group with feedback about an observee as described under "Triad."

Note: As a substitute for or in addition to observers of dyad and fishbowl behavior, use video sweep and playback. Participants then evaluate their own nonverbal responses.

Points for Reflection
(Elaborate in response to each of the following questions):

1. Was the amount of your nonverbal behavior a surprise to you? Explain.
2. Which of your specific behaviors were surprising to you?
3. Associate specific behaviors with specific feeling states that you experienced during the course of the discussion.
4. Identify those observed behaviors that are habitual mannerisms of yours.
5. Which of the subjects under discussion raise your anxiety level more significantly than others?
6. What have you learned from this exercise that will help you to recognize your own patterns of anxiety?

Verbal Communication

In the problem-solving approach, counselor responses are oriented mainly toward knowing and doing. This contrasts with client-centered counseling, in which responses are almost exclusively related to feeling. In problem-solving counseling, the counselor's verbal contributions are greater in number, more direct, and more varied. The counselor assumes the major responsibility for the climate and character of the relationship, as well as for the directions taken as the relationship progresses. In the initiation phase, as in that of the client-centered approach, continuing responses are used to establish trust and, consequently, ease of self-disclosure. Leads, or leading responses, are called into play then and later when needed. Whether continuing or leading, each verbal response is intended to serve a specific counseling purpose. Otherwise, silence is the preferred response.

In employing leads, the practitioner takes the initiative in moving the client from one point of thought and discourse to another in the direction of a specific goal (Chapter 7). The practitioner is thus in control of the amount of responsibility allotted to the client from moment to moment. More specifically, leads serve to stimulate and clarify communication, to allay anxiety, and to reinforce and enhance self-esteem. As problem solving progresses, leads encourage the client to discover alternate solutions to problems and to make judgments necessary for decisive action.

The various forms of continuing responses are described in Chapter 4. Leading responses as used by the helping professional are dealt with in the remainder of this section.

General leads Liberal use is made of general responses that stimulate discussion of feelings and facts directed toward agreed-on goals. From the client's first statement of the presenting problem, the helping professional requests further data as the need arises. A simple continuing response such as *Go on* often suffices. At times it is necessary to lead into specific information with definite instructions. For example: *Tell me more about your feelings at that time. I want you to tell me all you can about your ideas on that* (*on what you expect to happen; on what you might do;* and so forth). Leads of this kind may be formulated as questions and are discussed in the following section.

Questions Problem-solving counseling uses questions as often as necessary to gather data pertinent to its central problem-solving purpose. This contrasts with the client-centered approach in which the question form is used only if an opening lead is needed or as a means of underscoring the tentative nature of the counselor's reflection of feeling. Whatever the philosophy underlying the counseling method, the helping professional is warned against using purposeless questions. Every beginning counselor undergoes the experience of conducting at least one interview that quickly deteriorates into an aimless question and answer session. Its temporary effect, which wears off before the interview has proceeded very far, is an easing of the helper's anxiety by avoiding gaps in the conversation; its net effect is frustration for both helper and client. There is a real danger that a pattern may be set for both participants at subsequent meetings.

In any approach to counseling, questions are useful as general leads to open discussion at a first or later interview. They may be needed at any point to help an inarticulate client. In the following examples, the client-centered counselor would omit or avoid emphasizing the *me* in order to keep the focus on the client. The problem-solving counselor, as expert, may wish to retain it.

- *What do you particularly want to talk over (with me)?*
- *Will you tell me some of the things you find particularly difficult?*
- *What would you like (us) to work on today?*

Examples of continuing questions, universally useful, are:

- *Would you explain that a little further?*
- *What else comes to mind?*
- *Just what were you thinking of along that line?*

Although the examples cited as invalid below are so in most instances, there may be occasions when the helper's response serves an intended purpose.

Several precautions with questions:

1. Avoid questions that do not lead in a growth-promoting direction for the client or are merely socially oriented:

Client: *Before we were married we used to go dancing quite often. Now we never go.*
Helper: *Do you like dancing?*

A continuing question such as *Marriage changed things for you?* is conducive to more data about the current problem or to an expression of the client's feelings about it.

2. Avoid interrupting the client's train of thought:

Client: *It's hard on my wife, my being in the hospital.*
Helper: *Did your wife come to visit you yesterday?*

Here also a continuing response would be more emphatic:

You're worried about your wife.

3. Generally avoid closed questions—those requiring a yes or no answer. They gain little information about the client as a person and keep the initiative with the questioner. Closed questions, called leading in ordinary parlance, are worded to influence the reply. The metacommunication of such questions leads the client to please or agree with the questioner. For example: *Did you go because you thought you were needed?* or *You wouldn't say (do, like) that, would you?*

4. Avoid arousing anxiety by making demands that the client is not ready to meet:

Client: *I'll have to learn to control myself better.*
Helper: *How will you do that?*

A continuing response (*There's something to learn there...*) or a reinforcing response (*That's something worth learning*) is appropriate in this instance.

5. Avoid questions that probe motivation, either the client's or that of another person he or she may refer to. For example: *Why did you do (say, think) that?* or *Why did they stop speaking to one another?*

Although questions that explore the client's motivation have a place in deep psychotherapy, they are inadvisable for use by the average professional helper. The two examples above inquire into the causative factors of behaviors that are largely unknown to the behaving person. Such questions put the client at a disadvantage and, therefore, induce anxiety. The accusatory flavor attributed to any *Why did you?* question invites a defensive response. Concerning the behavior of a second person, such a question is still less appropriate because it makes impossible demands.

Note that some *what* and *how* questions are really *why* questions because they delve into motivation. For example: *What makes you feel that way?* or *How did you come to do that?* Usually, questions beginning with *who, what, when,* and *where* provide inoffensive means of obtaining pertinent problem-solving information. They also serve to bridge ideas. For example: *What happened then?* or *When did you see her last?*

It can be seen that considerable practice is needed to develop skill in using questions. Because the recommendations and precautions applicable in counseling are generally relevant to ordinary dialogue, opportunities for practice are easy to find. In both counseling and everyday conversation, strategic questioning can be an agent for developing interpersonal relationships and self-concepts of all concerned. Pausing to consider the purpose of each question and how best to word it can bring gratifying results.

Clarification and interpretation Clarification of attitudes is described in Chapter 4 as the one leading technique that is sometimes employed in counseling that is strictly client-centered. It is used more liberally in the problem-solving approach. As therapeutic measures, both clarification and interpretation involve decoding the underlying meanings in the client's communication. In each, a construction of meanings that is unrecognized by the client but comes through to the counselor is brought to the client's attention.

The difference between clarification and interpretation lies in the depth below consciousness of the client's unspoken message. In clarification, the attitude that is the subject of the counselor's inference is close to the surface of the client's awareness—so nearly conscious that it is discernible in the words of the client's own statement. Interpretation is variously defined by theorists (Singer, 1965). To the Sullivanian, it is a confrontation that gives the client, for the first time, a view of self quite different from his or her own conscious impression. The interpretation puts into words an observable tie between a current problem and an irrational attitude or motive that the client is unconsciously harboring.

In the case of Mr. C (Chapter 4), a professional counselor might use interpretation if the client had been in treatment over a considerable period of time to help him recognize his pattern of dependency and his distortion of reality in expecting others to divine his unspoken thoughts. For example:

> Mr. C: *Everything seems to be going wrong. If I plan anything it never works out. . . . I stewed for hours over whether to call her, and now she'll be mad because she must have expected me to do the calling.*
>
> Counselor: *Have you noticed that you make a habit of being disappointed when other people don't know what you want them to do?*

The counselor might continue by reviewing other instances of Mr. C's dependency and encouraging him to add to the list. The counseling purpose would be to reach consensual validation.

Professional helpers select those leading responses that they can expect to use effectively according to the needs of clients and their own knowledge and experience. Frequent use is made of the kind of clarification that occurs in everyday conversation. Whenever two people are trying to understand one another, they find it necessary to exchange feedback in order to keep literal meanings clear. Clarification of attitudes is used more rarely as a helping technique, and interpretation with consensual validation is seldom, if ever, used. Their value must be weighed against their potential for evoking anxiety. The helping person recognizes that the client is already contending with the disturbed state of mind that is an inevitable part of revealing and struggling with personal problems. Rather than adding to the client's anxiety, the helper is intent on allaying it, or, at least, keeping it within moderate bounds.

TA terminology provides clarifying and moderately interpreting responses that are not likely to arouse anxiety. For example: *You felt OK about yourself that time, didn't you?* or *So what you mean is that he is not an OK person with you? Am I right?* Preceded by discussion of the Parent, Adult, and Child within each of us, interpretation might take a form such as: *Your Parent was talking when you gave her that answer, wouldn't you say?*

Techniques that are particularly adapted to controlling anxiety are discussed under the remaining headings. They classify responses that come from the Parent ego state of the helper. An anxious client is likely to be temporarily in need of the nurturance that such transactions offer. In drug or suicidal crisis, their use may have life-saving value. Self-examination on the part of the worker is necessary to guard against any tinge of metacommunication that might be punitive or otherwise demeaning to the client. In other words, the nurturing attitude must be completely authentic.

Reassurance The term reassurance is used here to include many supportive attitudes and techniques that serve to establish trust, relieve anxiety, and strengthen self-confidence. In this sense it takes both implicit and explicit forms. In strictly client-centered counseling, explicit verbal reassurance is seldom used. Reassurance is implicit in the climate of the relationship, in the counselor's supportive characteristics of empathy, genuineness, and unqualified acceptance, and in the counselor's verbal and nonverbal skills of listening and responding. Regardless of the counseling method, indirect reassurance is supplied by giving needed information and by clarifying and explaining when necessary. The problem-solving approach relies on all of these factors and uses reassurance as an explicit verbal technique besides.

At various stages of counseling, direct offers of support may be given. In addition, guarded predictions, but not promises, about outcomes may be made. They function to abate initial anxiety and to establish and maintain faith in the helper as a person who is both confident and competent. Because overuse of the words *help* and *problem* may threaten some clients, they are avoided in the following examples:

- *I can look into this with you if you want me to. We'll go into this together and see what we can come up with.*
- *Maybe between us, we can find a way out of this. If you talk this out with me, it may become clearer.*

The sparing use of such supportive statements by client-centered counselors is consistent with their intention of fostering self-actualization and self-direction in their clients. Reassurance is a response offered from a sender's Parent ego state; a highly anxious client may be in need of such a nurturing response. But with an abundance of reassurance, there is a danger that clients will relinquish to their counselors the responsibility of finding solutions to their problems. The professional counselor therefore keeps this danger in mind.

The helping professional is likewise forewarned. The following precautions for using reassurance are recommended.

1. Avoid the liberal use of reassurance. It is possible to diminish anxiety to the point where the client expects to be relieved of all responsibility. A client's frequent demands for reassurance indicate proneness to dependency. They can be made a point of profitable discussion in relation to the problems that dependency creates.

2. Avoid making promises regarding outcomes. Reassurance that implies *Everything's going to be all right* is more likely to soothe the helper's anxiety than the client's.

3. Avoid expressions that belittle the client's problems (*There is nothing to worry about*) or expressions that make comparisons (*Other people have overcome worse troubles*). Such responses betray the helper's inability to enter into the client's frame of reference. Anxious people are most in need of the certainty that someone else is fully present to them and willing to undergo *with* them, but not *for* them, the uncertainties and insecurities that they are enduring.

4. Avoid attempts at reassurance that imply judgmental evaluation:

Client: *I have hateful feelings about her sometimes.*
Helper: *You don't really hate her, do you?*

It is obvious that the helper considers hating something to be condemned.

5. Avoid meeting the helper's own need for progress or closure:

Client: *Nobody cares whether I live or die.*
Helper: *I'm sure your daughter cares.*

Here, the client needs an opportunity to express feelings of despair and rejection. The helper is intent on avoiding discussion of negative feelings and moves to another area that might offer an easier solution.

Practice in offering reassurance is almost as readily at hand as practice in asking questions. The young, the old, and the ailing are likely to have a greater need for the support that reassurance gives than the normal adult. But at times of insecurity, we all need it. Reassurance is conducive to becoming to the extent that it is realistic, empathic, and genuinely nonjudgmental.

Reinforcement In ordinary usage, reinforcing is synonymous with supporting and strengthening. As a counseling technique, secondary, or social, reinforcement has many similarities to reassurance. It can serve to allay anxiety and bolster self-esteem. Both effects are implicit in nonverbal counselor behaviors such as those identified earlier that convey liking or agreement, as well as in counselor attitudes of acceptance and empathy. When reinforcement is used as an explicit technique, it must, like reassurance, be positive, realistic, and genuine, and it must be used in a way that does not foster dependence. In addition, the helping person must be fully aware of its behavior-modifying effects. This topic is discussed in detail in Chapter 8.

Setting limits In a general sense, limit setting is a reminder of the central aim of the counseling relationship. Client and helper come together to collaborate in resolving the client's difficulties. Prolonged discussion of trivialities, repetitive or circumstantial content, or content that is contrary to reason serve no useful purpose toward that end. They are likely to be partially conscious delaying tactics used to ward off serious discussion. The helper may choose to confront the client by clarifying this insight or may subvert the tendency less directly with a comment such as *Let's get back to our real job—discussing your problems.*

Limit setting can often be effected indirectly by using attention to positively reinforce desirable interview content and ignoring content that is undesirable. If nonessentials are regularly met with silence and serious matters invariably received with attention and concern, most clients soon learn to discriminate according to the worker's expectations. Habitual emphasis on the negative may be similarly discouraged. Circular talking may be intercepted as the helper picks up and follows threads of feeling or action that it contains. For example: *What could he do that would make you feel less neglected?* or *What do you think you should do about Mary's behavior?* Responses of this kind lead the client away from pointless rumination and back to problem solving.

There are occasions when setting a limit on weeping is in order, especially if it has continued to the point of being out of control. Ordinarily, crying is an expression of feeling that is welcomed, as is any other, but sometimes a supportive statement is needed—*I'm afraid that more crying won't help you. Let's ease back into our discussion now*—to bring the client back to present reality.

When encountered in the work of some helping professionals, a psychotic client may introduce delusional or hallucinatory material. If ignoring such irrational content is not effective in countering it, it is recommended that the helper suggest, and insist if necessary, that the conversation be confined to subjects that both participants perceive to be real. For example:

> Helper: *Some things you talk about seem to be real to you but not to me. Let's stay with things that both of us believe to be so.* (constructive limit setting)

Decidedly, this is not the time for a response that might imply agreement with, or in any other way reinforce, irrational thinking. For example:

> Client: *... so I got through to her on my thinking machine.*
> Worker: *How long have you had this thinking machine?* (reinforcing irrationality, therefore to be avoided)

Similarly, such content is not to be made the subject of argument, advice, or persuasion, all of which will prove to reinforce irrationality. Threatening or destructive behavior by a child or an irrational adult may require immediate physical restraint—if possible by means that have been determined in advance.

Advice and suggestion Among those who seek help from counselors or from experts in any human services, there are some who expect counsel in the form of instant advice, suggestion, or opinion. Beginners at counseling, in turn, react with frustration at not having a ready answer to each of the problems that clients identify. Especially in health services and the ministry, there is a fairly pervasive idea both among professionals and the public that there should be a drug specific to every discomfort and an answer to every question. There is also a widespread and erroneous belief that people who ask for advice are likely to act on it once it is received.

A little thought on the subject of advice giving and advice taking will expose the fallacies that lie at the basis of such views. A request may be worded in such terms as *What would you do if you were in my place?* Whether or not that question is asked, the advice giver, by the very act of giving advice, attempts the exploitative and impossible operation of thinking for the client. Meanwhile, the receiver of the advice may discount it then or later as not fitting the facts of the situation or the temperament of the seeker, or may blame the helper later for undesirable outcomes. It is likely, too, that the person who seemingly wishes advice or opinion is also a person who shares in our general cultural distrust of, and resistance to, authority in any form. On the other hand, the client may be so dependent in nature that the tendency to rely on others is reinforced with every suggestion or opinion received. Advice giving is a Parent response that often leads into *"Why Don't You?"* game playing.

Even when factual advice seems appropriate, such as information regarding a social, health, or educational referral, it is important to exchange feedback with the client to ensure that there is no misunderstanding on either side. The question remains: Is it information that the client really wants, or is the request a means of testing the helper's sincerity and skill before bringing an underlying problem to light?

Advice in the form of persuasion is seldom appropriate as a counseling technique. Especially in the form of coaxing, it invites either dependency or antagonism. In a few instances persuasion is appropriate: to encourage a child or a depressed person into essentials of physical health or acceptable grooming or as a bid for time with a suicidal client.

When the need for advice seems to present itself, it must be evaluated with reference to the existing client-helper relationship. In a single interview with no preexisting bond, it is important that:

1. The client's feelings about the point in question be explored
2. The problem be thoroughly clarified
3. Alternative choices available to the client be evaluated cooperatively by client and helper

If a relationship has already been formed, the helper is in a better position to estimate the possible meanings behind the client's apparent need. With reflection of feeling and clarification of the problem, and possibly of underlying attitudes, the client either revises the basis on which the helper's input is needed or evaluates choices and selects the most feasible one with the collaboration of the helper when required.

Whenever advice, opinion, suggestion, or persuasion seems called for, the helper is cautioned to maintain silence for the length of time it takes to think through the client's need at this point. Impulsive responses of the kind exemplified in the following interchange are unlikely to serve valid counseling purposes.

Aide: *I can't get Jimmie to do anything I tell him.*
Nurse: *He has never been away from home before. He'll adjust if you give him time.* (opinion)

or

You should keep your commands to a minimum. (advice)

or

Maybe I should give his mother a call. (suggestion)

Before any problem solving is attempted in response to the aide's complaint, her here-and-now feelings of frustration should be reflected. Further expression of feelings, together with some factual information to illustrate the problem will probably result. With further thought, the aide may begin to recognize that the problem originally brought up for discussion is her own problem, not Jimmie's. It will broaden the aide's understanding of the situation to try to see the relationship from the child's frame of reference and to visualize the problems that it poses for Jimmie. Once Jimmie is viewed more as a person and less as a problem, the aide may be able to see a new and less frustrating way of relating to him.

In the preceding discussion of communication skills, much that goes into the process of problem-solving counseling has already been outlined. The following chapter presents and explains the intervention procedure in a more organized and detailed form.

References

Auden, W. H. 1947. *The age of anxiety.* New York: Random House.

Benjamin, A. 1974. *The helping interview.* 2nd ed. Boston: Houghton Mifflin.

Freud, S. 1936. *The problem of anxiety.* Translated by Henry A. Bunker. New York: Psychoanalytic Press.

Jacobson, E. 1964. *Anxiety and tension control: A physiologic approach.* Philadelphia: Lippincott.

May, R. 1950. *The meaning of anxiety.* New York: Ronald.

Mehrabian, A. 1972. *Nonverbal communication.* Chicago: Aldine Atherton.

Peplau, H. E. 1963. A working definition of anxiety. *Some clinical approaches to psychiatric nursing.* Shirley F. Burd and Margaret A. Marshall, editors. New York: Macmillan, pp. 323–327.

Peterson, M. H. Understanding defense mechanisms: Programmed instruction. *Am. J. Nurs.* 72:9, 1651–1674. (Reprints available.)

Scheflen, A. E. 1972. *Body language and social order.* Englewood Cliffs, N. J.: Prentice-Hall.

Schulman, E. D. 1974. *Intervention in human services.* St. Louis: Mosby.

Singer, E. 1965. *Key concepts in psychotherapy.* New York: Random House.

Sullivan, H. S. 1954. *The psychiatric interview.* New York: Norton.

CHAPTER 7

The Process of Problem-Solving Intervention

Students and practitioners of counseling often find it useful to visualize the process in a series of chronological stages. A number of related modalities employ a well-defined sequence of steps. This can facilitate setting goals, planning action, and evaluating progress toward the designated goals, and thus ensure the necessary counselor awareness and control. The steps are formulated in different terms between and within professions, but essentially they include problem identification, data gathering and processing, and evaluation of results.

The various helping professions use numerous adaptations of the problem-solving approach. Nurses, for instance, may recognize the similarity between the problem-solving model and that of the nursing process. The nurse-patient relationship itself is described as developing through a series of stages identifiable with those of the problem-solving method. The phases of the interview, which is at the heart of social work practice, are usually set out in similarly logical sequence.

The term **problem-solving intervention** is used here to signify all those processes used by the helping professional to assist the client to move in a goal-oriented direction within the counseling relationship. Because counseling is a dynamic interpersonal process, the demarcation between phases tends to shift somewhat in actual practice. In spite of this, the helper must remain conscious of the purposes to be accomplished at each step, and direct progress accordingly. Theorists in the helping professions who use a step-by-step format in presenting methods of counseling and interviewing variously identify three, four, or five stages of progress. The titles given to the steps also vary considerably. In order to introduce an element of purpose into each of the titles, the following nomenclature is used in this book:

Stage 1. Initiation of the relationship

Stage 2. Assessment and planning

Stage 3. Implementation

Stage 4. Termination

A problem-solving approach to counseling is appropriate for a well-prepared helping professional to employ with a client who is able to recognize a counseling problem as such. Further, the client must be able to make a commitment to the work involved in moving successively through the problem-solving counseling stages. A categorization of the problem of daily living typically encountered in counseling situations appears under "Problem Identification." Also under that topic, conditions under which the approach is justified are amplified.

A type of problem-solving that lies outside the counseling function is used in numerous other aspects of the work of any helping professional. A nurse, a teacher, or a social worker, for example, encounters a variety of problems in working with clients that are recognized and systematically solved by the worker without the cognitive participation of the client. But if the required problem-solving activity has the potential to offer a growth experience that is acceptable to the client, mutual involvement of client and helper is desirable.

The client's acceptance, or owning, of the problem and his or her commitment to working toward its solution do not necessarily have to be verbalized. As implicit factors in the client-helper relationship, they can be detected by the competent professional in the early phases of the general assessment of the client's needs, capabilities, feelings, and attitudes.

Each of the four stages of intervention is detailed here with relation to the purposes and tasks of intervention characteristic of that stage, and the skills, techniques, and methods best adapted to that stage.

INITIATION OF THE RELATIONSHIP

The three overlapping tasks of the first stage are to:

1. Reduce the initial anxiety and develop the beginnings of mutual trust
2. Provide an appropriate climate and structure for the relationship
3. Begin to define the problem or problems

The helping professional is responsible for the first two tasks; the third responsibility is shared with the client.

At the beginning of any relationship, the two participants come together as strangers. Strangeness, a change of any kind from the familiar, brings an element of risk, or threat. Here, the risk is to one's previously earned self-esteem and to one's security in being able to gain acceptance. The threat to each participant, and the resulting anxiety, are multiplied in the counseling relationship. The client must submit to self-disclosure without the normal protection of gradually attained intimacy. For the helper, the relationship presents a new test of humanistic principles and professional skills.

Because the helper's own anxiety is readily communicated to the client, it requires anticipatory attention. Anxiety will be lessened to the extent that the helper has grown in tolerating ambiguity, in being able to let others simply be, and in trusting in the capacity of others to change in the direction of fullness of human functioning. The achievement of a personal success by reaching a gratifying closure with the client is not the helper's objective. The aim is rather to help the other person to move toward appreciating difficulties as opportunities and toward adequate ways of dealing with them within the context of more satisfying human relationships.

Mitigation of the client's anxiety begins in the climate of the helper's attitudes of quiet self-assurance and supportive acceptance. It is furthered by the continued attention given to the atmosphere and structure in which the encounter takes place. The ideal emotional climate is described as client centered in Chapter 4. It is maintained throughout the relationship by the helper's deeply held empathy, sincerity, and positive regard. The requirements of the physical setting are outlined in Chapter 5 under "The Context," and are appropriate for any counseling interview. Elements of problem-solving structure that require particular emphasis are explored in the next three sections.

The Opening

The inception of the first, and perhaps the only, helping interview differs according to whether help is sought by the client or offered by the helper. When counseling is only one part of a broad range of services offered by an agency, the possibility that a counseling relationship will come into existence may hinge entirely on the sensitivity of the helper. This was the case in the nurse-client relationship illustrated in Chapter 5. Such a relationship can be formed in a variety of settings other than the client's home: a school, a factory, a health agency, a clergy office, or on the street.

Generally, the person who recognizes the need opens the discussion with some reference to it, although a client who seeks an interview may not necessarily find it easy to state the reason. When this becomes evident, the helper may find a moment's weather or traffic talk justifiable as a means to ease tension. The point of the visit should not be deferred beyond that because a pattern of engaging in small talk might inadvertently be initiated.

The client may have given the helper a previous intimation of the problem to be discussed. If so, it is not advisable for the helper to move in by attempting a restatement from an earlier perspective. The real problem may turn out to be quite different. An open invitation provides the client with an opportunity to offer a here-and-now, personal perception of the situation. For example: *Where would you like to begin?* This opening may actually be anticipated by the client with a question or comment such as *How do we go about this?* or *I'm not sure I know where to start.*

When the helper is the instigator of the interview or if the client has been referred by another agent, it is incumbent on the helper to make an immediate statement of the reason for the interview. A student might be told, *I wanted to talk with you about that fracas this morning,* or an employee told, *I asked to see you about the possibility of a lay-off before long.* In an impromptu or informal setting, the helper's opening may be more tentatively directed toward the apparent need: *You look worried. Is anything wrong?* or *I was sorry to hear that your vacation (hospital discharge, promotion) was postponed.*

In any of these instances, the helper's next thought is to give the client the opportunity to express any negative feelings that accompany thinking about the difficulties of daily living. There may be an immediate overflow of feelings, or feelings may come in response to verbal or nonverbal continuing cues. A lead that reveals the helper's concern for the client may be needed: *How would it be if we talked about it for a while?* Clarification of facts and reflection of feelings will bring new aspects of the problem to the surface and thus lead to an increasingly accurate version of it. The helper will also receive clues concerning the client's attitudes toward self and others and his or her degree of motivation for action or change.

For clients who close off discussion of their difficulties, Lazarus (1969) has developed an **inner circle strategy**. He draws a diagram for the client consisting of five concentric circles and labels them from A (smallest) to E (largest). Circle A is described to the client as representing the most private areas of a person's life, containing thoughts that are not shared with anyone. Circle B contains those thoughts that are exchanged with one's closest intimates; C and D with an increasingly wider audience; and E with even the most superficial acquaintances. For some of us, circle A is so large that it takes in part or all of B, and perhaps C and D also. This means that the individual keeps everything of moment private, and otherwise interacts only superfically within a narrow circle of people.

Counselors who use the inner circle device find that not only timid or embarrassed clients, but also those who are initially belligerently defensive, respond with openness to this diagram. At first there may be only a third-person discussion about the varying tendencies to share found among individuals and about the types of problems that people have difficulty in discussing. Whatever the level of the client's participation, the counselor fully accepts his or her right to be at that level. In the open climate that this acceptance creates, the client gradually becomes less defensively evasive and begins to claim thoughts and feelings that were previously denied expression.

As an exercise in self-awareness, counseling students diagram their own personal circle arrangements, jotting in the different types of problems that they are able to expose to different audiences. The results that they are willing to share are then discussed in dyads.

Time Factors

If the problem is complex and the relationship extends over several interviews, the first two steps, problem identification and assessment, may be combined and spread over a number of contacts. When only a single meeting is possible, the two steps must be telescoped into the space of a few minutes. During that short time, a significant reorientation of thought and behavior may occur in an especially open client. With those whose attitudes are more rigid, less can be accomplished. Small personal compromises with existing circumstances may be all that can be attempted, or the personal limitations may be such that compromises must be sought in the situation rather than in the person.

If the meeting occurs in connection with an official agency, the client may need to be given an explanation of agency policy regulating the length and number of interviews. This should be taken care of as early as it logically fits into the first interview. Although agency policy often sets limits on the freedom of both participants, it has the advantage of giving a structure to the situation, which usually acts as a spur to progress. Under less formal circumstances, limits are set by mutual agreement.

An interview of forty-five or fifty minutes usually allows sufficient time for concentrated discussion between two people. Under acute time pressure a good deal may be accomplished within a shorter period. Whether further meetings are needed depends on the nature of the problem and the human and material resources available to deal with it. In the interchange about Jimmie between the aide and the nurse (Chapter 6), the problem is one that might be moved toward a solution within a few minutes. This presupposes openness to change on the part of the aide, and skill and experience on the nurse's part with the uses and abuses of advice giving.

Role Definition

The establishment of roles is implicit in the structuring of the initial phase. A simple statement indicating the worker's availability and willingness to work with the client usually suffices. According to the needs of the client, explicit reference to roles may be made. An insecure client may gain confidence from a brief sketch of the problem-solving process and from knowing what is expected of each participant. If the client asks direct questions about the worker's position or credentials, they should be answered briefly but cordially. Personal questions about the worker usually stem from anxiety, and serve to postpone the substance of the interview. A reflection of the feeling underlying the question, rather than an answer to the question itself, changes the focus to productive discussion.

If the client seems inclined to rely completely on the helper for answers and actions, the working-together aspect of the relationship will need to be emphasized. Perhaps as a result of defeating experiences in the past, an exceptional client may seem to mistrust the ability of the helper. A gentle reflection of the apparent lack of confidence and a reference to the cooperative nature of the task may provide the necessary reorientation. For example: *You seem to be uneasy about this arrangement. Perhaps if you and I work together, we can come up with a reasonable way out of any difficulties you may be having.*

The helping professional's alertness to the participant-observer aspects of the helper role is essential. Close attention is given to both client and helper participation and to the effects that each is having on the other. Anxiety content is particularly noted. The client's anxiety is likely to be signaled by defensive reactions to introducing and discussing problems. The helper's own feeling states are likewise monitored. The observation of the effects of verbal and nonverbal helper responses in stirring up or diminishing the client anxiety is a vital aspect of the helper's role.

If the helper is on an interview schedule, time must be allowed between interviews for sufficient note taking to allow for detailed recall. Only on the basis of prompt recall can progress be made in responding effectively to the needs of the individual client. As areas requiring improvement are recognized, recall comes about not only from a careful mental review of each interaction, but from talking over perplexing aspects with experienced colleagues.

It will be recognized that elements that are dealt with here under one phase of the helping relationship are, to a considerable extent, applicable to the other stages. The helper role, for instance, must be thought of as continuing unchanged throughout the relationship, short or long as it may prove to be.

Problem Identification

The earliest stage of problem identification was described in this chapter under "The Opening." It occurs with the first allusion to the presenting difficulty, however indirectly it is made, whether by helper or client. This is the juncture at which the client is given an opportunity to comment on the various ramifications of the problem and openly express the feelings with which it is charged.

Anyone who undertakes a problem solving process finds it necessary to isolate and define the problem, as well as delimit it to manageable proportions. In a helping situation, the professional person assumes responsibility for this cognitive task. The work of categorizing is expedited if the helping professional has in mind a general classification of problems to work from. A list of typical problems provides the worker with a cognitive handle for mentally lifting the problem from the general to the particular. Further limitation is attained through a process of clarification with the client.

Reid (1972) devised a system of classification consisting of seven major groupings for use in the field of social work. The five groupings that have been adapted in the following list are appropriate for classifying psychologic problems that come to the attention of workers in the various helping professions.

1. Interpersonal conflict (family, employer-employee, teacher-student)
2. Dissatisfaction in interpersonal relations caused by the client's personal characteristics (hostility, nonassertiveness)
3. Difficulties in role performance (parent, spouse, student, patient, employee difficulties due to role confusion, unrealistic role expectations, interrole conflict, inadequate role performance, and so forth)
4. Problems of potential or actual social transition (marriage, parenthood, divorce, ethnic incompatibility, dependence caused by age or disability)
5. Reactive emotional distress (occurring as a normal psychological response to any acute crisis)

Two other categories in Reid's list pertain to the functions of some helping professionals, but not of others:

6. Problems with formal organizations (school, hospital, court, welfare organizations)
7. Inadequate resources (money, housing, food, clothing, transportation, employment)

If at first hearing the matter seems to fall outside of the purview of the helper, it should not be summarily dismissed. Members of the helping professions are obligated by virtue of their inclusion in this group to have complete, up-to-date information at hand on material and psychologic resources available in the immediate community. If a need is urgent, a recommendation or a referral may be indicated. But these, like other forms of advice, may be premature at this point, and are subject to the precautions to be observed in advice-giving.

A possible exception to this general rule is a case of acute crisis. The subject of crisis intervention is treated briefly at the end of this chapter. There, as well as here, it is recommended that the professional helper obtain specialized, practical training as a volunteer in a community center designed specifically to provide crisis intervention on a 24-hour basis. The fact remains that any professional may encounter a person in **reactive emotional distress** in the course of a day's work or in any other normal pursuit: for example, a client, a co-worker, or a friend shortly after a death in the family or shortly before major surgery. The counseling measures delineated in this chapter and summarized for crisis intervention at the end of this chapter are applicable in any such instance.

When a client's problem is obviously one of psychologic crisis, or reactive emotional distress, it may be necessary for the helper to make a referral to external support systems on the client's behalf without delay. In cases of threatened suicide, victimization by violence, or presenting symptoms of neurosis, for instance, the client may be willing to accept help in finding a continuing source of professional psychologic treatment. Meanwhile, the availability of systems of psychologic support is looked into as part of the problem identification and assessment to follow. Support may be found among family members, friends, or organized self-help groups or other community services. Sources of material assistance are located as needed.

Matching of problems to Reid's categories is usually conjectural at first. It is refined as clarification with the client proceeds. A specific problem may span two or more categories, or may seem at first to fall into one category but later prove to belong in another. Clarifying and delimiting the problem or problems begin from the client's first problem statement. Questions are necessarily asked by both client and worker. The worker's questions should be kept

to a minimum until it is evident that the client is able to answer them without undue pressure from anxiety. The principal aim of clarification is to bring to the surface those facts of the situation that are necessary to give the problem a shape recognized as valid by both participants.

It is essential that client and worker agree on a definition of the problem or problems before much progress in intervention can be made. Although the definition may be modified several times during the progress of the relationship, work must begin from something that the client views as important. If the worker has a target in mind that does not coincide with the client's perception of the needed outcome, cooperation is impossible. Furthermore, it is preferable to adopt the client's wording rather than to define the problem in helper or agency terms.

Two additional conditions must be worked with before systematic problem solving can begin: (a) the client must own the problem and (b) he or she must sincerely intend to work on it cooperatively with the helper. It is expected that continued discussion may lead to a redefinition of the problem or to reversion to another problem that mutual inquiry has uncovered. If the preceding qualifications do not obtain, problem solving must be postponed or, possibly, referred to another agent or agency.

Referral does not necessarily terminate the helping relationship, at least from the worker's point of view. Unless circumstances are prohibitive, the client can benefit from a continuing client-centered relationship. A pertinent example may be found in Rosalyn's case in Chapter 5. There are undoubtedly numerous problems that Rosalyn and Dick might select to work on together, but postponement of that aspect of their relationship is obviously essential.

Case Example: Jeremy Goes Home

This case example illustrates problem-solving counseling as used by helping professionals. The case is somewhat typical in that a client-centered helping relationship has already been initiated, but a problem has arisen that has practical and time-related dimensions. These seem to call for the addition of problem-solving measures.

Jeremy Harburg, the proprietor of a fairly prosperous garage, is a patient in one of the medical-surgical units of a metropolitan hospital. He is making a satisfactory recovery from a second surgical procedure following a pneumonectomy necessitated by lung cancer. Since his hospital discharge is imminent, Jeremy is being encouraged to progressively resume self-care and other light activities.

Four days a week, Jeremy's bedside care is assigned to Vivian, an undergraduate senior in nursing, who comes to the unit as part of a group supervised by an instructor. The students are interested in their assigned

patients, not as medical cases, but as persons who merit the full scope of their nursing skill. Following each day's clinical experience, a group conference is held on the hospital unit. Each student offers items of clinical interest and concern for the consideration of the group.

At the first conference of the third week of her care of Jeremy, Vivian brings up a new nursing problem for discussion. Jeremy was formerly quite easy-going and companionable, but has become plaintive and demanding. He has known his diagnosis of carcinoma since shortly after the first surgical intervention and has seemed quite confident in the surgeon's hope of an entirely favorable outcome. In addition he took pleasure in reporting signs of his returning vigor. But he now insists that he is still too sick to spend time out of bed or to attend to the unskilled aspects of his care. He says that neither the staff nor his wife, who is a daily visitor, understands the seriousness of his condition. Vivian adds that she read about this change in Jeremy's behavior in the problem-oriented medical record, and it was reported to her on her arrival by Jeremy's primary care nurse. His attitude today has amply corroborated the reports.

Vivian tells the group that she checked the record for coincidental factors that might account for the change. It was first noted the day following the surgical resident's notation that the necessity of limiting future work activity was discussed with Jeremy. Vivian's remark that Jeremy will want to be able to do things for himself when he gets home met with the response: *You're just like the others. You all think I'm faking.* Recognizing the anxiety underlying the accusation, Vivian replied: *It seems to you that we are asking you to do more than you can manage just yet.* With verbal encouragement and repeated reflection of his feelings of apprehension, Vivian was able to persuade Jeremy to bathe, shave, and settle himself in a chair to await his wife's visit.

Conference participants agree with Vivian that Jeremy's anxiety was the most urgent nursing problem of the day for Vivian to deal with. With suggestions from the group, Vivian tentatively identifies his underlying problem as role confusion. He is expected to discard the dependent sick role and make a difficult transition to new and uncertain roles as responsible husband, father, and worker-employer. Group discussion relates Reid's fourth and fifth categories to the problem thus identified. Jeremy sees the impending social transition as a threat, and is reacting to the crisis with mild emotional distress. Vivian plans to test Jeremy's readiness to explore these questions on his own terms the following day. She reports this intention to the primary care nurse, who is happy that Vivian is free to spend the time with Jeremy that exploration will require.

As a somewhat experienced helping professional, Vivian recognizes

that she is called on to initiate a new phase of the client-helper relationship. In this phase, she has found that continuing, client-centered responses are indicated, with reassurance when needed, until the client's anxiety is at a level tolerable to him. At that point, questioning and clarification can be used, but with careful attention to their effect on the client's anxiety level.

ASSESSMENT AND PLANNING

The assessment of the problem is a continuation of the investigation that began when the relationship was initiated. If the client is in an identifiable difficulty, preliminary discussion tends to reveal aspects of the problem, as well as to renew the anxiety connected with it. Using appropriate measures to reduce anxiety, the professional helper guides the discussion with a view to problem identification and delimitation in terms that are meaningful to the client. Once the problem is defined, the lines to be investigated can be drawn out to give focus to the assessment that follows. This is the stage at which the helper and client analyze the problem and its various ramifications and identify possible goals and methods for the ensuing implementation.

The assessment process focuses on the dynamic relations among client, problem, and factors operating in the problem situation. As correlations among data are recognized, objectives for the amelioration of the problem can be identified, and viable ways of reaching them considered. Conjectures are made about possible outcomes, and one or more alternatives are selected. These predictions, which signify intentions, become the goals of the problem-solving endeavor. They may be clarified or changed as the work of planning moves along. Finally, a plan is proposed for the strategy to be used in the next phase.

The nature of the problem determines the personal, interpersonal, social, and material factors that should come under investigation in the problem analysis. Client characteristics such as intelligence, education, social background, interpersonal relationships, and material resources may or may not be germane to the situation. The analysis takes into account as many of these elements as directly bear on the task at hand. If persons or groups other than the client are centrally involved in the problem, a decision may be needed as to whether discussion should include them directly or whether contacts external to the counseling relationship should remain with the client.

If the relationship of psychologic counseling is to continue over a period of several interviews, a thorough assessment of the psychologic milieu of the problem may be indicated. Snyder and Wilson (1977) designed a tool for nurses to use for this purpose. Sample questions for eliciting content under each heading follow the authors' list:

1. Response to stress: coping and defense mechanisms

2. Interpersonal relationships
3. Motivation and life-style
4. Thought processes and verbal behavior
5. Nonverbal behavior
6. Awareness of and handling feelings
7. External support systems
8. Talents, strengths, and assets
9. Physical health
10. The interview and the self of the nurse

Remember that the client's strengths (item 8), as well as weaknesses, should be assessed. The questions suggested for item 10, used here as examples, are applicable, not only to nurses, but to anyone who undertakes a counseling role. They are:

1. How do I feel like responding to a patient? With sympathy? Anger? Distress?
2. How does the patient seem to respond to me? Do I have any clues to how much he or she trusts me?
3. What personal experiences am I reminded of as the patient talks to me?

In a brief contact, the psychologic assessment must be effectively condensed. Whatever the duration of the relationship, the assessment must include an analysis of the meaning that the problem holds for the client and the helper. Disparate attitudes, feelings, and values must be brought into workable alignment. Strong feelings on the part of either client or helper distort the problem in his or her thinking. A difference in values between the participants creates a division in their ways of looking at the situation—a possibility the helper must be aware of.

Case Example: Jeremy Goes Home (Continued)
Before her appeal to the conference group, Vivian was engaged in a continuous assessment of Jeremy's changing nursing needs. This both coincided with and followed the initiation of their relationship. Although Jeremy required carefully planned physical care and reassurance regarding various problems and procedures. Vivian found him quite able to deal with his own feelings throughout the crisis of his surgical experience.

On the day following the conference, Vivian watches for an opportunity to gain Jeremy's cooperation in defining his present problem. She finds it in his apparent pensiveness, which she reflects in the remark *You seem to have something heavy on your mind today.* Jeremy responds by referring to the fact that the second bed in his room is empty: *Mervin went home last night, and it will be my turn soon, I hear.*

During the exchange that follows, Jeremy automatically accepts Vivian's nonverbal cues about undertaking various aspects of his own care. He proceeds quickly, and when he is comfortably seated in his armchair, Vivian seats herself partly facing him. Meanwhile, Jeremy has been voicing his worries about leaving the hospital with less strength than he had before his hospitalization.

Vivian listens intently, using an occasional continuing cue, as Jeremy thinks aloud about the difficulties that he is likely to face. Recognizing that his willingness to confide in her indicates an openness to learning, she uses every occasion for health teaching that occurs. She is thus able to correct her patient's minor misconceptions about his future capabilities and to offer suggestions concerning the availability of medical advice and other aspects of health care when needed.

As the interview progresses, Jeremy himself begins to identify assets in his position: the cooperativeness and reliability of his wife, his two teenage sons, and his three employees, and the relative security of his financial position. But as the time nears for Vivian to leave, he reverts to a complaint about the uncertainty of the date of his discharge and of the preparations that will have to be made.

Before she leaves, Vivian uses prompting to help Jeremy focus on the obvious need to begin from the present. He moves into practical matters connected with his discharge, which he anticipates discussing with his wife and with the resident who will be coming in. He agrees that he will then be in a position to consider what immediate decisions must be made and move from there into tactical details concerning his home and his work.

This reminds Jeremy of one particular area that will be especially difficult for him. He must plan for his employees to continue the heavy physical work that he formerly enjoyed doing. Here Vivian reflects Jeremy's evident pride in his former prowess and his anticipated regret at its diminishment. She reinforces his confidence in the understanding and helpfulness of his employees in this respect. The interview ends with a cooperatively formulated summary of the assets of Jeremy's position as presently viewed and a decision to come back to it the following day.

This example demonstrates, progressively and in capsule form, the processes of problem identification, assessment, and planning. The patient's problem was stated and analyzed in terms acceptable to both participants, an objective was agreed on, and a plan was devised to direct the implementation to follow. In this instance, participation between client and helper was fairly evenly distributed. With a client less able to proceed from step to step so fluidly, assessment would be a more prolonged and complicated process. Alternative goals would be offered with both participants contributing. Positive and negative consequences would be weighed, and goals selected with a view to minimizing the risks involved. The development of strategy would require a similar process. The exercise of a variety of counseling skills would be brought into play along with a judicious mix of continuing and leading responses.

At every stage of problem-solving or client-centered counseling, spontaneous verbalization on the part of the client is desirable. It is inspired as much by the helper's attitudes and expectations as by the use of specific techniques. Keeping leads to a minimum, the worker uses continuing responses to encourage expression of feeling. With the feelings that are ventilated, an intermingling of factual data vital to assessment, planning, and implementation occurs. Support and reassurance are used only to keep excessive anxiety under control, and questions for information and clarification are put forward only when necessary. Pertinent inferences are made and validated when needed to establish problem priorities and to assist in planning the action to be implemented.

Summarizing is a device that is indispensable to problem-solving counseling. Used at intervals during the entire process, it provides a periodic review for the client and worker to test their degree of consensus and evaluate other aspects of their progress toward stated goals. Once a pattern of summarizing is introduced by the practitioner, the client is likely to participate in, and even to initiate, further evaluative summaries.

IMPLEMENTATION

The third stage, the implementation stage, is where most of the direct work of problem alleviation is accomplished. It involves making decisions based on an evaluation of the proposed tactics, and acting on the results. Although some of the activities of implementation belong essentially in the cognitive domain, they can be radically affected by the feeling states of the individuals involved. According to Ruesch (1961), decision making involves scanning input against a background of memories. The accuracy of both the interpretation of input and the operation of scanning is distinctly reduced in this complex process by preoccupation with self or with a particular problem.

It is evident that the anxiety component of communication between client and helper must be monitored continually by the helper during implementation, as well as in previous stages. Measures of control are instituted when they are needed to render emerging decisions and actions as fully rational as possible.

Outcomes are determined in the light of the data assembled on the needs of the client or client group and the resources that are or can be made available.

Decision Making and Action

Assessment tasks were found to include tentative agreement on problem-solving goals and methods of attaining them. To insure the effectiveness of any operation, a definite strategy, or plan of action, must be formulated together with tactics—the precise action or set of actions to be employed (Ruesch, 1975). The implementation phase therefore comprises positive decision making on the strategies and tactics to be used in action, as well as the action itself. In psychologic counseling, the action taken is likely to be, for the most part, interpersonal or social, rather than physical. Decisions about tactics are reached by consensus between client and helper. The actions must fall within the client's capability, unless they are carried out by the helper as the client's agent or advocate.

In the process of growth toward fullness of functioning, our development achieves its most powerful impetus from purposive, autonomous action. Imposed reliance on others can retard this growth and foster emotional patterns of guilt and resentment. The professional helper, in accordance with these principles, supports the client's independence of functioning at every point of the problem-solving relationship. When deficiencies of resources—physical, emotional, intellectual, or material—render clients incapable of acting on their own behalf, helpers either act for them, or influence action on the part of other agents. A nurse makes necessary choices and gives care to a patient incapable of self-care; a teacher helps a child through the step-by-step rudiments of reading; and a social worker approaches welfare authorities on behalf of a powerless client. But in each instance, the client is involved in the attendant decision making and in the action itself to the maximum extent possible under the given circumstances.

As proposals that evolve from the assessment are examined, the decisions made must be satisfying to all involved. It is important that both client and helper be thoroughly committed to any course of action that is accepted. It may be necessary to find ways of obtaining the agreement of others, such as family members of the client, who may be affected by the action.

Whenever a choice is under discussion, the professional helper exercises particular caution regarding the pitfalls of advice giving. In areas where the helper has superior knowledge or experience, assistance is not withheld; it is offered in the form of suggested alternatives. The client is left free to choose among them or to augment them with additional alternatives until a consensus is reached.

Ruesch (1975) further defines a decision as "an event that takes place when an input of information is combined with memory material to produce an output or action that alters the parameters of a given social situation." With every alternative that comes under discussion, memory material is shared between client and helper to form a rationale for or against the suggested course of action. To the extent that human interaction will later be involved in the proposed strategy and tactics, information about possible outcomes will inevitably be incomplete. An insecure client finds it particularly difficult to risk proceeding on a set of assumptions that may later be discarded. Continuing responses to encourage ventilation of feelings will be needed from the helper, as well as reassurance and reinforcement of any signs of self-confidence. As options are narrowed on the basis of both negative and positive predictions, the prospect will seem less hazardous, and decision making will seem possible.

Each of the various types of problems encountered in psychologic counseling involves a demand for change on the part of the client, as well as a need for choice. In Jeremy's case, both a role modification and a shift of attitude are demanded. He is called on to relinquish practical aspects of his former roles and move from a temporarily imposed dependency to an attitude of shared responsibility. His future prospect requires that he change as a person—take on a role with functional activities and attributes that are new to his repertoire. This requires changes in body image and other integral elements of self-identity.

Changes of attitude and behavior may be expected to come about as a result of four factors: dissatisfaction with present conditions; confrontation with promising new conditions; practice in new attitudes and action; and satisfying feedback. In the case in point, Jeremy has experienced dissatisfaction in his patient role; he has begun to recognize potential assets in his new situation. From Vivian, he has received help that leads him to verbalize new attitudes and feedback that reinforces his new outlook.

Before carrying a problem-solving action into effect, it is usual to engage in some form of rehearsal. This testing may take place in the realm of thought, conversation, or simulated action. Once we are committed to following an unaccustomed course, we look for an opportunity to try it out under secure circumstances. This is as true of a change of attitude as of a new activity or skill. The counselor recognizes every client's need for rehearsal as problem solving progresses and provides for the needed practice.

In most instances, the discussion of tactics constitutes a symbolic rehearsal that proves to be adequate. Role playing may be used to help a client who feels insecure about finding the right words to express unfamiliar ideas and sentiments. In either case, the feedback received by the client in the form of satisfaction in new learning acts as reinforcement to encourage further trials. If the counseling relationship is a continuing one, repeated tryouts in the form of homework may be undertaken in the real world of relationships and problem resolution. Confirming or corrective client-helper evaluation affords positive feedback in the interim.

With or without the benefit of contrived rehearsal, the process of problem solving culminates in action. The client usually expects to implement the tactics that were selected as a solution to the target problem. Joint effort is indicated in some instances, or it may be necessary for the helper to act alone on behalf of the client. Regardless of the agent, it is desirable for the client and counselor to meet at least once more for an overall evaluation after action has been taken.

Any residual anxiety that exists is usually relieved by the commitment-action combination. Relief is not entirely contingent on successful problem resolution. Depending on such factors as the emotional maturity of the client, the quality of the counseling experience, and the severity of the situational threat, the client may emerge from apparent failure into enhanced ego strength for facing life problems in the future.

Case Example: Jeremy Goes Home (Continued)
In the microcosm of Vivian's experience in problem-solving counseling with Jeremy, their third interview of the week is in progress. To Vivian, this interview should carry them into the implementation phase. Jeremy is waiting in his chair when she arrives, his toilet already completed. He begins immediately to tell her about yesterday's events. His wife, who spoke with the resident on her way in, reported that he can be discharged on the coming weekend if his present progress continues. Noting Jeremy's emphasis on **if,** Vivian resists a momentary impulse to underscore the optimism that evidently colored the resident's message. At the same time, she is aware of the danger of reinforcing Jeremy's doubts and apprehensions. She chooses a noncommital cue:

> Vivian: *Mhm.*
> Jeremy: *I'll be an invalid. A hospital is the best place for that.*
> Vivian: *You're not looking forward to the weeks of restricted activity ahead.*

Jeremy goes on to review the resident's instructions about: delaying his return to work until the effects of radiation therapy can be determined, not climbing stairs at first, and resting whenever his breathing is difficult. With only an occasional question from Vivian, he begins to discuss the practical details of the necessary planning, such as having a bed moved temporarily to the ground floor and having the telephone cord lengthened so that he can talk to the men at his garage from the living room. This planning revives Jeremy's feelings of frustration as he remembers his diminished capacity for work. Vivian again reflects the feelings he expresses. Jeremy then returns to practical planning, this time for the continuing delegation of heavy tasks to his associates after he returns to work. Vivian seizes the opportunity to review the physiologic warning signs that Jeremy must be prepared to recognize and the actions to be taken.

Vivian knows from the problem-oriented hospital record that the resident has outlined for Jeremy symptoms that may possibly indicate metastasis. From past experience, she can assume that Jeremy may need further explanation and an opportunity to ventilate his feelings about that eventuality. She realizes that a person as generally knowledgeable as Jeremy must have had media exposure to the subject, and she hopes that he will bring his inevitable anxieties into the open.

Jeremy's irritable comment about the prospect of being deprived for life of the pleasure of smoking gives her the chance for clarification to validate her inferences:

Vivian: *It's hard to have to figure that this surgery may not be the end of your lung problem.*

Jeremy: *Yes, damn it! The smoking isn't the only thing. There's the radiation, and then maybe more cancer, whatever they do.*

Vivian: *That's a real worry just now for you.*

Jeremy stands up, walks to the window, and repeatedly pounds both fists on the sill. Recognizing the depth of his grief, his mixed feelings of loss and foreboding, Vivian says nothing until he speaks after returning to his chair.

Jeremy: *I didn't mean to load it all on you. I've taken other setbacks in my stride. I'll have to do the same with this one. But it will take time.*

Vivian: *It's a heavy thing to have on your mind all right. But getting the feelings out once in a while makes it more bearable.*

Jeremy: *That's the way my wife feels, but she's going to get more than her share for a while.* (pause) *I'll see you tomorrow, won't I?*

Vivian knows that she will be late for the conference, but stays for a little more conversation on less emotional topics.

Decision making has proceeded for Vivian's client, with commitment to the immediate essentials of a tactical plan. Priorities have been established, and the long-term risks of the situation have been faced realistically. With the completion of the implementation stage of counseling well under way, attention can be devoted to what remains to be done in the areas of evaluation and termination.

Evaluation

Evaluation is integral to each stage of the problem-solving process. It consists of a series of summary reviews of the progress made up to that point, with a view to measuring its effectiveness against established criteria. In problem-solving counseling, the goals set in the assessment stage provide criteria for use at each subsequent step. Early in the implementation stage, alternative choices are tested against these goals, and one or more are selected as most promising for their achievement. Proposed strategies and tactics are accepted or rejected on the same basis. Rehearsals of tactical actions, in whatever form they are carried out, are used to test desired outcomes. At each step, evaluation constitutes part of the sequential process of decision making. Results may include modifications of minor decisions along the way or of the major decision for action.

If the problem-solving sequence must be accomplished in a single interview, the joint summary that preceded the action must suffice. In either instance, the evaluation sets the stage for future problem solving and action. It abstracts something of what has been achieved in the way of new learning and what is still to be done. Discussion in this vein, however brief, reinforces the client and serves to consolidate the growth-promoting effects of the total experience.

A final evaluation of each counseling experience is essential for the helper's own professional development, and an evaluative summary made in collaboration with the client benefits his or her personal growth. The action itself may have required a modification of strategy and tactics. A redefinition of the problem may even be necessary, with a new problem-solving sequence to follow.

Case Example: Jeremy Goes Home (Continued)

In Vivian's counseling intervention with Jeremy, her implicit goal has been to help him emerge as quickly as possible from his temporary role confusion and begin to orient himself to the role changes that he must make following his discharge. In evaluating Jeremy's early progress, she finds substantial evidence that Jeremy has fully accepted this goal as his own.

Their combined evaluation of their progress toward this goal has also been implicit. They found that Jeremy is capable of assuming responsibility for both present and future role adjustments, and they have supplied each other with verbal and nonverbal feedback to this effect.

Vivian continues to use the opportunity for evaluation and feedback afforded by group conferences and by individual conferences with the primary care nurse, both of which occur on a daily basis. Periodic and final evaluations of her clinical experience in the unit, carried out as a joint activity with her instructor, serve as a reliable guide toward improving her nursing effectiveness in counseling, as well as in other nursing functions.

TERMINATION

Although the topic of termination is placed, in this section, within the context of problem-solving counseling, its various elements can appropriately be applied to the other approaches and methods described in this book. Factors involved in the termination of a single interview are considered, as well as those involved in the termination of intervention and/or the client-worker relationship.

Closing the Interview

Leave taking is an art that is not easily learned. As children, we find that a mere exit is not socially acceptable, yet what should precede it is not clearly defined. Some of us, including some clients and counselors, continue to find the process disconcerting. We must choose among or interpret a wide variety of signals. Expressions of thanks or references to future meetings are sometimes used. Nonverbal signs of leaving include partly or completely rising from a chair or placing one's hands on chair arms or on knees as if to rise. Other ways of showing a shift of attention include lessening eye contact, leaning back or to one side, allowing conversational lapses to become longer or more frequent, using elongated transitional *Uh's* and *Mhm's,* and glancing at the clock or one's watch.

In a professional interview, the counselor chooses only those indicators that are necessary and, at the same time, will not carry a threat of rejection to the client. If the length of the interview is regulated by agency policy or must be compressed because of work load or other considerations, this fact should be mentioned early in the first interview and repeated, if necessary, at the start of subsequent sessions. A statement such as, *The time allotted for our interview is 45 minutes,* or *We have only twenty minutes together today,* sets the stage for a smooth termination, which may then be initiated by the client independently. If the client shows signs of forgetting the time, the worker uses reminders such as, *We have only five minutes more, so let's review what we've accomplished,* thus leading into a closing summary.

It is desirable for each interview to close at a point that is relatively comfortable for the client. The helper therefore guides the discussion toward nonthreatening topics during the last few minutes, and attempts to end on a reasonable hopeful note. As reported in Jeremy's case example, Vivian adheres to this principle in closing an eventful interview with him.

Termination of Intervention or Relationship

The completion of the worker's problem-solving intervention may or not coincide with the termination of the helping relationship. There are situations in which the professional helper's agency assignment or some aspect of the client's status automatically limits the duration of the helping relationship. The contact may be broken when a school term ends, a hospital discharge or transfer is scheduled, or a period of employment is terminated. In problem-solving counseling, agency policy may decree that the relationship end within a stated time period or when agreed-on goals are satisfactorily met. If such restrictions are known beforehand, they are made the subject of discussion in the early structuring process.

Appropriate termination, in the sense in which it marks the end of the client's reliance on the helper for assistance with problem solving, is an objective of counseling from its inception. If the client shows a tendency toward clinging dependence at any point of the relationship, it is treated compassionately but matter-of-factly as a problem to be solved like any other. The separation anxiety from which dependence arises is reflected and clarified when necessary, and handling anxiety is discussed in a way that enhances rather than retards becoming. Meanwhile, the client's strengths in the areas of self-esteem are the focus of the present endeavor as insurance against later uncertainties.

At the last few interviews within a relatively protracted problem-solving relationship, the worker attends to manifest needs for anxiety abatement, reinforcement, and reassurance about the future. The final interview is largely made up of an evaluative summary of accomplishments and of preparation of the client to take further problem-solving action, either independently or with recommended support. The worker uses the opportunity to draw the client into a shared review of the new learning that took place. If done without any hint of patronizing, it serves to consolidate changes in the client's self-concept as well as to build self-esteem. It can be directed toward preparing the client to follow similar problem-solving procedures when needs arise.

If the client shows a tendency to obsessively linger, the helper may find it advisable to bring a note of finality into the leave taking. Realistic commendation for the client's part in the problem-solving task can foster independence and form an upbeat closing. The worker must judge whether it is in the client's best interest to invite him or her to report by telephone or visit at a later date.

Case Example: Jeremy Goes Home (Continued)

Their next interview terminates Vivian's counseling-intervention and her relationship with Jeremy. Before going to his room, where a new patient now occupies the second bed, Vivian learns from the record that Jeremy will be discharged the following day. Her hope that he sustains the confidence that he reached in his ability to cope with the future is justified by his cheerful greeting.

> Jeremy: *Here's my student I was telling you about, Craig.* (proceeds with introduction) *This is the young lady who has been psyching me up to go home.*
>
> Vivian: *You sound as though it worked.*

If it seemed desirable, Vivian would have arranged to see Jeremy alone in his room or in a visiting room. Under the circumstances, a three-way conversation ensues in which Jeremy leads in summarizing his plans for the near future. Vivian reviews with him the schedule for clinic visits that has been set up, and explains aspects of the radiation therapy about which he has questions. Craig turns his attention elsewhere while Jeremy, thanking Vivian for her help, makes a reference to his "blue spell." Craig calls out a goodbye after Jeremy and Vivian have exchanged good wishes for the future.

LABORATORY EXERCISES

The student of counseling needs monitored practice in amalgamating client-centered and problem-solving approaches. Supervised role playing with students acting in pairs provides a safe milieu for early rehearsal. If the student who assumes the client role offers as the subject of discussion an actual past or present problem, it will lend itself particularly well to the exercise of the student-helper's skill. The expression of the student-client's feelings will be genuine, and the relationship will approximate reality.

As an alternative or additional method, outside practice may be assigned or sought, either with a friend portraying the client or with a client who is receiving other services. The student keeps a detailed process record, which is discussed in supervisory interviews with the teacher or another experienced counselor.

Hypothetical openings may be used for role playing with role reversal. If two students reverse roles for a second round of problem solving, each has the opportunity to experience the process of intervention from the vantage point of both counselor and client. Again, if the openings are suggested by the participants, real feelings are likely to be evoked. Otherwise, the role players must try to throw themselves into the parts intensely enough to feel as they might in real-life situations.

Some examples of hypothetical client openings follow. The helper role in each case is that of the learner's own profession.

Parent: *I am almost sure that Mary* (high-school-aged daughter) *is taking some kind of drug that she gets at school. I am out of my mind trying to decide what to do about it.*

College student: *My grades are so poor that my adviser says I should go to the counseling service. Why should I go through that hassle? I think I'll just tell my parents I want to get a job next year.*

Young mother: *The man at the corner store says he has caught Jennifer* (10 years old) *stealing candy several times lately.*

Middle-aged man or woman: *The doctor says Mother is not capable of living alone any longer. She needs more care than we can give her, but she won't hear of going into a nursing home.*

PROBLEM SOLVING IN PRACTICE

The present chapter offers an approach to assisting clients who are faced with a problem to be investigated before a decision can be made and action taken. Any human circumstance that leads us to depend, even marginally, on the assistance of others awakens a measure of anxiety. Before rational problem solving can be undertaken, the complex of negative feelings to which the total situation gives rise must be diminished to the extent that we can think clearly and logically.

With a client such as Rosalyn (Chapter 5), who is incapable of openly facing the responsibility of acknowledging and working through the ordinary problems of living, the relationship must continue on a feeling basis. A reluctant client's seemingly impervious negative attitude may persist for a long time. If the helper can continue to absorb the repeated outpourings of hostility, the steadfastness of his or her attitude of unconditional acceptance may eventually instill the beginnings of trust in the client. Work on specific problems can then follow. Meanwhile, a referral for professional counseling is indicated, provided that the total situation makes it feasible.

In Mrs. Gregory's case, counseling is offered as an integral part of the nurse's full range of services. The combination of the nurse's sensitive responsiveness and Mrs. Gregory's mature openness to change makes it possible for Mrs. Gregory to modify a temporarily negative attitude toward her daughter in the course of a single interview. Open expression of negative feelings gives place to a balanced view of the problem. Finding some of its threat dispelled, the client is able to face the problem unaided. Although the relationship may continue as an aspect of the nurse's work assignment, Mrs. Gregory may not need the nurse's intervention with other personal problems she may encounter.

When a client who makes a direct request for help, as in the case of the aide who could not gain Jimmie's cooperation (Chapter 6), demonstrates a healthy outlook in the course of a balanced expression of feelings, the way is clear for making a problem identification. Discussion in the course of incidental services given to another client of similar strength may reveal the existence of a problem that fits into one of the categories listed in "Problem Identification" earlier in this chapter. If the client signifies an acceptance of the proferred assistance, the process of assessment normally follows. Whether the call for help is made directly or indirectly, the decision-making and action stages of problem solving flow naturally from identifying and completely assessing the problem and its context.

A client who obviously needs all the help delineated in the foregoing presentation of short-term problem-solving counseling is undergoing psychologic crisis. In the following paragraphs, the essential connections are briefly outlined to aid the professional helper in making the necessary applications.

Crisis Intervention as Problem Solving

At any given moment, the helping professional can expect to be brought into contact with another human being who is in the grip of psychologic crisis. The person in crisis may be an actual or potential client, a fellow worker, a relative, a friend, or perhaps a stranger who has been victimized in an accident or by intentional violence. When helpers are engaged in a service that is specifically set up for crisis intervention, there is a normal expectation that clients need such assistance. But for others, the helpers' ability to offer effective crisis counseling depends, from the start, on their ability to recognize that the presenting problem is a state of crisis.

A **situational crisis** is precipitated whenever the self is perceived to be severely threatened by an actual or an anticipated loss. Loss, or bereavement, involves factors such as: possessions or livelihood; health, safety, or intactness of body image; position, status, or reputation; or the presence or regard of a significant person or persons. On the other hand, the stressful circumstances may be connected with a **developmental crisis**—symbolized in Erikson's psychosocial crises or by another type of change-related state that makes threatening demands for personal growth. For some, crisis points occur with a new school or work adjustment or with impending or actual marriage, childbirth, desertion or divorce, menopause, or old age. In such cases, the perceived loss is likely to be a valued source of love, security, freedom, or personal satisfaction.

The helper's immediate aim in intervention is to help the client work through the acute anxiety of mourning that the loss precipitates and to restore the individual's ability to cope with the required situational or developmental transition. In either type of transition, both attitudinal and practical change is demanded. Predominant in the client's inner experience of crisis is a feeling of helplessness in the face of dangerously unstable circumstances. Helplessness and hopelessness may be extreme to the extent that the individual may be impelled to consider or to attempt suicide. For helping professionals, opportunities are widely available to gain skill and confidence in dealing with emergencies of this type. After qualifying as trained volunteers, they can man centers set up for intervention in crises of suicide, drug dependence, or violence.

In any crisis situation, the well-prepared professional can effectively use the skills of problem-solving counseling to alleviate the psychologic pain of crisis until, with appropriate referral when necessary, personal and community support systems can be called into action. Meanwhile, the helper enters into a relationship made strongly supportive to the client through realistic ego reinforcement and reassurance. All of the recommended measures for the control of anxiety are brought into play. Ventilation of feelings is encouraged by authentic helper attitudes of unconditional acceptance and empathy and by responsive listening and reflection of feeling.

Once anxiety has been brought within more moderate limits, problem assessment and planning can proceed. The variables to consider are primarily: the severity of the actual stress, the accuracy with which it is perceived by the victim, and the internal and external coping mechanisms that are available to the victim. For example, an adult who has reached a relatively high degree of self-reliance and who is part of a close-knit system of mutual support is likely to face a stressful situation with more competence than a child, a teenager, or an emotionally dependent adult who has no circle of friends, relatives, or peers capable of lending supportive assistance. Another variable occurs when a loss or bereavement has been anticipated for a period of time. In this case, some of the work of mourning necessitated by the actual event may have been accomplished beforehand.

Further stages of problem-solving intervention are outlined in the present chapter under "Implementation" and "Termination." With supervision, students and practitioners can achieve skill in adapting these stages effectively to crisis as one among many typical problems of daily living. Alternative courses of action must be identified, and choices and decisions must be made in this area as in any other type of problem solving.

Every choice we make initiates or furthers a change in ourselves. Because the prospect of change is threatening, the skillful counselor provides a climate for the client that is conducive to expressing feelings at every step in the course of the counseling relationship. The problem-solving approach becomes humanistic and therefore humanizing only insofar as the client and helper encounter one another as persons. Both positive and negative feelings are appreciated; both are put into the service of the problem-solving venture rather than being allowed to impede it. To the extent that this occurs, their collaborative effort furthers the becoming of each participant.

References

Aguilera, D. C., and Messick, J. M. 1978. *Crisis intervention.* 3rd ed. St. Louis: Mosby.

Compton, B. R., and Galaway, B. 1975. *Social work processes.* Homewood, Ill.: Dorsey.

Erikson, E. 1963. *Childhood and society.* 2nd ed. New York: Norton.

Hoff, L. A. 1978. *People in crisis: Understanding and helping.* Menlo Park, Calif.: Addison-Wesley.

Lazarus, A. A. 1969. The "inner circle" strategy: Identifying crucial problems. *Behavioral counseling: Cases and techniques.* John D. Krumboltz and Carl E. Thorensen, editors. New York: Holt, Rinehart and Winston.

Reid, W. J. 1972. Target problems, time limits, task structure. *J. Educ. Soc. Work* 8:2, 58–68.

Ruesch, J. 1961. *Therapeutic communication.* New York: Norton.

——. 1975 *Knowledge in action.* New York: Jason Aronson.

Sheehy, G. 1976. *Passages: Predictable crises of adult life.* New York: Dutton.

Snyder, J. C., and Wilson, M. F. 1977. Elements of a psychological assessment. *Am. J. Nurs.* 77:235–239.

Yura, H., and Walsh, M. B. 1978. *The nursing process: Assessing, planning, implementing, evaluating.* 3rd ed. New York: Appleton-Century-Crofts.

CHAPTER 8

Behavioral Approaches in Helping Relationships

Behavioral counseling, which utilizes numerous modalities of behavior modification, is a type of problem solving instituted for the purpose of helping people solve problems of daily living. It is modeled on the experimental method. The two statements also apply to the problem-solving approach to counseling explored in Chapters 6 and 7. The essential difference between the two approaches lies in the counselor's frame of reference. The therapeutic goals examined so far have related to the client's inner growth toward self-actualization. The behaviorist's focus is behavior that is overtly perceptible to the client, the counselor, or both.

Quite apart from implementing a planned behavioral program, the helping professional uses aspects of behavior modification both unwittingly and by design. The worker's spontaneous smile or frown may act, respectively, to positively or negatively reinforce the client behavior that occasions it. Verbal reinforcement is mentioned in Chapter 6 as one of a number of communication skills in counseling. This chapter enlarges and applies the notion of reinforcement and other concepts of respondent (classical) and operant (instrumental) conditioning in order to open up possibilities for their wider and more programmatic use in short-term counseling. Applications of behavioral methods in short-term helping relationships are explored and illustrated.

BEHAVIORAL AIMS

The general aim of behavior modification is implied in the term itself: to weaken or extinguish undesirable behavior and to initiate or increase desirable behavior. Definitions of specific outcomes or target behaviors differ with individual clients or groups of clients. The identification of explicit goals therefore becomes an indispensable initial segment of the process of intervention.

Behavioral counseling is often instigated at the request of the behaving person. Exceptions occur when counseling programs are offered to institutionalized groups who are willing to work with a staff member to correct a behavior problem they have in common. For very young children and severely retarded persons, modification procedures may be planned and employed without the full knowledge of those subjected to them. Although means of strengthening motivation may enter into the **reinforcement program**, it is usually important that clients be capable of cooperating in the selection of target behaviors and in the reinforcing measures used to attain them.

CONCEPTS OF REINFORCEMENT

Beginning from the work of J. B. Watson in the early part of the present century, and the later development of theory led by B. F. Skinner, a terminology specific to the field of behaviorism has evolved. Although its most commonly used terms are somewhat familiar to the average reader, a more precise understanding of those that may have particular application to counseling is needed by the helping professional. A brief review follows.

Operant or instrumental conditioning is carried out in a planned sequence **(schedule)** in which a predetermined environmental consequence **(operant stimulus)** is made contingent on a specific behavioral response **(operant response)**. In other words, an operant stimulus (reinforcer) emitted from the environment is used as an instrument to modify the specific unit of respondent behavior (behavior affected by its antecedents). The relationship between the environmental reinforcer-response bond and its behavior consequence is called a **contingency**.

Contingency management is the process of changing a subject's response by controlling events that precede or follow it. In **positive reinforcement**, the response is strengthened (accelerated) by making a rewarding (positive) stimulus contingent on a desired response. In **negative reinforcement**, the wanted response is strengthened by making a negative (aversive) stimulus contingent on an unwanted response; an increase of targeted behavior avoids or escapes the noxious stimulus. In other words, wanted behavior is again accelerated as unwanted behavior is decelerated or extinguished.

The contingencies that might be used to bring about reinforcement are shown in Table 8-1. Taken together, the two under "Positive Reinforcement" represent the key techniques employed in behavior modification. Of the three contingencies of negative reinforcement, only punishment by cessation of a positive operant stimulus is widely applicable in planned programs of behavior modification. A discussion of the uses of each of the five contingencies follows.

Broadly conceived, the stimuli used in the five contingencies are connected either primarily or secondarily with the satisfaction of such fundamental drives as those for food, rest, activity, and social interaction. In the practice of behavior modification, every human situation is looked on as distinct. The reinforcing stimuli that are selected are those that are found to be most appropriate to effect the desired response in the individual client. The effectiveness of any stimulus cannot be determined in advance. Until it brings about the desired consequence in a particular instance, it is not properly called a reinforcer of a specific unit of wanted behavior.

POSITIVE REINFORCEMENT

There are two classes of techniques (contingencies) by which positive reinforcement, with resulting increase (acceleration) of wanted behavior, is brought about. They are identified in Table 8-1, in which a contrast is drawn between positive and negative reinforcement. Some ways in which the two contingencies of positive reinforcement are used in human behavior modification are described below. Because the emission of a positive operant stimulus following an opera-

Table 8-1 Comparison of effects on behavior of positive and negative reinforcement

Positive reinforcement	
Positive stimulus	**Effect on behavior**
Positive operant stimulus following an operant response	Reinforcement of operant response
Cessation of negative operant stimulus*	Reinforcement of operant response
Negative reinforcement	
Aversive stimulus	**Effect on behavior**
Punishment following operant response	Temporary cessation of operant response
Punishment preceding operant response	Avoidance of operant response
Punishment by cessation of positive operant stimulus*	Extinction of operant response

*Cessation of a positive reinforcement acts as a negative; cessation of a negative reinforcement acts as a positive (Skinner, 1938).

tive response is by far the most commonly used contingency, it is predominant in the following discussion.

Positive Operant Stimulus and Response

The operant stimuli used in positive reinforcement may be primary or secondary reinforcers. Both terms were originally used in classical (Pavlovian) conditioning, which is concerned with the pairing of stimuli to modify behavior. **Primary reinforcers** satisfy basic drives such as those for food, fluid, oxygen, rest, muscular activity, and human interaction. **Secondary**, or acquired, **reinforcers** take on strength from being combined with already potent reinforcers. They include individual and social rewards such as attention, approval, respect, or praise; and indirect rewards in the form of money, grades, promotions, or privileges.

As positive operant reinforcers for children, primary and secondary stimuli are regularly combined. Candy is commonly dispensed as a contingent stimulus following a unit of desired behavior. A point system may be used, with candies or some other tangible reward given for accumulated points. As secondary stimuli, verbal expressions of approval are more effectively linked with the desired behavior if the behavior is specified. For example: *Good! You tied your own shoe,* rather than *Good!* alone. Nonverbal expressions include signs of affection such as a smile, a pat, or a hug, and they are paired with a similar verbal label. Adult patients in mental health facilities who are in behavioral programs of resocialization training receive tokens as stimuli, again accompanied by social approval. The tokens are negotiable for food snacks or privileges such as attendance at an entertainment function.

The scheduling of reinforcement may be an important consideration. With a **continuous schedule**, the reinforcing stimulus is emitted with every appropriate client response. This is both necessary and possible at the beginning of a program such as the toilet training of a child. At first, there is a continuous schedule of both primary and secondary reinforcement. As conditioning proceeds, the primary reinforcers are shifted to an **intermittent schedule**, while social reinforcement remains continuous. Next, the primary reinforcement is gradually discontinued, and social approval becomes intermittent. Finally, even social approval is no longer necessary.

In group treatment of patients in a psychiatric ward, an intermittent schedule is used. It may be regular—a token is awarded for every five successful performances—or irregular. When patients are able to respond to it, the irregular method is preferred. The unpredictability of the positive stimulus keeps the patients' performance at a relatively high level of appropriateness.

The principles of scheduling have many applications in behavior modification. In general, the use of a continuous schedule is an effective measure at the beginning of a program, but becomes less so later. Although it expedites operant conditioning, it prolongs client dependence. Furthermore, it does not prepare the client for the realities of everyday life. One does not normally encounter rewarding responses for behavior that is merely appropriate. Achievement of self-control by the behaving person is the ultimate aim of intervention.

In counseling a single child or an adult, reinforcers are individualized. Some clients react with suspicion to counselor approval, or they consider the use of checklists childish. They may respond positively to self-reinforcement when wanted new behavior is followed by a favorite food, an enjoyable activity, or a rest or a relaxing change of focus. This is an application of the **Premack Principle**. Premack (1965) states that high-probability (high-preference) behaviors may be used to contingently reinforce low-probability (low-preference) behaviors. A parent who wishes to reinforce a child's music practice, for example, makes a specified amount of television watching contingent on each hour of practice.

Several generalizations, including the Premack principle, may be made to guide the choice (control) of positive reinforcers. To be effective, a reinforcer must be attractive to the individual client. It must also be immediately available. Delay in receiving a reward tends to lessen its value. In addition, there is danger that the delayed stimulus might reinforce coincidental behavior that falls outside the intended program. Finally, previous deprivation of a reinforcer is conducive it its effectiveness, whereas satiation lessens its usefulness. Social approval, for instance, should be withheld except as an intentional reinforcing response. The profuse or insincere use of counselor approval is likely to render it ineffectual as a reinforcer.

The preceding general principles are illustrated in the following case example:

Case Example: Emily at Dinner

At dinner, Emily leaves her carrots until last, and she shows her repugnance for them. The toddler is told that she may have her ice cream only if she eats the vegetable. Emily slowly complies. Her mother seldom serves ice cream at meals because she believes that fruit is a more healthful food.

Although her parents plan to eat their dessert with coffee later, Emily is given ice cream, with an approving pat on the head, as soon as the vegetable is gone. When coffee is served, Emily is teasing her crying baby brother. If Emily's serving of ice cream had been deferred until coffee time, it could have operated as a reinforcer of teasing. Immediately after the vegetable consumption, it was a potential reinforcer of carrot eating, obedience, or both. Emily will soon be expected to empty her dinner plate without reward or punishment.

Operant shaping The preceding section explained the use of positive stimuli as antecedents to the repetition of a learned or unlearned operative response. Shaping, or successive approximation, is a procedure that adapts the emission of positive operant stimuli to new learning. The stimulus follows each approximation of the desired activity. This method is used in training stage and domestic animals and in teaching children. It has specialized applications in teaching retarded and autistic children new behavior in communication, self-care, and social interaction. Both shaping and modeling, as described in this section, demonstrate a principle that is generally applied: as progress in the reinforced activity is attained, standards of performance are gradually raised.

An infant in an ordinary family is rewarded by approval of its first attempts at forming words. Without consciously applying the principles of operant conditioning, parents use positive stimuli in graduated measure as the child more closely approaches the correct pronunciation of *Daddy, baby,* and so forth. In treatment programs for children with language handicaps, shaping is used according to a minutely devised program of approximation. Retarded and autistic children are similarly trained to carry out activities such as self-feeding, tying shoelaces, buttoning jackets, and washing hands and faces.

In teaching a severely autistic child to feed herself, for instance, a detailed program is drawn up that breaks the skill down into its many components: touching a spoon, grasping the spoon in the dominant hand, holding the spoon by the handle, touching food in a dish with the bowl of the spoon, and so forth. The child is placed in a tray-equipped chair, with a spoon lying on the tray. When the child's hand randomly touches the spoon, an M&M candy is popped into her mouth, and the worker says *Spoon. That's good!* in an encouraging tone. The reinforcers are repeated each time either hand comes in contact with the spoon. The child eventually clutches the spoon, at which point the reinforcer is used—and thereafter only for clutching. After this, the candy and the comment are withheld until the dominant hand is placed on the spoon. This action is reinforced each time it is repeated until the child has learned to hold the spoon with the dominant hand. When she next grasps the bowl of the spoon, the reward is not given. It is reinstated when she uses the dominant hand to grasp the handle. The same procedure is repeated with every identified component of self-feeding until the complete skill is achieved. The duration of each lesson is, of course, adapted to the child's tolerance.

Modeling and behavior rehearsal Modeling, or observational learning, is also used to promote learning of new and, in some instances, modified behavior. The worker initiates the operant sequence by demonstrating the new actions or by using visual materials or sound. Such demonstration acts as an environmental operant stimulus to evoke imitation as the subject's operant response, which the worker immediately reinforces. In ordinary life, the learning of speech and language is expedited through this sequence, as are the elements of self-care and many other behaviors. Because modeling has been recognized as an effective teaching vehicle, television advertising and programming for child viewers continue to be controversial public issues. The modeling effect of parental and teacher behaviors, with their subtle *Don't do as I do—do as I say* implications is less widely appreciated. Instruction, whether formal or informal, in a motor procedure, such as the use of a manual tool, a machine, or a musical instrument, regularly combines demonstration and explanation with subsequent social reward. Hand, or contact, modeling may be added to guide the subject through the motions of the new skill.

A problem typically amenable to modeling is poor posture in school-age children or young adults. The worker initiates the operant sequence by showing the client pictures or drawings displaying good posture. The tilt of the head may be featured first, and approval subsequently may be offered as the client sits, stands, and walks with the head at an attractive angle. Videotaping is an ideal adjunct to the modifications of posture problems because it provides feedback that has a self-reinforcing impact. A mirror is a good substitute. When practice shows that reinforcement of the first step is adequate, attention is transferred sequentially to positioning the shoulders, hands and arms, chest, abdomen, legs, and feet.

Behavior rehearsal, a form of role playing, may be combined with modeling or used separately as an operant procedure. Feedback by way of helper commendation and client self-reinforcement constitute the positive operant stimuli. For example, a child who is to undergo surgery is sometimes taken into the pediatric hospital unit to become acquainted with the setting. Role playing is carried out in play in which a nurse enacts her own role to make the child familiar with procedures. Role reversal is encouraged as the child plays the nurse part and freely handles equipment.

With some role playing, homework is prescribed. The client's assignment is to practice in real situations the skills that have been rehearsed. The depth of the client's learning is similarly increased by role reversal. Symbolically stepping into the other person's shoes gives the client the opportunity to anticipate the fact that the other person in the real situation will be someone with feelings and attitudes that humanize the actual event when it occurs.

Most of the current adaptations of behavior modification involve cognitive as well as conditioned learning. This is true of modeling insofar as conceptualization is encouraged. Much that goes into behavior rehearsal is cognitive in nature. In both methods, a considerable amount of identification, or unconscious imitative learning, also takes place.

Cessation of Negative Stimulus

In the second contingency (Table 8-1), a negative (aversive) stimulus acts as a positive reinforcer when it is terminated. As a result of the relief from unpleasantness that its cessation brings, the stimulus becomes instrumental in effecting positive reinforcement. The particular response that terminates the aversive stimulus is thereby strengthened.

The principle is operative, in combination with negative reinforcement, in withholding attention during a temper tantrum and in isolating a noncompliant prisoner or an excited psychiatric patient or child. In such cases, the cessation of the aversive treatment (stimulus) becomes temporarily a positive reinforcer of ensuing quiet or compliant behavior.

NEGATIVE REINFORCEMENT

Behavior modification employs a number of direct punishment contingencies (negative reinforcement) that parallel positive reinforcement techniques but here decelerates or extinguishes unwanted behavior. In Table 8-1 they are classified under three headings that represent the different ways in which punishing (aversive) stimuli are used. Each method is briefly discussed below.

Punishment Following Operant Response

Punishment that follows unwanted behavior (operant response) is listed first in Table 8-1 as a direct deterrent. This principle is applied in human behavior modification when signs of counselor disapproval act as a punishing operant stimulus. Punishment by mild electric shocks has been used in the treatment of head banging and other self-mutilating behavior of seriously disturbed children.

As indicated in Table 8-1, punishment that follows an operant response brings about, at best, only a temporary discontinuance of the unwanted target behavior. There is a commonly held belief that because reward strengthens a response, it must follow that punishment weakens it. Behavioral research has shown otherwise (Blackman, 1974). Instead of extinguishing a response, subsequent punishment merely brings about a temporary cessation. When the punishing circumstance is lifted, the behavior is likely to be resumed in its full strength; little weakening effect can be observed. The judicious use of punishing stimuli in human behavior modification may have the limited value of demonstrating that the client is capable of suppressing the unwanted behavior. In the case of self-mutilating children, the values involved in the use of punishing stimuli are carefully weighed. The administration of an aversive stimulus can provide the child with a needed rest from self-administered abuse. The effects on the person who deliberately applies the punishment are unknown.

Punishment Preceding Operant Response

In the second type of negative reinforcement listed in Table 8-1, the aversive stimulus precedes the operant response; it is an avoidance response that is triggered. This has the effect of removing or preventing the punishment (negative reinforcer), making it a prospective reinforcer of avoidance behavior. An example that comes readily to mind is the parking ticket. Its imminence prompts a chain of behaviors such as: selecting a legally sanctioned place, depositing the required coin, and returning to claim the car within the allotted time. Unwanted, or in this case, less wanted, behavior is suppressed, but not necessarily extinguished. In a planned token or point system, subjects learn that certain behavior will bring a **response cost**: repayment of tokens previously earned or the forfeiture of points. They avoid the costly behavior, at least intermittently, in favor of one that promises a positive operant stimulus.

Cessation of Positive Operant Stimulus

The third type of aversive stimulus, the cessation of a positive operant stimulus, is the preferred method for use in negative reinforcement. The underlying principle is that a response that is not reinforced will weaken in strength and frequency and will eventually be extinguished. The example of temper tantrums is particularly applicable here. Relatives such as parents or spouses commonly respond to displays of temper with excessive attention. Because attention serves as a positive operant stimulus, it reinforces the antisocial behavior. If attention is withheld during the tantrum and used instead when peace is restored, the former pattern may be extinguished and the latter strengthened.

Removal from positive reinforcement, or **time out**, refers to an effective procedure that also falls under the third type of aversive stimulus. Contingent on unwanted behavior, the subject is removed from or otherwise denied a positive operant stimulus. Time out becomes an aversive stimulus that leads to deceleration of the unwanted behavior. A child, a psychiatric patient, or a prisoner whose behavior is troublesome or dangerous to others is removed from the group that constitutes reinforcement, and he or she is placed in temporary isolation. This mode of treatment involves controversial values. To be placed behind a locked door can be frightening or infuriating. Furthermore, it is seldom necessary. Isolation without companionship, occupation, or diversion may result in worse behavior than that which it is intended to correct. This concept is discussed further under the topic of intervention. Also within the time out category is the withholding of tokens, points, or other tangible rewards. The subject is deprived, for a time, of a reinforcing stimulus. Cutting down on television watching is another example of time out–also of response cost.

The general principles of negative reinforcement are similar to those that apply to the choice and use of positive reinforcers. An effective negative reinforcer must be perceived as aversive by the client. To be separated from a given group, for instance, may be viewed as either a positive or a negative factor by a particular individual. The principles of immediacy and satiation also apply to both types of reinforcement. Delayed punishment may become associated with responses other than those it is intended to avert. Punishment used indiscriminately is likely to lack any connection with a specific response. It may even be sought as a means of gaining a sense of being worthy of notice.

A planned reinforcement program includes measures to control antecedent conditions that currently operate as stimuli for the nonadaptive behavior. In countering overeating, for example, taking meals in restaurants is ruled out, and only nonfattening foods are kept in the home. With both positive and negative contingencies, the standards set for client performance are increased as the program of reinforcement continues. In the above example, the client can eventually be expected to choose both voluntarily and circumspectly from a menu or from a normally stocked refrigerator.

It can be recognized that contingencies involving positive and negative reinforcement represent devices that we are conditioned to use to modify our own behavior. Most of us, most of the time, reinforce our good intentions with intervals of relaxation in the midst of tedious work. We silence or isolate ourselves when we note signs of boredom in our listeners. We avoid illegal parking, overeating, and numerous other behaviors because of the expense or embarrassment of their response costs.

The following two behavioral approaches draw on principles of classical (respondent) as well as operant conditioning. They fall significantly within the cognitive realm. In the first instance, the technique of counterconditioning is used: a stimulus that has become conditioned to an anxiety response is paired with a response that is incompatible with anxiety.

SYSTEMATIC DESENSITIZATION

Joseph Wolpe, a psychiatrist-professor, has pioneered in the behavioral treatment of neurotic phobias. He uses a process of progressive counterconditioning (systematic desensitization) combined with deep relaxation. Underlying his method is the respondent **Principle of Reciprocal Inhibition**: *If a response that inhibits anxiety can be made to occur in the presence of anxiety-evoking stimuli, it will weaken the bond between these stimuli and anxiety* (Wolpe, 1973). The inhibiting response in this instance is deep relaxation. The anxiety-evoking stimuli vary with each client.

A client suffering from a fear of heights may become acutely anxious at the thought of entering an elevator or climbing a stairway that is open on both sides. If the client learns to pair the imaginary occurrence of such stimuli with deep relaxation, which is inhibiting to the generalized muscular tension of anxiety, the anxiety reaction can be weakened and eventually overcome. Wolpe and others who use systematic desensitization as a method of treatment follow a well-defined procedure. The client is first given a full explanation of the method, then is trained in the process of deep relaxation according to a model such as Jacobson's (1964). Concurrently with the training, data is obtained from the client about specific incidents of phobic anxiety. This is used for the construction of an anxiety hierarchy, in which the anxiety-producing stimuli are ranked from the least anxiety-laden to the most anxiety laden.

After the hierarchy is established, the procedure of progressive desensitization follows. Having first entered into a deeply relaxed state, the client is assisted in living out, as vividly as possible, a series of imaginary versions of scenes associated with the least threatening stimulus. For a client with a maladaptive fear of heights, this might include standing on the first step of a ladder. When the relaxed client can imagine, without anxiety, each of several scenes in which he or she stands on the first step of a ladder, the second stimulus in the hierarchy is presented, and the process, starting from an initial state of relaxation, is repeated.

Each treatment session repeats the first stimulus and proceeds as far as possible upward through the hierarchy. For the client who fears heights, the last scenes might represent the experiences of riding in an airplane and looking over an open cliff at the sea below. When a situation does not evoke anxiety in fantasy, it is unlikely to do so in reality. The client is encouraged to accomplish, within the realm of possibility, each of the hierarchical steps under relaxed conditions in real-life (*in vivo*) circumstances. In some cases, *in vivo* rehearsal is possible. Whether *in vivo* or under imagined conditions, behavior modeling may be used. Positive reinforcement comes from the counselor's reassurance and commendation and from the client's own successes.

ASSERTIVENESS TRAINING

The teaching-learning approach called assertiveness (assertive, or assertion) training is a behavioral method of helping clients overcome problems of self-assertion in social relationships. A number of techniques of both respondent (classical) and operant conditioning are employed, as well as cognitive instruction. The training may be combined with another treatment program such as systematic desensitization, or it may be offered alone on either an individual or group basis.

Some people find it difficult to express their feelings and thoughts in a forthright, yet inoffensive, way; some express themselves so strongly that they antagonize or frighten others; some are unable to discriminate between situations requiring assertiveness and those in which discretion is necessary. Because there is a marked anxiety component in problems of this type, specific training in progressive relaxation is often used. There may be discussion of authority relationships and conceptual differences between assertive self-expression and hostile aggression. Modeling, role playing, and behavior rehearsal are usually included in the program of behavior modification. In the following example, several techniques are combined to modify a lack of assertiveness in behavior.

Case Example: Jason Asserts Himself

When Jason presented himself for training, he appeared dejected, his head and shoulders bowed. He spoke in an almost inaudible tone and avoided eye contact. At twenty years of age, he saw as his main problems the inability to ask girls for dates, to answer questions in college classes, and to talk with his father on any topic without acute discomfort.

Jason's training included a modified form of Jacobson's progressive relaxation, cognitive learning experiences, modeling, role playing, positive reinforcement, and real-life rehearsals. The counselor examined with Jason a sampling of the latter's experiences of relating to others and their behavioral consequences. With each incident, he was encouraged to imagine more desirable outcomes. For homework, Jason was assigned to select, from his reading, from television, and from other people, examples of behavior involving appropriate assertive responses connected with each of his problems. Counselor and client then role played situations in which Jason used responses similar to those selected. When he found response behavior particularly difficult, Jason and the counselor reversed roles, and the counselor modeled the difficult parts in the Jason role.

Jason's appropriate role-playing responses, both verbal and nonverbal, were reinforced by the counselor's encouraging comments and his own satisfaction with his progress. As the training continued, Jason was able to rehearse his newly acquired skills in actual situations of gradually increasing difficulty. He reported the incidents in detail and reenacted them with the counselor for their combined evaluation. After ten weekly training sessions, Jason moved and conversed with improved assurance and was able to perform with a degree of assertiveness in the three problem areas originally presented.

THE CLIENT-HELPER RELATIONSHIP

The helping professional who aspires to develop a humanistically eclectic approach can appreciate the advantages of drawing on the insights and skills of behavioral counseling. The relationship between client and helper can center on the client and, at the same time, aid the client to solve crucial problems by making needed behavioral changes. Throughout the process of intervention, the helper is fully present and sensitively responsive to the client as a person who is capable of becoming. Feelings are regarded to be as significant as external behavior, and the client's freedom of choice is fully respected in each decision that is made. The contingencies of reinforcement that are put to use are selected and administered, insofar as possible, with the informed consent and cooperation of the client.

THE PROCESS OF INTERVENTION

When the professional helper deems it advisable to use behavioral techniques in intervention, an individualized reinforcement program is developed. The classification of counseling problems presented in Chapter 7 under "Problem Identification" is applicable here wherever a discrete unit of behavior can be chosen for acceleration and deceleration.

Also, the amelioration of the problem behavior must fall within the field of competence of the helping professional or of his or her teaching supervisor. Counseling education in a basic program of professional nursing, for instance, can be expected to prepare a practitioner to use behavioral techniques in dealing with problems in training an educable child in self-care, or in helping an adult client achieve a more assertive or less demanding behavioral style. But for a problem as pervasive and profound as autism in a child or a phobic or addictive complex of behaviors in an adult, specialized preparation in one of the psychiatric disciplines must be added.

If the client has sought help in bringing about a change in behavior, program planning is made a cooperative venture between helper and client. In other problem situations, the cooperation of others, such as personnel or family members, may be enlisted. The following general consideration of the process of behavioral intervention makes the successive phases consistent with those under problem-solving intervention in Chapter 7:

1. Initiation of the relationship
2. Assessment and planning
3. Implementation
4. Termination

Initiation of the Relationship

Because it constitutes a form of problem solving, a behavioral approach to helping has much in common with the more general problem-solving method discussed in Chapter 7. Much of the material to be found there under "Initiation of the Relationship" is equally applicable here. This is especially true of the suggestions included under "The Opening," "Time Factors," and "Role Definition." The concept of role is developed in this chapter with reference to the helper as change agent and role model.

At the initiation of any client-helper relationship, the client is likely to experience anxiety about having problems severe enough to require assistance with intervention. The helper who recognizes this attempts by empathic and attentive listening to structure a situation that is conducive to the expression of feeling. Reflecting and clarifying comments and periodic summarizing are used when necessary to facilitate the construction of clear statements of problems, troublesome behaviors, and goals.

The culminating task of the initiation phase, if possible a shared responsibility between client and helper, is problem identification. Even clients who voluntarily seek help may need assistance in this task. It is not easy to acknowledge behavior that we do not wish to own and to contrast it with behavior we consider closer to our ideal. The professional helps the client to arrive at a clearly descriptive statement about every problem to be worked on.

Some clients have difficulty in expressing their own personal view of the problem situation. The inner circle strategy (Chapter 7) is pertinent here. It was originally devised for use in behavioral counseling (Lazarus, 1969). From the behavioral point of view, behavior is evaluated only on the basis of its consequences, and then only in terms of the ultimate desirability of those consequences to the behaving person. This helper attitude enables the client to explore, perhaps initially in a defensive or evasive guise, but gradually more openly, the thoughts and behaviors that he or she finds most troubling.

The thoughts that are shared with the helper may convey feelings rather than specific problems, or problems may be stated in vague language. In such cases, the professional helps by translating ideas into behavioral terms. A global complaint about being afraid of everything and everybody, for instance, must be related to specific situations and specific people. The problem that surfaces may be a set of incapacitating phobias or simply a dread of having to open a conversation with a stranger at a party.

In many situations in which behavioral intervention is indicated, the helper is the one who recognizes the need for change in a client's behavior as a means of improving the client's relationships and general well-being. In a case example that fits into this category, the initiation of a counseling relationship between a licensed practical nurse and one of her assigned patients is introduced below. The behavioral intervention is carried out under the supervision of the head nurse, whose background includes preparation in counseling theory and practice. The situation also illustrates the necessity of involving a family member and others who form part of the interpersonal environment in every stage of the intervention process. The reinforcement contingency used is punishment by cessation of positive operant stimuli.

Case Example: Mrs. O'Connor Changes Her Behavior

Mrs. O'Connor is a newly admitted hospice patient who is in a terminal condition from a long-neglected carcinoma of the cervix. Until institutionalization became necessary, her widowed daughter Marian devoted herself to caring for her mother, also a widow, in the home that they shared. Marian stays throughout the day of the admission and attempts to help her mother accept the hospice patient role by sympathizing with her whining complaints.

In spite of Marian's solicitude, Mrs. O'Connor frequently puts on her call light for superfluous details of staff attention. Debbie, the young practical nurse assigned to admit Mrs. O'Connor to the nursing unit and attend to her other nursing needs, finds herself responding to numerous calls for services such as adjusting and readjusting the window shades and watering the plant that Mrs. O'Connor brought with her. At each call, Marian apologizes, saying that her mother would not allow her to carry out the service in question. Mrs. O'Connor detains Debbie to listen to a complaining recital of symptoms.

In a brief conference alone with Marian, Debbie and the head nurse learn that, although Mrs. O'Connor has withdrawn from almost all of her former activities since her physician informed her of the diagnosis, she does not tolerate any mention of cancer, but insists that her illness is caused by an infection. On a rational basis, she is aware of the nature of hospice care. She nevertheless talks of her stay there as temporary and necessary only until her daughter recovers from high blood pressure.

The two staff members tell Marian that Mrs. O'Connor's present need to deny the truth of her condition will be respected. They also recognize that the patient's demanding behavior is at least partly caused by her need to test the staff members' concern for her. On learning that her excessive bids for attention have been habitual since she became partially bedridden some weeks previously, the head nurse offers a suggestion. The others readily agree to cooperate in trying out a behavioral approach that has proved effective with other patients who were similarly overdependent at admission.

Marian is assured that her mother will be given the customary mixture of analgesics and alcohol in graduated doses to eradicate pain and, therefore, the fear of pain. After data is obtained on the frequency of her calls to the staff, Mrs. O'Connor will be informed of the plan to provide her with all the attention that she can realistically require, and her cooperation will be solicited. The head nurse predicts a rapid deceleration of the patient's demands. Once this is achieved, she will be better able to participate in the salutory social milieu of the hospice and relate comfortably with other patients, staff, volunteers, and visitors. In the general hospice environment of open awareness of terminal illness, Mrs. O'Connor may eventually find it possible to come to terms with the reality of her own situation.

The head nurse, who welcomed Mrs. O'Connor to the unit at the time of her admission, makes an early visit to further her acquaintance with Mrs. O'Connor. She shows genuine concern for the newcomer as a person and she succinctly explains the idea of the hospice as an alternative type of inpatient care, including the regimen of medication for pain prevention. She assures Mrs. O'Connor of the interest of the whole staff in making her stay with them as satisfying as possible.

On the head nurse's instruction, Debbie begins to obtain baseline data on the target behavior. She checkmarks a posted graph sheet to show the number of times per hour that Mrs. O'Connor's light goes on, without making any comment to the patient about the undesirability of her behavior. Instead, she chooses a moment when the light is not on to inform Mrs. O'Connor that she will be regularly responsible for the latter's care on the day shift. At every contact, Debbie avoids using leading questions that would elicit renewed complaints. She listens to those that are made with empathy, responding with cues that indicate acceptance of the patient's underlying anxiety. At this early stage of the relationship, she offers realistic reassurance when needed, reinforces expressions of positive feeling, and uses questions only as continuing responses.

Assessment and Planning

The principal purpose of the assessment phase of behavioral problem solving is to obtain baseline data about the undesirable behavior and to use the data in planning the goals and strategies of intervention. The information that is gathered also provides a standard for measuring changes in evaluating the effectiveness of the reinforcement program that is instituted.

Assessment sometimes results in the targeting of two or more aspects of behavior that are not closely related. Although they may be treated simultaneously, they may require different contingencies of reinforcement. If several problem behaviors are to be dealt with, a decision may have to be made about which behavior to treat first. Sometimes the problems are so closely related, as in aspects of a child's early training, that reinforcing stimuli need not be differentiated. When priorities must be established among problems requiring dissimilar types of reinforcement, determinations about the order in which they are to be treated depend on considerations such as the client's preferences, the relative significance of problems in the client's current life situation, and the resources of the client and the immediate environment.

Each targeted problem is stated as explicitly as possible in terms of behavior to be increased or decreased, and its response strength is measured. Assembling baseline information therefore centers on the problem identified and given priority during the initiation of the relationship. When unwanted behavior is to be decreased or extinguished, it is important that the assessment also include client assets that can be exploited in increasing appropriate behavior. To the extent that appropriate behavior is incompatible with unwanted behavior, chances of the desired extinction are increased.

Case Example: Mrs. O'Connor Changes Her Behavior (Continued)

At the afternoon shift-change report, the head nurse orients the nursing staff to Mrs. O'Connor's overall nursing needs and communicates the proposal to use behavioral problem solving as one aspect of Mrs. O'Connor's care. Based on previous experience, it is agreed that the behavioral goal of near extinction of the use of the call light is feasible. Except in emergencies, other patients on the unit seldom find it necessary to use their lights. The evening and night shift personnel will continue to collect baseline data, and Debbie will choose an appropriate time to solicit her patient's cooperation on the following day. Marian will be kept informed of the plan and its implementation, and her participation will be encouraged.

The next morning's report shows that, with the help of a sedative, Mrs. O'Connor slept most of the night. The checklist indicates that her calls averaged six per hour on yesterday's day shift, four per hour during the evening, and less than one per hour during the night. A provisional reinforcement program to cover the ensuing 24 hours is developed cooperatively by the staff. It combines negative reinforcement of unwanted behavior with positive reinforcement of desirable behavior.

Mrs. O'Connor's call light will be answered promptly, whenever possible by the staff member assigned to her care. During the day and evening shifts, the services she requests will be performed, but without any conversation initiated by the staff person. Mrs. O'Connor's comments will be responded to with noncommital cues such as *mhm* and *oh.* Any direct questions that she asks will be answered politely but briefly. On the completion of the service, the patient will be informed that the staff person assigned to her will be in to see her approximately 20 minutes later. The need for this visit will be called to the attention of the staff person concerned, and the visit will be timed to occur when the light is not on. If a call comes from Mrs. O'Connor in the interim, it will be answered as are her other calls, and the promised visit timed for 20 minutes afterward.

In addition to answering her calls, the assigned member from the day or evening shift will visit Mrs. O'Connor at 20-minute intervals until she is settled for the night. Timing these visits when the light is not on, the staff member will not only carry out any services that the patient needs or requests, but will spend time with her to get better acquainted. This will allow for information gathering for assessment, giving reassuring answers to her questions, and otherwise attempting to allay any anxiety manifest in her verbal or nonverbal behavior. Debbie will carry major but not sole responsibility for gathering data to round out the behavioral aspects of assessment. With the head nurse's help, she will use the data she obtains for further planning when occasion arises.

After she is settled for the night, Mrs. O'Connor will of course be included in the hourly observation rounds made to all patients. Since the level of her anxiety may be higher at night until she discovers effective ways to adjust to her new situation, she will be treated with as much open concern as any other patient when her call light is answered. Mrs. O'Connor's calls are to be recorded throughout the 24 hours, and an evaluation of the total plan is to be made at the next morning's report.

To start the 24-hour plan, Debbie does not go to see Mrs. O'Connor until Mrs. O'Connor is eating breakfast and her light is not on. She greets her patient warmly but does not ask any questions about how she feels or how well she slept. Instead, Debbie reintroduces herself and says that she will be Mrs. O'Connor's regular nurse on the day shift. She adds that she will be busy this morning until breakfast is over, but will come in immediately after that to plan the day's care with her patient. As she is leaving Debbie gently but firmly says, *It won't be necessary for you to put on your light. I'll come back within 20 minutes at most.*

After 20 minutes free of calls from Mrs. O'Connor, Debbie returns and draws a chair up close to the patient's bed. She briefly explains the

The preventive connotations of this principle are evident. A given setting, including the significant others within it, is an antecedent condition (secondary reinforcement) of behavior. Nonadaptive behavior is kept from becoming habitual in any setting in which it is not reinforced from the beginning. In the previous case example, the control of antecedents is carefully planned as a significant aspect of the remedial program itself. Also, we become conditioned to respond differently in the presence of different people in the same set of circumstances. This takes on special significance when clients must be readied to generalize the use of new responses from contrived counseling situations to those of real life.

Programs of reinforcement vary in complexity from the training of a normal or slightly retarded child in self-care to the eradication of a disabling addiction in an adult. In each instance, the contingencies that are employed are selected to fit the needs and values of the particular client. The client, the person whose life is most directly affected by the program, is involved in its conceptualization to the fullest extent possible.

As they participate in implementing contingencies of reinforcement, some clients face the prospect of uprooting response patterns that may be habits of long duration. Others assume a similar role secondarily in that they seek an instrumentality whereby to effect a turnabout in the behavior of another person. Marian's role in the example is a case in point, falling as it does between those of the head nurse and her mother. A parent or teacher may wish to bring about a corrective change in a child, or a health professional in a patient or client with whom a relationship is already well established. Change agents in such instances find that by modifying their own behavior in the relationship, modification in the primary client's behavior can be effectively brought about.

Implementation in any program of behavior modification may progress only with difficulty. One's own or another's change may not be accomplished without occasionally or frequently falling back into accustomed patterns. At such times, the helping person must be prepared to draw on the creative use of listening, reflection and clarification of feeling, ego reinforcement, and strengthening reassurance when the occasion demands.

Ongoing evaluation is an essential factor in the implementation phase. It may indicate, at any step of the process, a need to modify the goals or the contingencies of the program. The client as well as the helper participates in the evaluation insofar as possible. For a client who seeks counseling, every evaluation conference with the helper has in it a response cost factor that reinforces the target behavior. Keeping a graph, a checklist, or a diary has a similar effect. Sometimes a formal contract is cosigned by client and counselor.

Evaluation that is carried out strictly in terms of a stated target also increases one's objectivity in observing one's own behavior or that of another person. Its activities lend distance to one's perceptions of a problem situation by diminishing obstructions such as feelings of frustration, self-blame, and discouragement with results. They bring a sense of proportion to the perspective that the behavior is amenable to modification.

Case Example: Mrs. O'Connor Changes Her Behavior (Continued)
The implementation phase of the behavioral program designed for Mrs. O'Connor was advisedly begun coincidentally with the assessment phase. This served a preventive purpose in that responses of others that would have constituted antecedents to her unwanted behavior were avoided from the outset. If the continuation of the habitual behavior that she developed at home had been fostered by staff complicity, a complex plan of behavioral modification would have become necessary. Changes in the patient's behavior would have depended on prior modification of the behavior of involved personnel.

That this eventuality was circumvented is evident in the evaluation that took place at the morning report on the second day after Mrs. O'Connor's admission. The 24-hour record of her calls shows a reduction to an average of one call per hour around the clock. A review of the various reasons she summons staff assistance indicates that, with few exceptions, they relate to the recency of her admission. As Mrs. O'Connor becomes more familiar with the hospice routine, she can be expected to respond to its built-in antecedents intended to diminish the frequency of patients' need to call for services. Their ordinary needs are anticipated from one hour to the next by a combination of the well-organized regimen of nursing care and the pervasive attitude of human concern.

Another of Mrs. O'Connor's behaviors that was reduced as an intended, but not specifically targeted, effect of the behavioral approach was her proneness to respond to workers with multiple complaints. Because the staff was already attuned to the regular use of negative reinforcement as a response to this type of stimulus, specific targeting was not necessary. Staff members report that Mrs. O'Connor now greets them quite pleasantly and seldom detains them with complaints. It is evident that their preventive controls yield results that are beneficial to client-staff relationships.

On the head nurse's recommendation, a plan is made to extend the timing of staff visits to half-hour intervals for the current day and evening shifts. If tomorrow's morning evaluation reveals no increase in hourly calls, the checklist will be abandoned. Debbie will inform Mrs. O'Connor and Marian, when she arrives, of program changes as they occur, communicating the reasoning behind them.

Debbie reports to the staff the assessment data concerning the patient's former interests and Marian's involvement in assessment and planning. Also reported is the success of yesterday's plan for an orientation tour of the unit and the later visit, with the help of the evening staff, to the dayroom. Although Mrs. O'Connor's verbal participation with other patients and their visitors was minimal, she stayed long enough to accept the food snacks, and she made no complaints afterward.

Staff members plan to participate in reinforcing any interest demonstrated by the patient in individual or social pursuits. Later, Marian follows through on her promise by bringing in a book and a crocheted garment that her mother started at home as a gift for a grandchild. Mrs. O'Connor shows no interest in either at first. But when Debbie admires the crocheted item at her next visit, the patient takes it from her without comment. She begins to work on it after Debbie leaves.

Evaluation and Termination

In a relationship that centers on behavioral intervention alone, a final evaluation is made cooperatively by client and helper as part of the terminal interview. But both evaluation and termination begin before that time. The ongoing aspects of evaluation have been emphasized throughout this section on intervention. That termination has similar aspects is brought out in Chapter 7 under "Termination." The section as a whole applies equally to problem-solving and behavioral approaches.

Problem evaluation begins with the beginning of the behavioral relationship. This is the point where the professional helper must judge the likelihood that the client will receive benefit from a behavioral approach. An essential aspect of this judgment is the evaluation of the worker's competence in utilizing behavioral procedures to assist the client toward problem solution. Clients' openness to change can usually be estimated on the basis of available information about their previous experiences with problems. This subject is pursued further under "Further Applications." Workers learn to evaluate their own professional strengths as a result of their continuing study and experience.

Behavior evaluation or assessment proceeds as baseline data is obtained. To the extent that the problem lends itself to measurement, the frequency, duration, and/or intensity of the unwanted behavior is recorded over a preset period of time: by hour, by day, by week, or by intervals between counseling sessions. The principal change agent—either the professional helper or, if a program of self-reinforcement is being devised, the client—is responsible for the measurement. The continuing record is used during implementation to determine the effectiveness of the reinforcement contingencies in increasing or reducing target behavior. Favorable feedback itself reinforces the desired modification. If the change falls short of the targeted level at the end of a specified time, a reexamination of the program is necessary. Either the reinforcement contingencies or the way in which they are carried out may need to be modified.

Termination, as indicated in Chapter 7, also begins early in the counseling relationship. Measures to minimize the client's dependence on the helping professional are suggested in the presentation of each approach addressed. In behavioral counseling, standards of performance are raised as the program progresses until the client's newly learned responses no longer need reinforcement. Control is gradually shifted from the environment to the client as the source of self-reinforcement. An understanding about the termination date can be reached as time limits are set in the planning for deceleration or acceleration of specific behaviors.

A final review evaluation can make the terminal interview reinforcing to the client's self-esteem. If the original goal has been attained, the client will enjoy expressing feelings that are intrinsically rewarding. Even limited success is a sign that the program has afforded the client a useful learning experience. Reinforcement comes from a positive view of the degree of self-control and control of environmental stimuli that the client has succeeded in exerting.

By bringing out the possibilities of preventing undesirable responses from becoming patterned into behavior, the helping professional can assist a receptive client to achieve further learning. Discussion is directed to the principles of positive and negative reinforcement, with particular reference to the problematic antecedents and consequences associated with the client's own environment.

The change agent's own summary evaluation of each case is an essential function of counseling practice. If the complete conduct of the case can be discussed with a knowledgeable colleague, the result will add to the professional growth of both participants. In the client-helper relationship with Mrs. O'Connor, behavioral intervention is incidental to a broadly-based, humanistic approach to nursing care. Termination of the behavioral program per se is tentatively decided on, on the basis of its demonstrated efficacy.

Case Example: Mrs. O'Connor Changes Her Behavior (Continued)
On the third day of Mrs. O'Connor's hospice stay, an evaluation of the behavioral program is again part of the morning shift-change report. Even with raising the time standard of performance from 20 to 30 minutes, the checklist demonstrates that Mrs. O'Connor maintains the modification of unnecessary calls. On a more general basis, it is noted that the patient visited with others during Marian's stay with her and showed spontaneous interest in their activities. After Marian left, she read a little, crocheted a little, and later asked to go to the dayroom, where she watched her

favorite television program. At the half-hourly staff visits, she was easily led into pleasant interchange on topics other than herself. Staff responses were directed throughout toward reinforcing each positive behavior change as it was noted.

The head nurse suggests that, on the basis of these reports, a suspension of the time program might prove to be feasible. Assigned staff members can try spacing their visits, as is done with other patients, according to Mrs. O'Connor's manifest needs. The plan meets with the assent of the group, and the head nurse asks Debbie to explain it to her patient. The head nurse's further comments carry positive reinforcement for the willing participation of all staff members, and especially Debbie.

When Marian comes in for her daily visit, the gratification that she expresses at the marked change in her mother's behavior serves as a reinforcing consequence of the staff effort as a whole.

FURTHER APPLICATIONS

In the previous case example, key premises and principles of humanistic helping are brought into relationship with applications of behavioral concepts. Although the identified problem has some similarities to Jeremy's problem (Chapter 7), Jeremy's previously demonstrated capacity for conceptual participation in solving his problem merits a different approach. In addition, his problem behavior is found to be a temporary reaction to change and loss for which he has the obvious capacity to compensate. Because it does not require precise scheduling and measurement techniques and does not target grossly deviant aspects of behavior, the present case is typical of the informal, everyday behavioral applications that can be made by helping professionals in a broad range of work settings.

In working with clients with varying needs, the helping professional finds that the individual who seems least appreciative of the worker's genuine recognition and concern is likely to be the one most in need of reinforcement as a person. Clients who have been alienated by circumstances such as permanent disability or stark poverty may defensively rebuff every display of friendliness. Consistent modeling of appropriate interpersonal responses by those in their environment may make an initial favorable impression on the behavior of disaffected clients. In a planned program, modeling is combined with reinforcement of every sign of social acceptability clients display. The ingenuity of change agents may be taxed to discover responses to positively reinforce. Attention is directed toward small elements of appropriate behavior, whereas client responses of truculence, peevishness, or demanding behavior are met with a studied lack of reinforcement. An expertly devised program of this type that takes into account reciprocal modeling and reinforcement involving peers might prove to be effective in drawing Rosalyn (Chapter 5) into mutually supportive interpersonal relationships.

Some fellow workers or parents may mistakenly believe that disgruntled or obstreperous individuals can be dealt with successfully only on their own behavioral level. When individuals act on this view, each party models similar behavior and thus reinforces that of the other. Although the cooperation of workers and parents may initially depend on modeling, reinforcement, and reassurance supplied by the helper, each experience of demonstrated success becomes a reinforcing consequence in itself.

In addition to using primary and secondary reinforcement, a program may be planned to include an application of the Premack principle, the use of time out, or both. Children and querulous elderly clients are two groups who generally respond well if their participation in preferred pursuits is made contingent on completion of program requirements. Clients in other age groups can usually appreciate the logic of the Premack principle and apply it in their own programs of self-control.

Unless time-out procedures are practiced with intelligence and compassion, they are likely to be self-defeating. Although they can bring about a temporary and hostile acquiescence, it is improbable that they will effect a long-lasting behavioral change if they are not acceptable to the client. Time out is useful if it is controlled to dispose the client to voluntarily modify a specific unit of behavior and if each emission of target behavior is immediately rewarded.

Children whose behavior is annoying to others are given the opportunity to leave the antecedent social situation with the assurance that they may return as soon as they are able to control their conduct. School-age children can understand the explanation that they are in better control of themselves in the absence of unusual external stimulation. A child who must be forcibly evicted is carried to a quiet place, preferably not his or her bedroom, and left with a toy or other object that affords security. The door may be left open or closed as the child prefers. If the child's own room is used as a place of banishment, it becomes associated with negative feelings rather than with comfort and happiness. In caring for a child who is removed in a highly emotional state, a trusted adult remains quietly at hand until the furor subsides and the child can be restored to the group situation. These principles are similarly observed in the care of mentally disturbed children and adults and with prisoners to an extent that is compatible with the safety of others.

Parents, nurses, and teachers may be helped to apply procedures of shaping and counterconditioning in promoting healthy development in young children. In some cultures, most of the early training of children is conducted through a combination of modeling and hand shaping, with minimal verbalization. This method contrasts with the constant parental use of commands and admonitions that characterizes child rearing in Western society. Comfort and security are communicated by gently holding the child's body still and gently guiding the child's limbs and fingers in movement. An expectation that learning and becoming are experienced in relationships and are part and parcel of a shared humanity is conveyed by such practices.

Children can be gradually desensitized to irrational fears if the frightening object or experience is paired with feelings that are incompatible with fear. For example, to be held by a trusted adult when a dog is briefly introduced into a room by another trusted person has an initial counteracting effect on a child's fear of dogs. Counterconditioning proceeds as the change agent combines the techniques of modeling and shaping with the use of reinforcing presence and equally reinforcing verbal cues. The modeling of the desired behavior by their age peers can be effectively used in modifying the behavior of children and adolescents, but this is not effective if demeaning comparisons are made. The fearful child client is enabled by degrees to observe an animal from a distance without an untoward reaction, then to be held near while others pet it, and finally, to touch and hold it. Once it is understood by parents and teachers, this approach can be applied to a variety of problems in the training of children.

An adolescent or adult can be taught in direct counseling to use the principle of desensitization to overcome minor fears of everyday life. Role playing in an anxiety-free context is a means of conditioning the individual in anticipation of events such as public speaking or participating in a dreaded interview or encounter. The intrinsic reward of a successful simulated performance creates an expectation of achievement antecedent to the real situation. Extrinsic reinforcing consequences come from the helper's verbal and nonverbal responses.

Role playing combined with techniques of anxiety relief can involve a worker-client in controlled responses to imagined aversive stimuli: an angry supervisor or an indifferent or rejecting fellow worker. This may be followed by preparing the client to try out similar responses in a series of situations less threatening than the one eventually to be faced but that gradually approximate its threat more and more closely.

A client who is having generalized difficulty in relationships or difficulty in a particular relationship may be helped by using behavioral learning techniques. With a client with whom a dependably strong relationship in connection with other services has been established, the helper may ask, in response to complaints of difficulties with people, *Would you like to know how I see you as coming across some of the time?* This is followed by objectively but empathetically reflecting the client's general hostility, pessimism, negativism, or whatever attitude underlies the complaint, using examples of the client's behavior. Techniques of modeling, role playing, and other programs of reinforcement are then in order if the client is receptive to the idea of commitment to behavioral change. An approach of this kind can be safely employed only when the worker's expectations of people are not stereotyped under labels such as hostile, stupid, immature, spoiled, uncooperative, and so forth. Such expectations can only become antecedent conditions for the type of behavior that is so labeled.

Before the theories of modern psychology became widespread, people, other than the frankly psychotic, were expected to find ways to modify unacceptable behavior by their own efforts. The method was called self-control, a term that is currently revived in the literature of behaviorism (Nay, 1976; LeBow, 1976). A program of self-reinforcement is appropriate for the client who is consciously committed to changing behavior as a means of achieving a highly valued goal. The behavioral change agent's functions are to guide the assessment and to help in the selection of reinforcement contingencies and the evaluation of their effectiveness.

When the client takes on the function of implementation, the helper's overall role is that of consultant: monitoring progress and providing intermittent reinforcement of the client's efforts. Added to that is a significant teaching function. It is necessary for the client to understand and accept as valid those principles of behavior modification that are operative in the program that is devised. The language used is adapted to the client's level of comprehension. But a working knowledge of a few basic behavioral concepts confers a certain amount of flexibility in the client's adaptation of principles to specific situations.

Self-directed programs of self-control can be successful with diverse behavioral problems such as shyness, poor work habits, and overeating in its early stages. Environmental factors of time, place, and person are identified in the assessment as significant, to varying degrees, in the necessary control of antecedent conditions. In subsequent goal setting and planning, the client, for instance, who is harried by what could be considered a normal work load begins by organizing tasks and planning time; an overweight client restricts eating to certain times and places; a shy client plans to exercise assertiveness first with persons whose presence poses the least threat. But in each case, it is likely that the three types of antecedent stimuli—time, place, and person—must all be brought under control. In each instance, too, implementation involves a gradual raising of standards of behavior until desired performance is no longer contingent on contrived conditions. This also holds true for the reinforcing consequences of the emission of target behavior.

Regardless of the fact that the client may be motivated to change, the deceleration of habitual behavior and the substitution of more desirable behavior is not simple to implement. In our early years of growth, conditioning reinforces traits and tendencies that constitute integral elements of our personality structure. If the associated patterns of response continue to be strengthened by reinforcing circumstances, those responses become habitual elements of our behavioral repertoire.

Eventually, some persuasive intrinsic or extrinsic experience may provide us with an incentive to change. We come to recognize that, in the long run, we can gain more by altering our behavior than current behavior provides in the form of immediate satisfaction or relief. Or it may be that modifying our responses qualifies us for a type of gratification that has been previously excluded from our experience. The consequences of smoking may become more aversive than smoking is pleasurable; or the revision of a particular pattern of social assertiveness promises us new intimacy, competence, or prestige. Although the process of change may be difficult in either instance, the hope of reward may make present deprivation or embarrassment endurable.

The client looks for opportunities to rehearse the target behavior in natural settings. Those chosen first are free from antecedent stimuli that predispose him or her to the problem behavior. The target behavior is eventually carried out with confidence in situations that were originally threatening to the individual or, in cases of habituation, that tended to reinforce problem behavior.

The expectation that a person can change to the extent of exerting self-control in an area of habitual behavior may well be a value in itself. Our growth in humanness is proportionate to our increase in self-reliance and our balanced control of self in relation to others. In assessing the client's capacity to implement a program with little or no further assistance, it is important for the helper to recognize that self-reliance and self-control are not generalized characteristics. Persons who are painfully lacking in self-confidence in social situations, or perhaps only in social situations with either the same or opposite sex, may be thoroughly self-directed in their work and work contacts. Others may be strongly independent in most aspects of their lives but find that without assistance they are unable to bring certain responses under control. To seek help in such circumstances is likely to be a sign of strength rather than weakness. In assessing the client's capacity for self-management, the helper exercises the client's areas of strength and fosters their development. With client self-control as a mutual aim for client and helper, the resources of both are oriented as completely as possible toward that end.

LABORATORY EXERCISES

Students and others who wish to acquire a working acquaintance with behavioral counseling skills will need monitored practice with increasingly complex behavior modification. Students may begin by working in pairs, first on hypothetical problems, and then on aspects of their own behavior that they wish to modify. In either case, they begin by identifying a specific element of the behavior that might be amenable to modification at their level of skill.

Working alone at first, each develops on paper an appropriate strategy of intervention, carrying it through the steps of initiating the relationship, assessing and planning, implementing, and terminating. They then compare notes and reach agreement on a strategy that combines the best of what each has suggested. Each plan receives supervisory amendments and clearance from the teacher or another experienced counselor.

With the other as client, each applies in guided practice the behavior modification plan that has been cooperatively developed. They are expected at this point to bring into appropriate operation the principles and skills of communication and relationships they have learned from both client-centered and problem-solving counseling. Detailed recording forms the basis for periodic supervisory conferences.

It is worthwhile homework for students or helping professionals to successfully undertake programs of their own self-management or self-control. The improvement of work or study habits is illustrated in the following case example:

Case Example: Karen's Insomnia

Karen, an insomniac, conjectured from her study of behavior modification that her tendency to wakefulness was regularly elicited by a variety of antecedent stimuli. She retired at irregular hours. Whenever she spent an evening alone, she prepared for bed early in the evening and, comfortably seated in her dormitory bed against a backrest of pillows, performed a series of work and leisure activities until she felt tired enough to settle down and wait for sleep to come. She prepared for the next day's classes in this posture; she also worked on embroidery, read, listened to records, and watched television.

Karen's modification program included setting a regular bedtime and using rooms other than her bedroom for evening activities as a means of stimulus control. She immediately found herself less prone to stay awake mentally reviewing her schoolwork and incidents from her reading or television viewing. Another facet of her program consisted of the counter-conditioning practice of deep relaxation when she retired and again if she found herself wakeful during the night. As soon as she became aware of her thought processes, she substituted gentle attentiveness to her breathing sensations for the patterned thinking that previously reinforced her wakefulness. Knowing that if she dwelt on the timing of her sleeping and wakefulness she would reinforce an unhealthy tendency to think about the problem itself, she made an exception in her own case with regard to recording the progress. Intrinsic reinforcement of her new behavior came from realizing that insomnia was becoming less and less a problem and would eventually be a thing of the past.

It is evident that behavioral concepts and methods add a significant dimension to the professional helper's preparedness to meet clients' short-term counseling needs. Humanistic values can in every instance pervade their use. Generally, clients are seen as capable of choosing whether to change and what to change in their behavior. Their cognitive collaboration is enlisted in designing and directing their program of learning experiences and in evaluating the degree of achieving desired changes. More exceptional cases are those in which a child or adult is incapable of accurately discriminating between socially acceptable and unacceptable behavior. The helper then seeks consultation and cooperation from family members and/or co-workers who also have the client's best interests at heart.

Behavioral elements that are incorporated into client-helper transactions are considered to be only one aspect of the client-helper relationship—a relationship that is client-centered and interpersonal. Whether or not unwanted behavior is effectively modified, the client is still esteemed as a person who is unique and is therefore uniquely valued.

References

Blackman, D. 1974. *Operant conditioning: An experimental analysis of behavior.* Methuen's Manuals of Psychology. London: Methuen.

Fuhriman, A. 1969. Structuring for academic success. In *Behavioral counseling: Cases and techniques.* John D. Krumboltz and Carl E. Thorensen, editors. New York: Holt, Rinehart and Winston.

Gentry, W. D., editor. 1975. *Applied behavior modification.* Saint Louis: Mosby.

Hooper, M. H., and Scoresby, A. L. 1969. Commitment to change: Structuring the goals and ground rules for counseling. In *Behavioral counseling: Cases and techniques.* J. D. Krumboltz and C. E. Thorensen, editors. New York: Holt, Rinehart and Winston.

Jacobson, E. 1964. *Anxiety and tension control: A physiologic approach.* Philadelphia: Lippincott.

Krumboltz, J. D. and Thorensen, C. E., editors. 1976. *Counseling methods.* New York: Holt, Rinehart and Winston.

Lazarus, A. A. 1969. The "inner circle" strategy: Identifying crucial problems. *Behavioral counseling: Cases and techniques.* J. D. Krumboltz and C. E. Thorensen, editors. New York: Holt, Rinehart and Winston.

LeBow, M. D. 1976. *Approaches to modifying patient behavior.* New York: Appleton-Century-Crofts.

Nay, W. R. 1976 *Behavioral intervention: Contemporary strategies.* New York: Gardner Press.

Premack, D. 1965. Reinforcement theory. *Nebraska symposium on motivation.* D. Levine, editor. Lincoln, Nebraska: University of Nebraska Press.

Schaefer, H. H., and Martin, P. L. 1969. *Behavior therapy.* New York: McGraw-Hill.

Schwitzgebel, R. K., and Kolb, D. A. 1974. *Changing human behavior: Principles of planned intervention.* New York: McGraw-Hill.

Skinner, B. F. 1938. *The behavior of organisms: An experimental analysis.* New York: Appleton-Century-Crofts.

Sundel, M., and Sundel, S. S. 1975. *Behavior modification in human services: A systematic introduction to concepts and applications.* New York: John Wiley & Sons.

Wolpe, J. 1973. *The practice of behavior therapy.* New York: Pergamon.

PART III

Helping People in Groups

CHAPTER 9

The Group and the Helping Professional

GROUP INFLUENCES AND THE INDIVIDUAL

A large part of any individual's life experiences takes place among groups of people. Our early nurturance and socialization are provided in the context of a family group or in a group setting designated by society as a substitute for the family. Ordinarily, we continue to learn, work, and play in groups. Only through relationships formed in groups of various sizes and types is the individual enabled to exercise the human potential for achieving a distinct identity and becoming a fully functioning person. Conversely, experiences in groups can exert a destructive influence, resulting in distortions and impairments in personality formation.

The professional helper has many opportunities to grow in self-knowledge and self-actualization, and to help others grow, through the medium of structured group experiences. All the material in previous chapters that is pertinent to humanistic intervention within the client-helper dyad has implications for small groups of more than two persons. This chapter deals more specifically with the understandings and skills needed by the professional helper in growth-promoting intervention with small groups. Chapter 10 centers on the family as a special group whose structure and purposes are particularly adaptable to the growth of each of its members.

In order to facilitate the integration of group intervention concepts with those previously presented, the organization of this chapter is kept as consistent as possible with that of preceding chapters. First, a selection of relevant theoretical principles on which practice is based is presented. In this instance, concepts from the related perspectives of group dynamics and group counseling and psychotherapy are blended to highlight their application to the professional helper's humanistic interaction with people in small groups.

The main body of this chapter identifies specific skills that are called on in group intervention. All of the skills and techniques of intervention with individuals are also brought into play. The process of leading a group through an effective experience of learning and growth is described and illustrated using the stages already familiar from problem-solving and behavioral approaches to short-term counseling.

THE GROUP DYNAMICS MOVEMENT

Group dynamics as a field of study originally grew out of research undertaken by psychologists. In the 1930s, Kurt Lewin gained prominence from his studies of the processes observed in the behavior of small work groups. His name is linked with the group dynamics movement, which developed rapidly through the mid-century period. The movement was structured into a laboratory type of training in group processes. The experience is called *T-group* (training group) or *sensitivity training.* A recent outgrowth is the **encounter**, or **human potential, movement**, spearheaded by humanistic psychologists such as Rogers and Maslow and featuring various types of consciousness-raising group experiences. This latter movement, which is described briefly at the end of this section, draws from the fields of both group dynamics and group therapy.

Laboratory (T-group) training in group dynamics has proliferated since the late 1940s and has become widely available in a variety of forms. Regular courses are offered in most colleges and universities. Residential workshops for leadership training of key personnel in industrial and governmental organizations are scheduled for periods varying from a few days to several weeks. Educational, religious, and social agencies engage group dynamics experts to provide their staff members and influential citizens with experiential learning in the dynamics of social change.

If a large number of trainees in involved, a trainer, or facilitator, is assigned to each one of several component problem-solving groups of from eight to fifteen members. Much of the small group experience consists of laboratory practice of group functioning in a free discussion format. The training is experiential in that it focuses on the group's own modes of interaction and their results in the efficacy and growth of the group. Trainees are both subjects of observation and objective observers. Trainer and trainees collaborate in helping the group to translate basic democratic values into the skills of participation in functional group processes (Appley and Winder, 1973).

The facilitator interacts as a member of the group, functioning as a combination role model and participant-observer. Engaging in the ongoing discussion as a sharing member, the facilitator models participation observation by pointing out recognizable cues to progress in, and obstacles to, effective group functioning. Throughout, members are encouraged to provide each other with feedback concerning the feelings that evoke, and are evoked by, their interaction with one another. Conflicts that arise in the group are identified as such, and rational means of resolving them are chosen. Group members themselves gradually acquire skill in taking on observer as well as participant roles. With progress, they develop not only new skills in group functioning but also an increased sensitivity to the force and influence of the feeling component of human interaction and relationships.

Toward the end of the training experience, action sessions are held in the small groups. Methods such as role playing are used to help participants test the various uses of their new human relations skills as change agents in their back-home situations.

Sensitivity Training and Encounter Group Therapy

At the present time, the *sensitivity* aspect of human relations training is often given precedence over task-performance and change-agent functions. The aim of such groups is to provide a consciousness-raising and thereby a therapeutic experience for normal people who expect to benefit from it. The focus is kept directly on developing awareness of, and responsiveness to, the feeling content of interpersonal interaction. Some groups meet in order to concentrate on increasing their sensitivity to a single area of group behavior such as racism, sexism, or consumerism.

Encounter group therapy is offered severally under the leadership of psychiatrists, clinical psychologists, and psychoanalysts. The experience is sometimes recommended as an adjunct to individual psychotherapy. Encounter group members are impelled into intense, short-term relationships within the group, with the aim of increasing individual openness, expressiveness, and capacity for intimacy. The much-publicized **marathon** type of encounter group meets for an extended number of hours, commonly over two or three consecutive days, with prescribed, and sometimes short, breaks for rest and sleep.

Members are encouraged to express their feelings freely but to keep their attention focused on the present situation and on behavior of current concern within the group. Feelings soon tend to be vented in the form of assertive and, at times, aggressive confrontations between them. As a gesture of intimacy, physical contact is encouraged by some therapists, as well as acting-out behavior such as pounding a pillow to release rage. During group interaction, the therapist may remain passive for the most part and intervene mainly to model sensitivity to the feelings of overanxious members. Distress is expected to evoke enough sympathy within the group to provide adequate support for the distressed member. Members help each other not only to tolerate the encounter situation, but to learn from it how they affect others and are affected by them. Some therapists use supplementary explanations to further the development of insight.

As encounter group members feel increasingly safe with one another, self-disclosure assumes the depth of emotional catharsis, and self-evaluation is carried out on a healthier level than before. Warmth and empathy develop among members, some of whom succeed in carrying these attitudes into their everyday relationships (Mintz, 1974).

PROFESSIONAL COUNSELING WITH GROUPS

A growing body of theory and methodology supports the practice of professional group counseling and psychotherapy. Skills and principles are borrowed in part from group dynamics and are drawn as well from professional practice with individual clients. From long experience in providing treatment through a group discussion approach, the field of social work also contributes.

One obvious advantage of group methods is that the counselor's time can be used more economically with groups than with individuals. A more telling distinction is that counseling with a group makes the exchange of feedback possible among several individuals. As members of a group, clients can learn to see themselves and their difficulties as they appear through the eyes of others who have similar difficulties. Each person can be summoned by other group members to reexamine and reassess feelings, attitudes, and values in relation to needs, problems, decision making, and action. As the group develops in purpose and cohesiveness, its members learn from one another, support one another, and offer each other a healing presence through their mutual acceptance and regard.

CONCEPTS OF GROUP PROCESS AND GROUP DEVELOPMENT

In this section, under "Humanistic Group Aims and Values," humanistic principles are recapitulated with reference to helping a group rather than an individual as an experiential unit. The three following subsections offer concepts of group process drawn from the somewhat overlapping fields of human relations training and group counseling. All have implications for the professional helper whose work involves interaction with groups of clients and groups of fellow workers.

Humanistic Group Aims and Values

An assemblage of people ceases to be a haphazard aggregate of individuals and becomes a group when its members are engaged in achieving a common purpose. If the purpose is enforced or destructive, the group is likely to be designated a gang, or if large, a mob. People grouped together in the expectation of learning and growing through the medium of the group share, at least implicitly, a common, humanistic purpose. They can only attain it by participating wholeheartedly in each step of the process of attaining it. Whether the methodologic emphasis is on the side of treatment or on an educational, task-performance outcome, major responsibility for its own development falls on the group itself.

Ideationally, the group functions and moves forward by a process of internal consensus. Every contribution of individual members is given careful consideration. Differences among individuals are assigned positive values. No member's opinion is overruled on grounds of expediency or merely because it is not accepted as factual by the majority. The group recognizes a corporate responsibility to explore every idea presented and to leave every proposition open to the possibility of further investigation.

The group's progress depends to a great extent on its understanding of the vital importance of emotional needs and the feelings and attitudes they engender. Feelings are recognized as forces that are at least as potent as ideas. Members accept responsibility for giving nonevaluative expression to their own feelings and for supporting others in similarly expressing theirs. The group as a whole can only develop as its individual members learn to trust one another and to help each other grow in self-esteem and fullness of functioning. Interaction that takes place within a climate of mutual acceptance encourages risk taking and interdependence in relationships. The individual's self-acceptance and openness to change are carried forward by the affectionate concern of others. Interdependence becomes esteemed as an indispensable quality of creative relationships: those in which one person helps another to grow.

Appley and Winder (1973) offer the following **metagoals**, or ulterior values, of group laboratory training:

1. A spirit of inquiry
2. Collaboration
3. Conflict resolution through rational means
4. Freedom to exercise choice

In writing about the mode of communication of groups that attain their full potential, Kemp (1970) characterized it as communication in love and in responsible caring: I-thou communication. Most group leaders do not introduce the subject of values as such; they expect that participants will derive from their lived experience an enhanced appreciation of the democratic, socioethical principles in which it is grounded as they are manifest in the authenticity, openness, and interdependence of relationships within the group.

Setting Norms

Any group, regardless of its composition or the purpose of its existence, develops informal, unstated **norms** through which it pressures its members to conform (Napier and Gershenfeld, 1981). These implicit standards of behavior regulate factors such as: the openness and force of emotional expression; the responsibility assumed and the respect accorded members for status, position, or achievement; and the bases on which subgroup relationships are formed. Official claims may vary considerably from the group norms that are actually in effect. For instance, the person who supervises the work of a group may declare that the group functions democratically, yet he or she may repeatedly announce decisions that have been made unilaterally without any group consultation. Some teachers who profess to use the Socratic method of discussion habitually propel debate toward their own conclusions rather than allowing it to move toward its own logical outcomes.

For effective functioning of a training or therapy group, certain preconditions are essential. As with underlying values, norms may be made explicit at an early stage or left to come to the surface as the group develops cohesiveness and a sense of purpose. Because the purpose of either group is fundamentally to provide its members an opportunity to become, the group adopts norms that are consciously directed toward that end. When every member of a group is committed to a set of standards that he or she has participated in selecting, there is a good possibility that the group will function cohesively in attempting to accomplish its goals. Whether goals are developed gradually as the group develops or are formulated early in the life of the group, leader and members repeatedly interpret recognized group values in terms of explicit or implicit guidelines for acceptable group behavior.

Implicit understandings evolve to the effect that: (a) expressions of feelings are desirable, but only with due concern for feelings that their expression evokes in others and (b) the self-actualization of every group member depends for its maturing capability on his or her openness to the richness of the here-and-now experiencing being shared.

If the group takes a formal approach to standard setting, it is asked to collaborate with the leader in formulating norms of group behavior that every individual can genuinely subscribe to. The standards may be enunciated by listing responsibilities that are consistent with leader and member roles, or they may constitute a contract agreed to by the leader and by all group members. With either format, the leader is required, for instance, to share leadership responsibility with members to the extent that self-direction is fostered within the group, while members are required to keep initiative fairly evenly distributed among them. Participation is likely to include both verbal and non-verbal interaction and the expression of feelings as well as of ideas and opinions.

Roles and Functions

In any group assembled to achieve a particular purpose, members are expected to take on specific roles. The roles combine to form the group into a productive whole. Each role imposes a set of tasks, or functions. It is anticipated that the concerted carrying out of functions will result in achieving the purpose for which the group was formed. Whenever an aggregate of individuals is organized into a formal or informal group, its members usually take on a mixture of formal and informal roles.

For example, several people may agree to meet informally at intervals to discuss a specific political issue. They decide that, because all are expected to participate on an equal basis, no specific group role designations are necessary. Before long, some individuals will fall into a number of appropriate roles without preplanning. A member who is addicted to note taking becomes the unofficial secretary. Another regularly calls for the opening and closing of meetings, suggests that topics be chosen for the next meeting, and keeps the discussion on track when it threatens to wander. Two or three members conduct searches between meetings for the answers to questions that are left hanging, and they bring reference material to substantiate or refute conclusions that have not progressed beyond the tentative stage.

In training group theory and practice, formally identified roles are considered to be group, or shared, roles. It is assumed that all participants, including the facilitator, will exercise leadership functions as participant-observers. All are expected to use their previously developed abilities and to acquire new skills in the functions that make up two group roles: the **group task role** and the **group maintenance and growth role**. As an element of the group maintenance and growth role, they will monitor the group interaction and the relationships that are formed as the roles are enacted.

Whether the group's purpose mainly emphasizes sensitivity training or training in leadership skills, the group experience is essentially one of cooperative task performance. Either type of preparation requires the participants to pursue a combination of cognitive and interpersonal-emotional goals. In each of these areas, subgoals must be identified, however informally, and projects must be carried out in a continuing effort to reach them. Cognitive functions may include establishing and selecting goals and carrying out related tasks: gathering information and finding resources; initiating, clarifying, and expanding ideas; identifying areas of commonality and disagreement in conflicting concepts; and summarizing progress in problem solving.

Efforts must likewise be put forward to maintain the group's existence and to further its growth as a functional unit. A group maintains cohesion and grows into fullness of functioning only insofar as it proves its capacity to meet the needs of all of its members. If it fails to do so, it loses the constructive participation of those whose needs the group does not meet. They may drop out completely or continue on a noncontributing or obstructively dissident basis. Members find that their emotional needs are met within the group when they learn to communicate their feelings without hostility or defensiveness and when they learn to understand the metacommunications of others. They also learn to accept that the group can grow in cohesiveness only if no one is permitted to divert the energies of the group by allowing his or her needs to repeatedly take precedence over those of other members. Group solidarity develops as ties of reciprocal concern and affection progressively bind the group together into an interdependent, organic whole.

Solidarity does not take place without intervening vicissitudes. The diversity of characteristics among group members leads them to informally assume those individual roles that they feel are most rewarding to them. Some of the accompanying functional activities will promote and some will impede the maintenance and growth of the group.

In the group as a whole, there is likely to be at least: one peacemaker and one troublemaker; a scene stealer and a scene thrower; one who makes suggestions and another who blocks suggestions; and one who monopolizes the discussion and one who seldom enters into it. Being human, all attempt to ensure that their own needs will be met.

In a conceptually oriented training session, ongoing group experiences with roles and functions are discussed, together with the usefulness of establishing norms and discovering inoffensive ways of exerting group pressure toward observing them. Methods of group self-evaluation are given continuing attention. The group uses them to obtain internal feedback concerning its progress in the maintenance and growth role that is enacted throughout the life of the group.

Individual competencies that contribute to group maintenance and growth are discussed and practiced as an experiential aspect of group training. One of the basic skills of communication in groups is **creative listening.** Its creativeness lies in allowing the listener to take into account not only the factual content of a remark, but its underlying metacommunicative components as well. Creative listening makes nonevaluative feedback possible (Chapters 3 and 4).

When a group's primary emphasis is sensitivity training, the uses of **confrontation** are examined. If combined with supportive measures, confrontation that inquires into the possibility of hostility or defensiveness can have an ego-building effect on the individual and, indirectly, on the organismic group. But confrontation that demands a member's agreement on a point at issue is destructive both to the individuals concerned and to the effective functioning of the group.

Evolutionary Group Process

Much study has been devoted to the changes that take place in small groups of people who come together for therapy or for human relations training. In recognition of the fact that systematic progress and growth is intended, courses offered for training purposes may be listed under "Group Process" or "Group Development." The **process** is the movement observed in a group as its changing attributes are identified. To the extent that a training or therapy group fits into an anticipated pattern of step-by-step progression, there is great value to the group leader in knowing the order and constituents of the various stages.

Various therapists and facilitators describe the process elements that they observe to be fairly typical. Barrett-Lennard (1975) describes, from several different perspectives, some of the processes that take place in intensive experimental groups composed of individuals whose personal and interpersonal functioning is not impaired. Using a **life-cycle perspective**, the author draws from personal research and from research reported by Carl Rogers in outlining three stages of progress that seem to be typical of groups that show significant growth.

In the **engagement phase**, members move from initial, awkward self-consciousness to tentative exploration of acceptable limits of self-expression. Communicated feelings tend at first to be anxiety-laden and therefore negative, and references are mainly to past experiences rather than to what is going on in the meeting. As the assurance of security and connectedness increases, the focus of group orientation moves from past to present and from negative to positive. When this happens, the group is ready to enter the next level of the cycle.

The second phase is characterized by a deepening **trust** that allows free, active, and sustained exploration of feelings and attitudes. Members listen to each other and communicate with mutual concern, exerting what Rogers terms a healing influence on one another. The group may settle comfortably into this phase or move into a third.

The last phase is **confrontation and personal growth**. There is a free exchange of feedback among members concerning the protective facades individuals present for public inspection. In an atmosphere of mutual support, face saving is no longer necessary, and there is increasing readiness to unmask and begin intimate sharing. Individual change comes about as new, more authentic ways of behaving are tested and found to be safe from rejection.

In ordinary life, groups that meet repeatedly over a period of time, for whatever purpose, progress at their own rates and go through some stages that cannot be anticipated at all, much less in any dependable order. Most groups begin by cautiously testing the limits within which alignments can be formed and openness of expression tolerated. In many groups that are formally organized or selected, such as work staffs, committees, or college classes, there is covert jockeying for status, which begins early and is continued indefinitely, regardless of the fact that it impairs the efficiency of task performance. Resentment of authority, unresolved sibling rivalry, and general competitiveness in relationships find frequent expression in rebellion, factionalism, and scapegoating. Feelings are not discussed during meetings but instead are communicated between sessions in ways that serve only to fan the flames of dissension.

The preceding circumstances bring leaders in education, government, and industry to obtain T-group training for themselves and for key staff members. Through training, they hope to acquire the leader and member skills necessary to carry a group from chaotic anxiety reactions to cohesiveness and from obstructing conflict into efficient task performance.

GROUP INTERVENTION

Most helping professionals find that they frequently need skills to enable them to work productively in both leader and member roles with groups of clients, peers, and members of other occupations and professions. Whereas the professional counselor can choose whether to work alone or as a member of a therapeutic or other staff group and can choose whether to treat clients individually or in groups, the helping professional is likely to work in an institution or agency as one member of a staff of co-workers and may also carry responsibility as status leader of groups of clients and groups of co-workers.

Health and social service personnel with a wide variety of occupations and personal lifestyles spend part of their usual day with groups. This is also true of teachers, residential counselors, correctional personnel, members of the clergy, and other such helpers. Although a philosophic framework of humanistic helping is applicable in group as well as in dyadic relationships, the processes of group functioning are complicated by an intricate network of dynamic interrelationships. As preparation for effective functioning in any group situation, human relations training that emphasizes group leadership skills is recommended, in addition to formal education in the basic theory and practice of counseling presented in this book. Training in the application of TA concepts, which, like human relations training, can be obtained on a continuing-education basis in many geographic areas, offers additional personal and professional advantages to people involved in helping others.

As group members, helping professionals whose background includes training and experience in effective group functioning bring attitudes and skills that are an asset to any small group situation that allows for general participation. They demonstrate genuinely motivated attentiveness to every contribution the other members make, as well as a trained sensitivity to expressions of thought and feeling. In consequence, members who lack confidence in themselves and others are inclined to become more trusting, and they generally respond well to the modeling influence of the helper's noncompetitive, accepting attitudes.

The Context

As status leader, the helping professional initially assumes more responsibility for the developing group climate and for necessary structuring than can usually be expected of group members. The ideal climate is open, not only to the ideational content of every contribution made, but also to its metacommunication. The attitudes of the well-prepared leader convey mental alertness combined with a relaxed self-confidence, as well as a warm, unconditional regard for every member as a person.

The physical environment is made as informally comfortable as possible. Chairs are arranged so that every member, including the leader, can see the faces of all the other members. So that no barriers, either literal or figurative, intervene, extra chairs, tables, desks, and so forth are moved outside the circle of seated members. Meetings are held in a quiet area, and the meeting itself is kept free of interruptions.

Unless the composition and lifespan of the group are determined by extraneous circumstances, considerations of group size, duration, and type of membership enter into the leader's preliminary planning. A group of five to ten adults or adolescents usually permits interaction that is optimally distributed. Young children work and learn together more productively in groups of three to six (Gazda, 1978). If the leader is presented with a large gathering for a training workshop, for example, subsessions can be arranged to make small group interaction and autonomy possible.

Time limitations can also be transcended. Napier and Gershenfeld (1981) suggest various ways of using time as a dynamic variable. The microlab, microlecture, and microdiscussion methods are presented as devices that increase individual and small group involvement over relatively brief periods. Optimum group process can usually be expected when the small size of the group and the frequency and span of meetings allow for gradual development of cohesion and collaborative problem solving. A meeting time of 1 to 1½ hours allows for a warming-up period followed by concentrated participation. Unexpectedly, circumstances that impose strict time limits on a rather large group may sometimes prove to be an incentive to speeding up these developments.

The worker may or may not be in a position to determine the composition of the group to provide for similarities or diversity among members. He or she may find it necessary at times to lead a group that is almost randomly selected from a heterogeneous population. The people who volunteer for training in crisis intervention preparatory to manning a telephone service represent such groups. Following their screening interview, those who assemble for training vary in age, education, occupation, and sexual orientation, as well as in past and current factors that motivate their participation. Some drop out after a meeting or two; others complete the series and do not use it as their original contract requires; still others make a long-term contribution as staff members of the telephone service.

Homogeneity, at least in terms of a commonly held view on a single issue, may be an advantage to people who come together to resolve difficulties associated with problems such as substance dependence, a particular form of physical or emotional disability, or a community concern such as those related to housing, energy, or rising crime rates. Although marked dissimilarities among values, interests, and backgrounds of group members make a rich experience in relationships possible, their movement toward mutual acceptance and appreciation may progress slowly and with difficulty. Compatibility or incompatibility within member relationships is a factor that a professional helper is unlikely to have any control over in forming a group. But the intimacies and conflicts they give rise to can often be used productively as intervention proceeds. Shared problems provide an ongoing focus.

The degree of individual motivation varies among members of groups that are homogeneous or heterogeneous in composition. If all who enter the group experience were highly motivated to reach a common goal, the group outcome would be promising in proportion to its attainability. Although it may seem to be desirable to place all such like-minded individuals together, the participation of the highly motivated in a group is stimulating to less involved members. In addition, it broadens the experience of enthusiastic members to be instrumental in engaging the interest of those who are less deeply committed.

It may be necessary for the professional helper to work individually with certain clients before they can be expected to participate constructively with a group. An adult or a child who is acutely anxious or whose behavior is disturbed needs the type of supportive intervention that cannot be provided amid the give and take of a group situation. At the height of a serious crisis, the practitioner's individual attention and concern must be available to the crisis victim. Group crisis intervention may have definite advantages over individual treatment in the later stages of crisis resolution. Added comfort and strength can be derived from sharing with others the experience of undergoing a painful adjustment to the difficulties of enforced role transition.

Leadership Skills

When working with a client in a dyadic relationship, the professional helper remains vividly aware of the ultimate goal of self-determination for the client, as well as optimal self-realization in relationships with others. These areas of need do not become less urgent in clients the worker meets in a group. The helper has a responsibility not only to intervene in group interaction in ways that provide freedom to grow for each individual member, but to gradually relinquish this function to the total membership.

From the beginning, leadership is a function that is shared by helper and members alike. It is neither autocratic nor laissez-faire in character. Democratic leaders demonstrate their own ability to benefit from as well as exert influence on others. Through the attitudes they express both verbally and nonverbally, they reinforce this reciprocal openness among members. They share with all the responsibility of tentatively presenting issues and ideas for consideration and inviting others to do the same. Dissent is both offered and invited and is fairly and objectively dealt with as an essential part of group development.

In order to implement and to help members implement these principles, the leader models skills that are particularly applicable to democratic group experience, as well as those that help the individual within the group. Group counseling skills needed in addition to all those previously presented for short-term counseling with individual clients are discussed under these headings:

1. Stimulating openness of communication
2. Promoting solidarity
3. Linking
4. Shielding
5. Using conflict constructively
6. Emphasizing immediacy

As may be expected, there is much overlapping among these elements. Whatever is of value in bringing about any of the listed variables is also instrumental in relation to the others.

Stimulating communication The group leader assumes primary responsibility for encouraging open communication within the group. He or she is aware of the primacy of *presence* in establishing trust and promoting freedom of expression and actively listens to every communication of clients within the group. Interruptions from others are temporarily intercepted, and continuing responses are employed to give each individual in turn an opportunity for full communication. The feeling dimension of interaction is reflected and discussed as a force to be given equal weight in interchanges with ideational content. In this way, individuals are assisted in finding their own meanings in their communications and in expressing their feelings in terms that are comprehensible and acceptable to themselves and others. Leader responses model unvarying, nonjudgmental receptivity.

There are usually one or two members in a group who are unable to verbalize freely, and there is at least one who tends to monopolize a portion of the time available for discussion of almost every topic. If, in the early consideration of group norms, underparticipation and overparticipation are brought forward as common problems to be avoided, they can be forestalled to some extent. Members are likely to allude to the norms when unevenness in the communication pattern becomes evident. They may remedy the situation themselves by drawing out the diffident member and by refusing to reinforce the participation of the overly talkative individual.

If group pressure is not effective, the leader may find it advisable to offer individual help to the members in question. The monopolizing offender may already be trying to be less talkative and may be interested in undertaking an informal program of behavioral self-control. When trust has been established with a shy individual, he or she may feel secure enough to communicate briefly from a seat near the leader, without the threat posed by distance and intervening members. The leader promises to help by asking questions at first that require only one-word answers, or leader and member may role play in advance some simple interchanges that the client can then feel confident in repeating in the group. Once the ice is broken, the client usually becomes involved in at least minimal participation.

Promoting solidarity In the early life of the group, the leader is intent on promoting the solidarity, or cohesiveness, that enables the group to view itself as a single, dynamic organism. This is the main function of the group maintenance role, which before long must enlist the combined efforts of all of the members. It is developed when every individual accepts every other as uniquely being and becoming and as playing a vital part in the total functioning of the group. If members of a voluntary group drop out, morale is impaired. Especially at first, but subsequently as well, the leader is alert to mounting tension among members. Particularly if they do not know each other, all are initially in the grip of anxiety aroused by the threat of facing a new situation. Survival and security considerations are uppermost. Some look for affiliation, others for approval, still others for a chance to dominate. Later, anxiety is aroused by the sense of dependence that sharing confidences engenders.

Anxiety may be expressed in conflict between the more aggressive members and by maneuvers of withdrawal or denial by those inclined to avoid open dissension. The leader takes measures that may be necessary to diminish the anxiety, using continuing responses and reassurance phrased to link group goals, norms, and roles with positive group outcomes. As progress is made toward mutual trust, members are able to respond to evidence of both the supportive and modeling aspects of the leader's sensitivity. Individual attitudes such as diffidence, embarrassment, hostility, or indifference are reflected as the universal reactions to anxiety that they represent. By offering and eliciting feedback on game-playing transactions that are exchanged, the helper moves the discussion from P to C, C to P, C to C, or P to P transactions to A to A transactions. This can be done with or without TA explanations as such (Jongeward and James, 1973).

At appropriate points, the leader draws on all of the supportive and insight-giving counseling skills. Continuing responses are employed to encourage the group as a whole to express and acknowledge the feeling trends that become apparent in interaction. Selective use of various positive reinforcement techniques increases unified movement as it occurs. When confusion or division threatens, the leader helps the group stabilize and reroute itself by the judicious use of leading responses: raising questions, clarifying, reassuring, suggesting, and summarizing when the need arises.

Group cohesiveness is reinforced if leader responses are addressed to the group as a whole, at least as often as to individuals within the group. Reflection, for instance, is used to mirror whatever feeling tone seems to be generalized throughout the membership (for example: satisfaction in accomplishment, warm friendliness, discouragement, or distrust). Consensus is sought from the group as a whole, not only with respect to prevailing feelings and attitudes, but regarding values, ideas, and courses of action suggested by members.

It may be expected that members will imitate such leader responses, as well as other aspects of leader behavior. One by one, members begin to assume responsibility for giving verbal recognition to group perceptions as such, and they begin to take turns in seeking consensus when consensus is appropriate. The leader meanwhile intervenes to ensure that no one is required to agree with ideas or opinions of others simply for the sake of group unanimity. If the group is action-oriented, however, decisions that are reached must be those that all members can commit themselves to implementing.

Linking Through the function of linking, the leader furthers both the maintenance and task roles of the group. The desired solidarity does not in any sense transform the group into an amorphous mass. Rather, it is a multiplication of the bonding that occurs between individual and individual, which can be strengthened or weakened by the intervention of other individuals. The leader is quick to observe pairing as it begins to occur, to reinforce the optimism that it awakens in the group, and to encourage each pair to share their openness with others. Thus the group as a whole gradually becomes a mutual support system.

In the interim before this occurs, it may be necessary to circumvent the maneuvers of a member who seems to be intent on preventing others from achieving any degree of intimacy. This may be accomplished by stimulating a general discussion of the value of the group experience in making not only one, but a number of helping relationships possible. What is learned about relating and helping within the group can be adapted to situations outside it. Also, the act of helping has a healing effect on both the helper and the helpee.

As bonding takes place, it may lead to an alignment of several members who begin to place themselves in opposition to others in the group. If more than one faction forms as an unconscious process, a power struggle is soon under way. The leader remains alert to opportunities to emphasize commonalities of thinking and feeling within the group as a whole and to opportunities to draw the subgroup or groups into open interaction with other members. Discussion can be channeled to the subject of group maintenance and task roles: how they may be furthered and how endangered and where responsibility rests for their fulfillment. Emphasis is placed on the value of a group situation that provides unconditional acceptance from several others for the individual member, makes new ways of relating immediately possible, and offers means whereby any problem can be viewed from a number of different perspectives.

This, too, can involve tacit or explicit use of TA concepts. The idea of the "I'm OK–You're OK" position, which is somewhat familiar to most people, appeals to most. Discussion to clarify differences of meaning between the terms *acceptance* and *approval* in interaction may be necessary.

Apart from the occurrence of pairing or factionalism, the linking function is still essential to furthering the group process. The helper bridges areas of meaning in member contributions and between two or more situations that are described or occur within the group, as well as between ideas, areas of feeling, and suggestions for action in pursuit of group goals. Summaries are used to link events in the life of the group and to demonstrate progress toward desired outcomes. At times, the leader may choose to take the lead in the review or to ask that the group summarize aspects of its work together. Linking in its various aspects serves to build trust and openness among members. Confidence in their ability to solve problems and to accomplish tasks is similarly strengthened (Kemp, 1970).

Shielding To be effective, the leader must be responsive to tendencies toward vulnerability or dominance among group members. Some are overly sensitive to any hint of rejection in the manner of others; some take an offensive posture at any indication of disagreement with their views; others attempt to manipulate both the leader and the group into satisfying their own need to exert control. Without singling out a specific culprit, the leader can appeal to the group norms, with an occasional, interim summary statement that draws attention to the various forces at work within the group. Much repetition of this type of leader response is usually unnecessary. Members soon acquire the knack of using a fairly gentle type of confrontation with each other as violations of the norms occur.

A member who stands out in some way, in temperament or background, for instance, may gradually be placed in the position of group scapegoat or group favorite. The leader's intervention in such situations is designed to reinforce the use of that individual's competence or sensitivity in appropriate facets of group process. As the member's concept of self in relation to others in the group takes on more realistic proportions, the group's perceptions of his or her role are likewise modified.

Some members of the group may find themselves cast in work roles that make them feel subservient or unappreciated. The leader encourages reviews of group activities and progress that allow for recognition of any discontent that may exist and for shifts of roles and tasks when indicated.

Using conflict constructively A thoughtful appraisal reveals conflict to be a necessary and useful part of relationships between individuals and within groups of people. To the experienced helper, conflict is expected as an inevitable part of group interaction. Every conflict presents group and leader alike with an opportunity to put it to creative use in a more fruitful experience than either winning or losing an argument. A disagreement can be taken as a signal to investigate a variety of alternatives and lines of thought that are new to the antagonists.

In order to be able to further this outcome, leaders must be able to maintain a balanced perspective in the midst of altercation, and they must be able to refrain from taking sides. Their function is to bridge the differences and tie in the commonalities discernible in the expressed points of view. At appropriate times they encourage exploration of possible alternative ways to resolve the differences. They may need to call upon the group to examine whether motives of factionalism or scapegoating underlie the conflict. A persuasive connection may need to be made between specific problems within the group and the metagoals or values essential to both effective personal functioning and group process: growth in awareness, an open spirit of inquiry, appreciation of differentness, recognition of individual choice and responsibility, and shared authority. A to A transactions focus on issues rather than placing others in "Not-OK" positions.

Emphasizing immediacy The helper is acutely aware that the progress of growth and becoming is successful only to the extent that an individual or group is much more fully oriented to the present and future than to the past. In guiding a group, therefore, the leader attempts to keep the attention of members focused on the here-and-now of their interaction and its relevance to the eventual attainment of their goals, as well as on their task performance. As segments of current interaction are related to both goals and norms, members can be brought to distinguish between effective and nonproductive or counterproductive forms of group behavior. Their awareness and understanding of the processes of their interactions are expanded if the leader interjects, from time to time, a query such as *What is going on in the group now?*

Exploration of the immediate feeling elements of interchange between individuals or subgroups is stimulated by helper questions that directly address the metacommunicative content. For example:

> *John, can you name your feelings now, after telling us you don't care what other people think?*
>
> *Brenda, how did you feel when Bill said that you didn't know what you were talking about?*
>
> *Neil and Evan seem to have a different view on this issue from most others in the group. Let's hear how they feel with so many lined up on the other side.*

Member feedback elicited by helper leads of this type are likely to be descriptive rather than defensive in nature. In an instance of circumscribed conflict or mutual support among a few participants, a concrete learning experience can be provided by introducing a role-playing or tape-recorded replay of what transpired. It is followed by the adroit use of questions, some of which are likely to come from the group in imitation of previous leader behavior that has proved to be productive of group progress. Discussion remains objective and so furthers self-awareness and self-knowledge in individual members, as well as mutual understanding and trust within the group as a whole.

The helper who is versed in TA principles and methods may elect to use early opportunities in the development of the group to introduce concepts that help members identify behavior motivated by P, A, or C and transactions as complementary or crossed. In addition, strategies of game playing provide material for discussion that is both interesting and informative. Leaders and members can thereafter draw on TA concepts as a vehicle for reaching further understanding of group interaction. TA terminology provides an inoffensive yet insight-giving method of confrontation.

As their recognition of the significance of metacommunication increases, members take over the responsibility of confronting one another with their perceptions of desirable or undesirable behavior. Group pressures keep interaction more substantially goal-directed and, at the same time, protective of the sensitivities of individual members. Conflict is given expression but is diverted into a search for creative solutions. The group is on its way toward autonomous, productive functioning.

Guiding Group Process

Whether the group is to meet only once or at intervals over a short or prolonged period, the orderly phases of problem-solving intervention prove to be useful in providing the worker with a dependable means of conceptualizing the tasks to be undertaken. Time and effort can be proportioned adequately to move as far as possible toward group goals. In each step (initiating group relationships, assessment, planning, implementation, and termination) much that is required of the helper as group leader is similar to that needed in individual counseling. The elements of each stage peculiar to the group situation are illustrated in the following case example through glimpses of a nurse's group experience with elderly residents in an intermediate care facility. The group leader is Jane Warren, nurse supervisor of several units, including those in which group members reside. She hoped to effect some improvement in communication among residents and so to lessen the self-centered preoccupation that narrowed their horizons.

Case Example: Jane Warren Guides Group Process

Recognizing that the success of a group endeavor depends in large part on the willing participation of each of its members, Jane invited every prospective member individually to attend the initial meeting. With the help of the head nurse on each unit, she selected a total of three men and five women. All were capable of self-care and were able to carry the thread of a brief conversation without forgetting its beginnings. Although Jane was acquainted with all eight members, she was not involved with them in a direct-care capacity. This would make it possible for her to remain somewhat detached from the immediate administrative functions of the units they resided in. It was her hope that other, less proficient residents might be enlisted later, with the original eight subdivided to constitute the nucleus of each of two or three other groups.

In issuing the invitation on the forenoon of the first half-hour afternoon meeting, Jane stated merely that the meeting would give a few residents an opportunity to get better acquainted and to share ideas with each other. She mentioned that the afternoon snack usually distributed at about that time would be served at the meeting. All of the eight accepted, and, after a reminder as the time neared, all were present at the stated hour.

Initiating Group Relationships

Jane chose a small, comfortably furnished visiting room as the setting for the meeting, and she served the promised snacks to members as they arrived. When all were seated in the circle of chairs, she took the place that was left and began by making sure that all knew the others by name. There was no one in the group who did not know at least one other member beforehand.

Jane formulated her own objectives for the first meeting in advance: to keep relationships group centered rather than leader centered; to encourage communication in a climate of mutual acceptance and support; and to help participants tolerate differences among them and provide ego reinforcement for each other. When group members, once settled, looked expectantly in her direction, she stated that although she had taken the lead in bringing them together, she hoped that they would consider the meeting theirs and use the time to discuss their own interests and concerns. She added that if they wished it at the end of the half-hour, she would plan with them for further meetings.

Mr. R responded cheerfully, with appreciation of the break in the customary monotony. Ms. C, who sat next to him, complained that monotony is what getting old amounts to. *You are put out of the way into an impersonal institution by the people you have worked for all your life.* Knowing that a certain amount of ventilation of negative feelings would provide relief for the anxiety aroused by the novel situation, Jane made no verbal response as others picked up and enlarged on Ms. C's theme.

When Mr. F mentioned his long years of high school teaching in contrast to his present uselessness, several of the others made similar comparisons. Jane used this opportunity to reinforce self-esteem by verbally acknowledging the past accomplishments of each speaker. She invited Mrs. N and Mrs. E, neither of whom had spoken, to tell the group what they had been engaged in previously. When *only a housewife* responses were offered, she used a leading question to prompt them to tell about their sons and daughters. As Jane complimented them on their effective parenting, the two women, already sitting in adjacent chairs, edged themselves closer together.

Jane summed up the variety of strengths made evident among the group as a whole, and she suggested that the members might eventually like to think of ways in which some of their talents might be used in their present environment.

Jane's move in the direction of goal identification led to a mild difference of opinion between Mr. R and Mr. B, who took a pessimistic view of the current possibilities. Jane impartially reflected their individual attitudes, stating further that it is always good to examine differing points of view. To support her effort at linking, she added that as the group progressed, they might like to identify some of the specific difficulties in their present situation and consider how they might cooperate in using their many capabilities to overcome them.

Ms. L, a former saleswoman in a busy department store, said that the greatest problem for her was the constant loneliness that she felt. When others echoed this sentiment, Ms. F volunteered the thought that a series of group meetings might alleviate this problem to some extent. Ms. F's suggestion was opportune because the half-hour was nearly up. Jane underlined Ms. F's idea, giving her full credit for it. As they separated, group members agreed with a suggestion that she arrange for another meeting early the following week.

Recalling her objectives for the first meeting, Jane felt that they had been attained to a reasonable degree. Leader-member roles had combined without formal definition. No occasion for assigning other roles or for setting norms had arisen, although Jane realized that some formal structuring of this kind might be needed as the honeymoon phase wore off. A beginning was made toward identifying a common goal that would further bind the members into a group. She knew that aimless discussion soon burns itself out and must be harnessed to some issue or issues that can be expected to lead to a meaningful outcome.

Assessment and Planning

At the beginning of the second meeting, Jane shared with the others the gist of her evaluation of the first meeting. She reminded the group of the impressive total of accomplishments they had revealed and of the suggestion that they might find current ways to use their talents. Mentioning the agreement within the group that Ms. L's reference to loneliness had engendered, she suggested that members might like to take an informal census of additional problems they might wish to work on. In response to their affirmative nods, she wrote *loneliness* at the top of a small chalkboard that she had brought in before the meeting.

With each successive topic volunteered, conversation about its significance became general. Examples were brought out to support most topics. Toward the end of thirty minutes, the list included "forgetfulness," "more outings," "nothing to hope for," "unacceptable behavior of some residents," and "attitudes of indifference among relatives and staff." The feasibility of including "increasing physical disability" was argued. As a result, it was modified to "increasing dependence."

Before the group dispersed, Jane promised to see that each member received a copy of the complete list. She suggested that they give individual thought to possible solutions to one or more of the problems before the next meeting. Mr. R added that they could talk about the topics in two's or three's when they met in the dining room or in the large common room. In her private evaluation, Jane noted the momentum gained in the first two meetings and its exhilarating effect on group members, including herself.

In anticipation of the next meeting, Jane classified the problem items in her own thinking. Most were personal or interpersonal in nature. "More outings," because it could lend itself to a practical solution, seemed the logical one to begin with. The sharing involved in planning for its implementation would promote cohesiveness within the group. Carrying plans into the kind of action that would yield measurable results would give the members a sense of accomplishment as a group and would serve to confirm their group identity.

After a brief review of progress at the beginning of the third meeting, Jane asked if anyone else had picked out, as she had, a particular problem that seemed to be most practical to work with. Mr. B said immediately that "more outings" was the only practical problem, but he doubted that anything could be done about it. Mr. S, who had worked in a managerial capacity before his retirement, said that anything can be done if you can get it across to the right people. With very little help from Jane, the group embarked on a discussion aimed at identifying desirable activities and a specific plan of action. Before the next meeting, a delegation consisting of Ms. L, Mr. R, and Mr. B would carry a definitely outlined request from the group to the director of social activities.

Implementation

While implementation of the "outings" action plan proceeded, the ad hoc group reported their progress at the weekly meetings. Gratifying evaluations of their efforts greeted their reports of the social director's successful negotiations in arranging for transportation and free tickets for interested residents to several entertaining and cultural events.

Jane's personal interim evaluations led her to judge that the other problems on the list called for implementation that could result in significant personal and interpersonal growth within the group. In subsequent meetings, she left members free to choose the order in which to discuss the topics and free to amend the list as they deemed necessary. Her own contribution to daily discussions consisted mainly of exercising her listening and clarifying skills, with the liberal use of reflection of feelings and attitudes.

In separate discussions of "forgetfulness" and "unacceptable behavior," Jane was able to provide useful information and suggestions drawn from her nursing background (Yurick et al., 1980). The latter topic also gave her an opportunity to involve the group in considering the various meanings that may be attached to the perception of individual differences. The uniqueness, or "different-ness," of persons came into focus as a value to be cherished. The same theme carried the group into examining the topic of "indifference of staff and relatives." Here, the members arrived at several techniques to be tried out as means of sparking interest by showing interest. Jane found a willing response when she introduced the idea of role playing. Group members achieved fresh insights by taking turns in acting out the parts of relatives, staff members, and of other residents. When Jane questioned them on the nature of their feelings as they enacted the various roles, some recognition of the function of seeming indifference as a cloak for other, more disturbing feelings emerged.

Discussion in any meeting seldom proceeded without intervening periods of conflict and stalemate. When necessary, Jane bridged gaps between differing opinions and recommendations, encouraged silent residents to give at least yes or no responses, and channeled disagreement into a consideration of alternative ideas or courses of action. Past grievances were brought up frequently as evidence of the difficulties that would complicate present and future efforts. Jane continued to draw on all of her counseling skills in an effort to build bridges between alternatives, shield more sensitive members, and reorient the group to present realities. Consistently and consciously, she tried to model effective member functioning in all of her responses.

"Nothing to hope for" and "increasing dependence" brought out a variety of attitudes concerning the imponderables of existence. Residents derived and offered mutual support as they told of the meaning given to their lives by attitudinal expressions such as: *One day at a time, God knows what is best for us, Everything changes,* or *Every adversity is a potential stumbling block or stepping stone.* These came to the surface only after much outpouring of depression and discouragement—feelings that were reflected by other residents as well as by Jane.

Evaluation and Termination

The group readily fell into a pattern of contributing to the evaluative summary by which Jane signaled that the meeting was drawing to a close. The process as well as the content of the day's discussion came under scrutiny. One day's progress was compared with another's. The relative value of different types of responses was also judged. When anger was expressed at one point about Mr. B's negativism, the group assented to Jane's suggestion that "feelings" be added to the list of topics. Group solidarity was strengthened through subsequent exploration of the members' own feelings as potent forces in their relationships both inside and outside the group. Mr. S introduced the term *feedback,* enabling Jane to engage the participation of members in a comparative demonstration of its judgmental versus nonevaluative forms.

Jane knew that a certain amount of anxiety would be aroused by the prospect of terminating the group experience. She was watchful, therefore, for opportunities to give recognition to that eventuality. During the summary evaluation at the end of the seventh meeting, Mrs. E paired a statement of foreboding with one of appreciation of the experience. A circle of apprehensive looks was cast in Jane's direction. In response, she suggested that the group might wish to consider how much longer it should continue to meet. Because the half-hour was up, members agreed to think about the question between meetings and to use part of the next meeting to discuss it.

Early in the following meeting, Mr. B, who had sounded tentatively optimistic of late, broached the subject directly.

> Mr. B: *Are you going to throw us over when we get through the list of topics?*
>
> Jane (reflecting his feeling): *You're thinking I might desert you?*
>
> Ms. L (breaking in): *He's not the only one. We have all been wondering what you meant about ending the meetings.*

Jane voiced her wish to give a similar opportunity to meet to other residents, whereupon the group began a general discussion of the pros and cons. Although no one entirely rejected the idea, there was definite opposition to enlarging the present group. The upshot of this discussion, which consumed part of the next three meetings, was that Jane would continue to meet with the present group, but only once a month. Two new groups would be formed to meet on a weekly basis. Each new group would include four members of the original group and four other residents invited by the four originals on a one-to-one basis. It was agreed that the head nurses whose units were represented would also be invited by those representatives.

The implementation of these plans effectively brought about a type of termination. Jane was comfortable in leaving the future of the group and that of the new groups in the ensuing state of ambiguity. She looked forward to helping the original eight members continue to grow, to meeting new challenges with other groups containing less competent members, and, in all of this, to forwarding her own personal and professional development.

References

Appley, D. G., and Winder, A. E. 1973. *T-groups and therapy groups in a changing society.* San Francisco: Jossey-Bass.

Barrett-Lennard, G. T. 1975. Process, effects and structure in intensive groups: A theoretical-descriptive analysis. *Theories of group processes.* C. L. Cooper, editor. New York: Wiley.

Bion, W. R. 1961. *Experiences in groups.* New York: Basic Books.

Cooper, C. L., editor. 1975. *Theories of group processes.* New York: Wiley.

Gazda, G. M. 1978. *Group counseling: A developmental approach.* 2nd ed. Boston: Allyn and Bacon.

Jongeward, D., and James, M. 1973. *Winning with people—Group exercises in transactional analysis.* Reading, Mass.: Addison-Wesley.

Kemp. C. G. 1970. *Foundations of group counseling.* New York: McGraw-Hill.

Kissen, M., editor. 1976. *From group dynamics to group psychoanalysis.* New York: Wiley.

Lakin, M., and Constanzo, P. R. 1975. The leader and the experiential group. *Theories of group processes.* C. L. Cooper, editor. New York: Wiley.

Lasky, R. G., and Dell Orto, A. E. 1979. *Group counseling and physical disability: A rehabilitational and health care perspective.* Belmont, Calif.: Wadsworth.

Milman, D. S., and Goldman, G. D., editors. 1974. *Group process today.* Springfield, Ill.: Thomas.

Mintz, E. E. 1974. Marathon groups as intensive psychotherapy. *Group process today.* D. S. Milman and G. D. Goldman, editors. Springfield, Ill.: Thomas.

Napier, R., and Gershenfeld, M. K. 1981. *Groups: Theory and experience.* 2nd ed. Boston: Houghton Mifflin.

Olmsted, M. S. 1978. *The small group.* 2nd ed. New York: Random House.

Rioch, M. J. 1976. The work of Wilfred Bion on groups. *From group dynamics to group psychoanalysis.* M. Kissen, editor. New York: Wiley.

Rose, S. D. 1977. *Group therapy: A behavioral approach.* Englewood Cliffs, N. J.: Prentice-Hall.

Sampson, E. E., and Marthas, M. S. 1977. *Group process for the health professions.* New York: Wiley.

Sheehy, G. 1976. *Passages: Predictable crises of adult life.* New York: Dutton.

Whittaker, J. K. 1974. Models of group development: Implications for social group work practice. *The practice of social work.* R. W. Klenk and R. M. Ryan, editors. 2nd ed. Belmont, Calif.: Wadsworth.

Yurick, A. G., et al. 1980. *The aged person and the nursing process.* New York: Appleton-Century-Crofts.

CHAPTER 10

Short-Term Intervention with Families

Psychologic intervention with whole families, together with growth-promoting and restorative work with other groups, became an accepted area of practice around the middle of this century. Specialists emerged who recognized the value of dealing with the family as a total unit, with the advantage of observing its interaction patterns *in vivo* instead of having to depend on the reports of a client or clients. Research was soon under way, and work proceeded on the development of a theoretic framework to encompass family life as a process and family therapy as such. Currently, several periodicals are devoted to these subjects. Specialized training in family therapy is offered at a number of centers that provide education in psychology, psychiatry, and related fields.

In this chapter, key concepts of the developing theory of family process are presented, and applications of theoretical formulations to the work of the professional helper are made.

CONCEPTS OF FAMILY PROCESS

The theory of family process and family therapy draws on sociologic as well as psychologic and psychiatric concepts. Because the family is a group, much that is discussed in Chapter 9 concerning processes that take place in groups pertains also to the specialized group that is the family. Whether it comprises only two members or more than two, a family is usually thought of as a group that is tied together by blood and marriage and that lives together as a unit for a period of time. The **nuclear family** may consist of a conjugal pair only or of a parent or parents with a child or children. Sharing the same residence, there may also be members of the **extended family**, who, although outside the nuclear family, are related by blood or marriage. In modern Western society, it is usual for the members of only two related generations to remain together while the children are growing. Whatever its composition, the members of a living-together family group are in close, dynamic interaction with one another.

Within, the family has all the features of a social system. Its members are linked together in a network of relationships. Their mode of interaction is based, for the most part unconsciously, on a pattern of interrelated social roles. Every role has a set of prescribed functions. If parent and child roles are trimmed to the individual capabilities and inclinations of each agent, roles are carried out to combine into a smoothly functioning, organismic whole. Ideally, the family is an open system that flexibly articulates with other kinship, work, recreation, and religious systems. It responds adaptively to new conditions and maintains an organization that is mutually supportive of its members.

The family has a shared, interlocking lifestyle with its own particular norm system—a complex set of rules that govern its behavior and relationships. To the extent that it operates effectively, this system of norms, rules, and functions furthers the maintenance of the family as a group. Family standards of behavior are introjected to form the Parent ego states of the children. They are replicated by the offspring in all of their future relationships (Bowen, 1978). When the children of one generation themselves become parents, they tend to unconsciously reproduce in the new family situation the patterns they learned to conform to in the old. Consciously, most parents try to improve what they perceive to have been amiss in their original family lives. The success of their efforts depends on the accuracy of their perceptions of past and present realities.

Although the family interacts from its beginnings with the society and culture of which it is a unit, the values and norms of the larger groups are mediated by the parents until the children reach adolescence. Added pressure tends to build up within the family system as the children begin to be attracted to standards that vary from those by which they have heretofore been guided without material question. Because the family is a living, dynamic system, it is subject to shocks and stresses from changes within it and from events impinging on it from without. Any change in one of its members produces reverberations throughout the system that affect all of its members.

In addition to individual roles, the family, like other small groups, must functionally fill a group self-maintenance role and a group task role. Its **self-maintenance role** is designed, theoretically, to preserve a dynamic functional equilibrium, or relative **homeostasis**, within its system. This is accomplished as members influence and support one another and repel or accommodate incursions from the outside, in order to adequately fulfill expectations and obligations internal to the family.

To the extent that the flexibility of its internal system of roles, norms, and functions fulfills both its self-maintenance and task roles, a family is **functional** in its patterns and operations. A **dysfunctional** family may be locked into a rigid condition of homeostasis that is maintained only at the expense of the growth toward functional autonomy and identity of its individual members.

The major functions of the family's **task role** as a group and as a social system are to provide *protection, basic need satisfaction, self-expression,* and *emotional support* for its members at all ages and stages of development as well as to carry through a process of *child rearing* appropriate to the given society and culture. The role is performed functionally to the degree that members achieve interdependence characterized by mutual giving and receiving in a climate of mutual respect and trust. The level of maturity of the marital relationship is determined by the ability of the partners to accommodate themselves flexibly and openly to the responsibilities that face them as they initiate the family unit. In the theory developed by Bowen (1978), the capability fundamentally essential in each partner is that of functioning autonomously under the domination of intellectual rather than emotional attributes. In times of stress, a minimum of reality distortion is needed, and the partners resort to cognitive problem solving.

If the partners are also capable of intimacy, with all that it requires in giving to as well as taking from a relationship, they can complementarily function with each other and subsequently with their children. If, on the other hand, either partner expects to find the other a submissive follower or a magic helper, the result is continuous conflict or mutual avoidance of intimacy. Conflict may be masked, and a **pseudomutuality** (Wynne, 1958) or a dominant-submissive pattern (Hoffman, 1976) may be maintained. In either event, the relationship is inauthentic and exploitative. As such, it cultivates a dysfunctional climate of mistrust that inhibits growth in personhood in the marital partners and in their children.

Serious dysfunction, when it exists, is inherent in family relationships from their beginnings. It originates in a dysfunctional marital relationship, which results in dysfunctional parenting. To borrow Bowen's terms (1978), the dysfunctional partnership is one in which at least one member has a need to **deself** the other. A **no-self** person is one who resorts to filling up the emptiness by pleasing others or by living vicariously through them. Because all of the roles within the family are assigned and developed as an outgrowth of the marital relationship, the nature of that relationship determines not only all the family roles and their functions, but the norms connected with the roles. Together, these constitute the pattern and processes of the family system.

If each marital partner begins their life together expecting to make the other over in his or her own image and thereby to get rather than give narcissistic supplies in the relationship, a pattern of mutual intolerance develops. Differences in characteristics and needs of one partner are seen as a rejection of those in the other. Each interprets even a slight disagreement as evidence of a lack of love in the other (Satir, 1968).

As the children learn to relate, they too become enmeshed in the system, which may include extensions beyond the nuclear family. Conflict occurs inevitably and frequently, with each opponent or group of opponents viewing the other not simply as separate and different, but as the enemy. Reactions and interactions are dominated by blind emotion rather than by intellect. Important choices are made on the same basis as a means of achieving relief from emotional tension and anxiety. In a climate of perpetual mistrust, communication is guarded at best. In endlessly repetitive game-playing transactions, each individual tries to compensate for a lack of self-esteem and self-identity by destroying the self-esteem and autonomy of one or more of the others. It often happens that the need to project guilt and shame leads some members of the system to stop speaking to others, sometimes for years or for the remainder of a lifetime.

The role allocation in a dysfunctional family is of the kind required to preserve homeostasis, however dysfunctional the state of equilibrium may prove to be. The rest of the family may be subservient to one who assumes a dominant role or to one who finds that a martyr role earns neverending payoffs in the form of sympathy and services. A role that is assigned quite commonly by others comes about through the use, largely unconsciously, of the mechanism of **scapegoating.** It binds all but one of the family members into a collective projection of hostility against the excluded member. The chosen scapegoat is used to explain and relieve family distress. In this capacity, the culprit is made the object of various forms of cruelty: rejection, blame, derogation, or derision. In extreme cases, neglect, deprivation, or violent abuse is inflicted on a child victim. Ackerman (1966) and others find three complementary roles that are often assumed by family members in interaction: **attacker, victim**, and **healer.** In the dynamic shifts brought about by circumstances in most families, one victim (attacker, healer) may be replaced by another, and a variety of alignments may occur.

In a functional family of several members, dyads and triads form and reform into mutual support systems. Bowen (1978) finds the triad, or **family triangle**, to be the smallest stable relationship unit. In calm conditions, two of the three members continue in comfortable closeness, with the third a somewhat uneasy outsider. When stress agitates the system, the three vie for the position outside the site of the tension. In any family of more than three, the members move among the possible triangles. A functional parental dyad is kept open for the children's entry to make triangles successively when needs arise. Under conditions of stress, the family often seeks to functionally or dysfunctionally triangle outsiders into the system. A therapist or counselor uses this tendency therapeutically but is watchful to prevent being incorporated into dysfunctional relationships.

In a dysfunctional family, breaking into dyads and triads may lead to schism, with one individual or subgroup pursuing dominance and another defensively or submissively aligned. A coalition may become rigidly patterned with members interacting in a **repetitive cycle** consisting of *conflict, emotional distance,* and *emotional closeness* (Hoffman, 1976). Symbiotic ties formed within an internal alliance may stifle individuation and development toward self-identity. Bowen's early writing (1965) describes a pathologic bonding that makes the whole family a tightly closed system, emotionally fused into an **undifferentiated ego mass.**

Weakland (1976) recognizes that many types of problematic behavior in families are perpetuated by a **vicious feedback circle.** The behavior that most needs to be modified often includes a game-playing payoff that reinforces the part of the transaction that precedes it. If the problem-maintaining response is not forthcoming, the circle can be broken. The circular nature of the problem is not likely to be recognized by the family without the help of outside intervention, as is exemplified in the case of the Wilson family described under "Process of Intervention" below.

Communication theory plays a prominent part among current concepts of family process and family therapy. It is through its internal transactions, or units of communication, that the observer seeks to understand the family as an interacting group. Parsons (1955) suggests that a family faces the task of performing two sets of functions: instrumental and expressive. **Instrumental functions** are those that insure the family's maintenance as a stable unit within a supportive social network. **Expressive functions** involve openness of communication and interaction within the family's internal system.

In a dysfunctional family, authentic communication may be entirely lacking between marital partners or among the family group as a whole. The factual or report level is commonly disregarded in favor of a command interpretation that is then given a command response (Satir, 1968). Adult members of the family provide no model of mature, reciprocal interaction for the children. The children may be denied the opportunity to learn to communicate. They may be interrupted by their elders before they can finish expressing a thought, often with a command or demand that blatantly denies their individuality and worth; for example, *Keep quiet and do as you are told! Go on out and shut the door after you. We're not talking to you. Listen to who's talking! Who asked your opinion?* Less obvious, but equally inhibiting is an attitude of complete disregard of what a child is trying to say, as adults continue their own conversation as if the child has not spoken or otherwise tried to participate.

THE FAMILY AND THE PROFESSIONAL HELPER

In the course of the work of most professional helpers, opportunities to helpfully intervene with a family usually come when the family is facing a maturational or situational crisis. A nurse, a teacher, a minister, or a guidance counselor, for example, may be acquainted with several members of a family. Only when the family is under unusual stress are any of its members likely to seek or accept emotionally supportive outside help. Even then, the opportunity to meet the family as a total group may not be open to the worker. The helper's sources of information about the family's problems, values, norms, and aims may be limited to the reports and appraisals of one or two of its members.

The helper remains cognizant of the fact that in almost every crisis situation, a family rather than an isolated individual is, to some extent, involved. And whatever affects one member of any family that is a closely associated group inevitably affects the others. Even though the actual practice of dealing with the whole family as the unit of intervention may not be attainable, the worker nevertheless keeps this ideal in view as a guiding principle. An attempt is still made to reach out to help the family as a group, even though it may be necessary to work with and through a few family members, or only one. The helper's immediate objective is to assess the depth and duration of the family's dysfunctional state.

Concepts of family process as well as those of group process are therefore relevant as subjects for discussion and application in the training of helping professionals. They enrich our awareness of the underlying motivations of our own and our clients' behavior, and they provide guidelines for the approach that we choose. If a suggestion or an actual referral for family counseling or therapy is indicated, the professional must have not only a factual knowledge and appreciation of such treatment, but information about the resources available in a given community.

When it is found that long-standing dysfunction, deeply rooted in the family's system of habitual roles, norms, and interactions, exists, referral for professional counseling is the most desirable outcome of the helper's intervention. A family that includes a psychotic or a seriously neurotic or addicted member may be capable of making only limited progress toward improved functioning, regardless of the mode of professional treatment used.

The helping professional who judges that referral is necessary may still be the only knowledgeable person the family has thus far been able to trust. Several meetings for supportive intervention with a family member or members may be required before the idea of seeking help from a mental health clinic or a private therapist can be broached.

Short-Term Counseling Skills

In circumstances that make it possible for the professional helper to work with a whole family or with a group of its members, essential counseling skills combine those of crisis intervention with those of group leadership as described in Chapter 9. Their use is adjusted to coincide with the worker's understanding of the concepts of family dynamics and process. In the remainder of this section, discussion of the skills of group intervention presented in Chapter 9 is amplified with reference to their use with families. In the present instance, the helper's immediate **aim** is to enable the family to become a mutual support system and thereafter to function effectively in coping with the situation of crisis. The overall humanistic aim in working with a family is to facilitate the growth of each of its members, and of the family as a whole, in the direction of fullness of functioning (Olim, 1978).

In order to help a family improve its capacity for expressive functioning, the helper tries to understand the subtleties of its interpersonal interaction. Attention is given to nonverbal as well as verbal communication and to both the report and command aspects of the latter (Chapter 5).

The importance of communication and its difficulties may need to be made a subject of the helper's discussion with the family. Only by communicating openly and genuinely with each other can family members succeed in identifying their goals and the roles and activities calculated to achieve them. Here, the worker may meet communication difficulties inherent in the family's habitual mode of functioning. Various members of the group may be unconsciously locked into long-standing patterns of game playing. One member may be singled out as the family scapegoat—the main recipient of blame and shame in the present crisis. Although not the object of blame, one member may be placed in a "Not-OK" position by some or all of the others, who may regularly answer questions directed toward their victim or discount any opinion that he or she might venture to offer. Another member of the family may dominate every avenue of discussion, arousing submissive agreement in some family members and resentment in others.

The helper intervenes directly in dysfunctional communication and indirectly as a model of its functional opposite. By being fully present to each individual regardless of his or her age or facility of expression, the helper affirms every person's worth and right to be heard in every instance. Benefit may be gained by discussing the importance and art of listening. Inequitable distribution of participation is called directly to the attention of the group, and reluctant members are drawn into every area of significant interchange. Reflective and clarifying techniques are used to bring metacommunicative aspects of interaction to the surface. References to the Parent, Adult, and Child sources of specific responses and to the ulterior content and crossing of transactions serve to enlighten and enliven comprehension and encourage the acknowledgement of feelings hitherto disowned. As members of a family group become aware of meanings they have not previously detected in their interactions, they gradually reach the point of being able to help and support each other in reaching still further awareness.

The measures that are used to promote **cohesiveness** in any goal-oriented group are equally applicable to the family. The helper addresses the group as a unit as often as possible rather than singling out individuals or subgroups for attention. This technique is employed in eliciting generalized feeling states—positive as well as negative. A question such as, *What is going on among you right now?* draws family members together in recognizing their common feelings and attitudes and keeps the **immediacy** of the situation in the forefront. A similar query can be used to lead the group as a whole into evaluating progress in goal setting, planning, and projecting the relative effectiveness of alternative actions.

The **linking function** of the worker is especially pertinent in helping a family move, as a unit, toward problem solving and crisis resolution. The strengths of dyadic and triadic alliances are used to identify areas of thought and feeling that may be common to the family as a whole. Bridges are built between persons and between points of disagreement. Disagreement itself is used as a path toward creative innovation in the family's ways of looking at itself and its methods of coping.

Shielding, when needed to reinforce self-esteem and self-confidence, is afforded any member being used as a scapegoat or any member who is particularly sensitive to the effects of the family's disruption in the crisis situation. The worker's sensitivity models acceptance of responsibility for another who needs help. As the feelings of the vulnerable member are reflected and as their expression and clarification are successfully elicited, the others respond with new awareness of the importance of drawing all of their members into the solidarity of a unified support system.

Conflicts among members are put to **constructive use** as the helper exemplifies the assignment of a positive value to "different-ness" (Satir, 1968). The problem of tacitly denying each other permission to exert autonomy may have existed from the family's beginnings and may now be a source of continuing conflict that involves all family members. The family's attention is drawn to the enriching effects of diversity in contrast to the destructiveness that results when members classify each other, on a feeling level exclusively, as either good or bad. The helper sets an example by identifying the obvious potentialities of various members and by relating their strengths to the goals that the family purports to hold as a group. Others are subsequently invited to help summarize the family assets.

The helper's responses consistently model the types of transactions that reinforce a feeling of self-worth in the individual. Discussion is directed to helping the group discriminate between the type of communication that builds up and the type that tears down the self-esteem and self-confidence of another. The hurt incurred by both senders and receivers of hostile messages is openly examined. Whenever the transactions between family members take on the character of defensive game playing or other defensive strategies, the helper questions the functionalism of such interaction and brings the group back to facing issues rather than deceiving or belittling one another.

The helper brings the group back to the immediate situation whenever members rake up old animosities, project blame to absent or nonparticipating members, or try to triangle the worker into a homeostatic configuration. For example: *Don't you think a husband (wife, child) should... ?* The obvious anxiety of the speaker or group is reflected, and cognitive attention is drawn to concrete problems under discussion in the here and now. Progress can be furthered if the family comes to recognize its dysfunctional lapses and returns to the pursuit of goals and activities to cope with its present crisis.

Process of Intervention

The first demand that a family crisis makes on the professional helper is to recognize it as such. It must be seen: (a) as a crisis and (b) as a crisis that threatens the total family system as well as the one or two members who may initially be identified as its victims. Even if the worker has no prospect of seeing the family as a group, it is still necessary to approach a given crisis situation with the likelihood in mind that it involves others in addition to the person whose claim to help is first noted. The quality of one's intervention is jeopardized if one's frame of reference is limited to a single member of a family. In order to avoid evaluating the crisis on the basis of the projections and other biased defenses of the informant, the helper must take into account the probable roles and goals of others in the system.

The Gregory family crisis (Chapter 5) is handled through Mrs. Gregory alone. On the basis of the client's response to the nurse's greeting, the community health nurse is able to recognize that a crisis exists. Instead of regarding Mrs. Gregory's opening comment as inconsequential, she sits down, thus indicating her openness to the fact that the client is troubled. With the skillful use of reflection of feeling, the nurse elicits a description of the family's disequilibrium. As she expresses her feelings in a climate of unconditional acceptance, Mrs. Gregory is able to identify the main problem as existing within the triad of which she, Elaine, and the baby are members. She is enabled to quickly move from the negative to the positive end of an emotional spectrum and thus to display the maturity of her own potential for functioning. It can be expected that she will lend strength to Elaine, who is evidently the chief sufferer in the crisis situation. It is likely that Mrs. Gregory will be able to draw the whole family together so that each member reinforces the others in combining their assets. Their task is to find ways of coping with the drastic change in their circumstances and to eventually resolve the crisis.

The opportunity for the helping professional to meet with a family or with some of its members may come only once. On the other hand, a series of meetings may be possible. In the following case, the intervention principles are applied by a nurse in a situation that makes several meetings possible. Mrs. Gregory's case demonstrates that adaptive changes in a family system that is only temporarily dysfunctional can sometimes be set in motion in a single interview with only one of its members.

Intervention with any family, as well as with an individual or another type of group, can be effectively conceptualized as a problem-solving process. Once the problem is identified in terms that hold comparable meanings for both family and worker, the family begins to evolve its own experiential goals. These can be dovetailed with the worker's underlying goals of enabling the family to become its own support system and, eventually, to use its problem situation as an incentive to growth in strength and unity. In the intervention described below, a professional helper organizes his plan of intervention in accordance with the customary steps of the problem-solving approach.

Case Example: John David and the Wilson Family

John, a graduate student in psychiatric-mental health nursing, is assigned to work with the Wilson family during his final clinical placement. The arrangement is made by his instructor in cooperation with the family clinic of the local community mental health center. The family is selected by the staff team that John has joined as a member. The team includes a social worker, a psychiatrist, a psychologist, and a clinical nurse specialist. On each of his clinical days, John attends the daily team meeting in which the group shares their progress in working with their families, exchanges insights, and provides each other with mutual support as family problems are worked through. John's instructor attends several of the meetings on John's clinical days.

The intake report provides the team with information on which to base John's assignment. Mr. and Mrs. Wilson applied to the center as a result of a referral made by a local police official. Ross Wilson, their ten-year-old son, had been brought home by an officer following his fifth runaway episode in as many weeks.

At the request of the team, the intake worker makes a first appointment for John to meet with Ross and his parents at the center. Ross's younger brother and sister are left at home with their aunt. They can be expected to share in the benefits resulting from favorable behavioral and role changes brought about in a significant part of the family system. The assignment of this particular family to John is made mainly because the dysfunction seems to be of recent origin and essentially located within the triangle formed by Ross and his parents. This limits the complexity of the interrelationships that John will be called on to deal with.

Initiating the Relationship

John prepares himself for his first interview with the family by engaging in an inner rehearsal. He anticipates that the parents will be anxious and embarrassed at having to explain their problem to yet another stranger. Their anxiety will be compounded by the prospect of being required to incorporate an outsider into the family's functional system. This, John reasons, might be offset to some extent by the fact that a state of psychologic crisis tends to create an unusual openness in its victims to accepting outside help.

John sees his immediate task as twofold: (a) to build the foundation of a relationship of mutual trust with the client family and (b) to work with them in defining the problem or problems that precipitated the present family crisis. Recognizing that his sensitivity to his clients' feelings will enable him to express genuine concern and a sincere desire to help, he also determines to keep the meetings family centered throughout. He plans to clarify his own role as catalytic but peripheral to the family's identification and implementation of new methods of coping. By these measures he hopes to reinforce the family's potential to function as a complete, interdependent system of mutual support.

Ross proves, on acquaintance, to be the least self-conscious of any in the group. He is an outgoing child, not overtly concerned about his problem behavior, but obviously eager to please his parents in other ways. When John issues a general invitation to all three to fill him in on the details of the problem that brought them to the center, all three participate about equally in the response. The parents tell of their worry over what might happen to Ross during his absence from home. Ross speaks sheepishly, but with a touch of pride, about having been repeatedly picked up in various public places by uniformed police officers late at night. John reflects the parental concern as inevitable under the circumstances, then to Ross his fascination with the police uniform.

Ross responds boastfully that his father also has a uniform and drives a truck. This leads to a description of the family's general lifestyle and, from that, to the particular events connected with the runaway episodes. The remainder of the first meeting and most of the next is taken up with the family's story. At first, John keeps it moving comfortably with only an occasional continuing response.

It develops that Mr. Wilson, who is employed to drive locally for a department store, is becoming increasingly discontent with the duties the job entails. At this point in the narrative, he and Mrs. Wilson engage in an argument that is a replay of one that, they admit, frequently breaks out at home. The husband says that he wants to transfer to a long-distance assignment, whereupon his wife complains to John that her husband's transfer would leave her with night and day responsibility for the home and family much of the time. Also addressing John, Mr. Wilson raises his voice in angry frustration at not being given an opportunity to explain how much better off the family would be if he could only take a better-paying job.

Mindful of the principles he has studied, John is alert to the danger of being triangled into the family conflict. He reflects Mrs. Wilson's apprehension directly to her and Mr. Wilson's anger to him, and he gently calls their attention to the fact that they are reliving feelings aroused in the past in the midst of the group's present information-gathering task.

With only an occasional outburst centering on the same theme, the sequence of events that typically precedes and follows Ross's leaving home is elicited as follows:

1. The argument about Mr. Wilson's proposed transfer begins in the course of a work-day evening meal.

2. Mr. Wilson shouts in frustration; Mrs. Wilson voices her fears and finally leaves the room in tears with the two younger children to put them to bed.

3. Ross remains with his father, who tells him of the joys of long-distance trucking.

4. On returning, Mrs. Wilson scolds Ross and her husband for lack of consideration for her and sends Ross to do his homework.

5. Mr. and Mrs. Wilson are uncommunicative with each other and with Ross for the next day or two.

6. One evening soon after, Mrs. Wilson prepares her husband's favorite dishes for supper. When Ross is again banished to do his homework, it is obvious to him that his parents are averse to having him present during their reconciliation.

7. Ross wanders off instead of going to school the next morning.

8. The police bring him home late in the evening.

9. His mother cries and scolds Ross, his father whips him with a belt, and he is sent to bed without any supper.

10. At supper the next evening, Mr. Wilson casually asks Ross where he went and what happened on the day that he missed school. He listens to the account with interest. Mrs. Wilson does not participate and, before long, suggests that Mr. Wilson would probably like to run away from the family too. The argument about the transfer begins again.

John recognizes that Ross, without being fully aware of it, picks up the metacommunicative approval and empathy in his father's questions about his escapades and identifies with his father's desire to see new places. Although Mrs. Wilson has come close to recognizing the command aspect of her husband's transactions, her feedback conveys criticism rather than understanding. With John's help, the three family members are able—the parents grudgingly at first—to identify the meanings that are thinly covered in their pattern of interaction.

Team discussion corroborates John's opinion that the family pattern currently displays a typically dysfunctional family triangle: a repetitive cycle of conflict, distance, and closeness; scapegoating to a minor degree; and the feedback circle that Weakland describes. These insights are not communicated to the family. The team is in agreement that the maladaptive pattern will be broken up and reassembled as family members move to assume the group task of defining their goals and accepting responsibility for each other in a unified effort at planning and implementation.

Assessment and Planning

At his third meeting with the family, it is evident to John that Mr. and Mrs. Wilson have done some homework between meetings. Mr. Wilson announces that, although Ross's running away from home is in no way excusable, he and his wife feel that their quarreling has made the child's home too hellish at times for him to want to stay there. Mrs. Wilson adds that the two younger children have been unusually fractious in the worrisome home atmosphere. She perceives her own impatience as both causing and resulting from the family's general state of disorder. Not to be outdone, Mr. Wilson says then that because his job is his own responsibility, he will see what he can do about it without bothering anyone else.

John observes, while Mr. Wilson is speaking, that Mrs. Wilson is becoming flushed and Ross is beginning to squirm. John briefly reinforces the start the parents have made toward defining their feelings about their present situation. He then points out in matter-of-fact terms the body language he noted, and he makes the connection between it and Mr. Wilson's statement about solving a significant family problem alone. Mrs. Wilson says emphatically that the problem concerns all of them and that she would like to have some say in how it is solved. Her husband concedes that she has that right, and they begin to discuss the pros and cons of the transfer.

This time, the parents address one another rather than attempting to involve John. Their argument is less heated than at the previous meeting. When they tend to move to positions at extreme ends of the issue, John helps them identify gray areas and calls attention to connections between judgmental opposites. Tendencies to blame or to dwell on the past are diverted into making plans to cope with present and foreseeable circumstances.

Ross's first attempt to contribute to the discussion is disregarded until John breaks in to reflect its underlying feeling. It shows that the boy is beginning to identify more evenly now and is trying to find ways of supporting his mother's point of view as well as his father's. John's response, although directed to Ross, serves to remind the parents that Ross's feelings are a significant factor in the problem as a whole. Thereafter they try, sometimes with John's help, to integrate Ross's comments into their overall assessment.

During the remainder of this meeting and the next, the family group is involved in action planning that is divided between the improvement of family relationships and a solution to the question of Mr. Wilson's transfer.

The problem of Mrs. Wilson being left to cope alone while her husband is out of town brings a response from Ross that signifies that, as the man of the house, he is quite able to protect her. It also leads to an assessment of resources outside the immediate family. Grandparents, an uncle, and two aunts who live nearby are identified as being closely concerned with the family's welfare. The parents admit that the relatives' interest in the children has recently been neglected.

As discussion proceeds, John continues to be aware of the importance of modeling clear and accurate communication in his own statements. He also gives and elicits feedback when necessary to clarify the contributions of the other three participants. Generalizations that the parents tend to make on the basis of untested assumptions are exposed and called into question, and interdependent, supportive interactions are strongly reinforced. Frequent summary evaluations of progress serve to reassure, as well as reinforce, the family as an effectively functioning unit.

Implementation

By the fifth meeting, a compromise plan has been reached on the question of the transfer. Implementation of the plan is clearly a family responsibility. The family agrees that Mr. Wilson will postpone making a change until both of the younger children attend school for a full-day session. Mrs. Wilson feels that she will be better able to cope with intercurrent difficulties when they are in someone else's care for a few hours a day. Mr. and Mrs. Wilson resolve to keep in closer touch with the relatives on whom Mrs. Wilson can depend for moral support. Ross promises to stay near his home and to spend some of his free time each day with the younger children.

Evaluation and Termination

John is able to utilize evaluation both as an ongoing impetus to the process of intervention and as a learning experience for himself. The three Wilsons soon participate with pleasure in the reviews, which highlight the steps of their progress in family collaboration as well as in problem solving. At staff team meetings, John reports each day's interaction with as much verbatim content as he can remember, and he joins the other team members in an evaluative exchange of questions, interpretations, and suggestions.

The team discusses the matter of termination midway in the series of six meetings. Progress to date gives every indication that the family will soon be functioning at a somewhat higher level than they achieved before lapsing into dysfunction. The shared prediction is that, if they agree to termination by the sixth meeting, it will be effected at that point without referral or planned followup.

Much of the fifth meeting is taken up by the members of the now-functional triangle in telling John how well things are going at home. John periodically expresses his observation of their sensitivity to each other's feelings and their supportiveness of one another. As the meeting ends, he indicates that they are now working together so effectively that there is little need for any help he can give. They assent willingly to his suggestion that the sixth meeting be the last and that it be used as a general windup. When his mother remarks that the children's aunt will be relieved to hear that her baby sitting chore is nearly over, Ross suggests that the other two children come along for the last meeting so that John can meet them.

With the two children aged five and six present, the sixth meeting turns out to be a little boisterous. John notes that Ross now identifies with his parents in monitoring the behavior of the younger children in keeping with his parents' commands. When he takes the others to explore a courtyard that can be seen from the window of the meeting room, the parents thank John for all his help, saying that they wish they had known sooner of the work of the family clinic. John uses this opportunity to reinforce their consciousness of new-found strength in their unified approach to problems, adding that there are sure to be more problems as time goes on. He assures them of the continuing availability of the clinic as a community resource. Ross proffers a gruff thank you when the children gather to add their farewells to those of their parents.

Whether a helping encounter occurs in a one-to-one relationship or in a work, family, or unrelated group, it gives each person involved an opportunity for an authentic view of self. Rogers (1951) quotes Emerson in an 1838 Divinity School address: *We mark with light in the memory the few interviews we have had with souls that... spoke what we thought...; gave us leave to be what we inwardly were.* Emerson put into words both the method and goal of the professional helper in short-term counseling. But the wise helper, like the experienced professional therapist, recognizes both as ends only incompletely to be attained but always to be striven after.

Throughout life, interaction with others continues to be the principal shaping influence of the self. Our sense of personal identity is derived cumulatively from the way others respond to what we do and say and are. The core of that identity lies in our meanings and values: in what we perceive to be worthwhile—to really make a difference in our lives. Each human encounter can help us recognize our valuing in the mirror it holds before our view.

Genuinely humanistic encounters can cumulatively allow us to transcend our being and move into becoming the ideal selves in which we center our most cherished meanings.

To help even in the most limited way in nurturing another toward this end is immensely satisfying. By giving us a sense of living up to our own professional values, it enriches our being and becoming. It moves us a step nearer to attaining a hoped-for integrity: that authenticity that lies in the proximity of the self-concept and the self-ideal. Once again we glimpse the possibility of becoming fully functioning, fully human.

To become part of a humanistic, person-centered movement on the world scene would be to participate in creating a quiet revolution. "Emerging persons" (Rogers, 1977), those who are becoming fully human, are beginning to raise serious questions within as well as outside the rigid authoritarianism of the institutions of modern society: government, business, military, church, school, factory, and family. With gathering momentum, persons who prize persons above status, "truth," power, or material possessions are exerting a significant influence on political choices—political in its broadest sense. There is a predictable backlash from people who prize tradition and conformity above individual freedom and self-determination.

It is unlikely that the influence of emerging persons will supersede traditionalist-conformist influences to our satisfaction in our lifetime. But a potent tool available to all of us is our vote. Through exercise of the franchise, as well as through participation in politically influential enterprises, we can work to mitigate some of the inequities underlying circumstances that precipitate everyday problems for many everyday individuals and families: unemployment, poverty, racism, sexism, and general ignorance and bigotry. No effort is wasted that is directed toward advancing that justice, freedom, and mutual respect that will allow every family and each of its members to become more fully functioning in personal authenticity, identity, and integrity, and in existential encounter with others.

References

Ackerman, N. W. 1966. *Treating the troubled family.* New York: Basic Books.

Bowen, M. 1965. Family psychotherapy with schizophrenia in the hospital and in private practice. *Intensive family therapy.* G. H. Zuk and I. Boszormenyi-Nagy, editors. New York: Harper & Row.

——. 1978. *Family therapy in clinical practice.* New York: Aronson.

Guerin, P. J., editor. 1976. *Family therapy: Theory and practice.* New York: Gardner.

Haley, J., editor. 1971. *Changing families: A family therapy reader.* New York: Grune & Stratton.

Hoffman, L. 1976. Breaking the homeostatic cycle. *Family therapy: Theory and practice.* P. J. Guerin, editor. New York: Gardner.

Okun, B. F., and Rappaport, L. J. 1980. *Working with families: An introduction to family therapy.* North Scituate, Mass.: Duxbury.

Olim, E. G. 1978. The self-actualizing person in the fully functioning family: A humanistic viewpoint. *Humanistic psychology: A source book.* I. D. Welch; G. A. Tate; and F. Richards, editors. Buffalo, N. Y.: Prometheus.

Parsons, T., and Bales, R. F. 1955. *Family, socialization, and interaction process.* Glencoe, Ill.: The Free Press.

Rogers, C. R. 1951. *Client-centered therapy.* Boston: Houghton Mifflin.

——. 1977. *Carl Rogers on personal power.* New York: Delacorte.

Satir, V. 1968. *Conjoint family therapy.* Palo Alto, Calif.: Science and Behavior Books.

Satir, V; Stakowiak, J.; and Taschman, H. A. 1975. *Helping families to change.* New York: Aronson.

Stefanics, C. 1974. My involvement with a young family. *Nursing of families in crisis.* J. E. Hall and B. R. Weaver, editors. Philadelphia: Lippincott.

Weakland, J. 1976. Communication theory and clinical change. *Family therapy: Theory and practice.* P. J. Guerin, editor. New York: Gardner.

Welch, I. D., and Flink, E. W. 1978. Humanistic parenting. *Humanistic psychology: A source book.* I. D. Welch; G. A. Tate; and F. Richards, editors. Buffalo, N. Y.: Prometheus.

Wynne, L. C., et al. 1958. Pseudo-mutuality in the family relations of schizophrenics. *Psychiatry* 21:205–220.

INDEX